SEASON OF GLORY

BOOKS BY ROBERT W. CREAMER

Rhubarb in the Catbird Seat
Jocko
Babe: The Legend Comes to Life
The Yankees (coauthor)
Stengel: His Life and Times

SEASON OF GLORY

The Amazing Saga of the 1961 New York Yankees

by

Ralph Houk and Robert W. Creamer

G. P. Putnam's Sons • New York

G. P. Putnam's Sons
Publishers Since 1838
200 Madison Avenue
New York, NY 10016

Library of Congress Cataloging-in-Publication Data

Houk, Ralph, date.
Season of glory: the amazing saga of the 1961 New York Yankees /
Ralph Houk and Robert W. Creamer.

p. cm.
Includes index.
1. New York Yankees (Baseball team)—History. I. Creamer,
Robert W. II. Title.
GV875.N4H68   1988   87-25058 CIP
796.357'64'09747—dc19
ISBN 0-399-13260-0

Printed in the United States of America
1 2 3 4 5 6 7 8 9 10

TO
MICKEY, WHITEY, and ROGER
and all the others who made
the 1961 Yankees
an unforgettable team.

CONTENTS

FOREWORD

In October 1960, after two years of trying, the New York Yankees fired Casey Stengel. The 70-year-old baseball genius did not go quietly but he went, and to fill the enormous void left by his departure the Yankees named in his place a Yankee coach, a down-home Kansas farm boy named Ralph Houk. Some of the most famous names in baseball—Mickey Mantle, Roger Maris, Whitey Ford, Yogi Berra—now called Houk the boss, the man they had to pay attention to.

Houk did have a certain notoriety. He was "the major," a baseball player who had been a wounded, decorated combat hero in World War II. But he had never managed a major league team, and as a big league player he had spent his entire career as a third-string catcher who seldom got into a game. He was a baseball nobody succeeding Casey Stengel, who had won 10 pennants in 12 years.

In 1961 the nobody led the Yankees to the pennant and victory in the World Series through one of the most extraordinary seasons in baseball history and through a year that was just as momentous outside the game—the first manned flight into outer space, the Bay of Pigs, the Berlin Wall, the threat of war.

What follows is an account of that amazing season, that tumultuous time, told from Houk's perspective—partly in the words of a general observer and partly by Houk himself as he watches his team stumble and falter at first, then gather itself and go on to a wild, record-breaking year that was dominated by the exciting, destructive chase after Babe Ruth's home-run record by Maris and Mantle.

PART ONE

Setting the Stage

1

For Ralph Houk, 1961 began 11 weeks before New Year's Day. In mid-October Casey Stengel's Yankees lost the 1960 World Series to the Pittsburgh Pirates when the Pirates' Bill Mazeroski hit a home run in the last inning of the seventh and deciding game. Five days later Stengel was dismissed. Two days after that, a week to the day after Mazeroski hit his home run, Houk was named manager of the Yankees. It had been a long time coming.

Toward the end of his playing career he had been taken off the active roster two or three times and made a coach in order to make room on the Yankee roster for one or another newly acquired player, and after the 1954 season he was asked if he would like to become manager of the Kansas City Blues, the Yankees' principal farm team. Houk quickly accepted the assignment, although he never actually managed in Kansas City; that winter the Philadelphia Athletics switched their franchise to Kansas City, and the Yankee farm team moved farther west to Denver, where Houk took over.

The Denver assignment made Houk in baseball. At the end of the 1954 season, he was nothing, a 35-year-old, washed-up ballplayer who even when he was on the coaching staff was at the bottom of the totem pole, a bullpen catcher. At Denver, he flourished. He was a powerfully built man (5 feet 11 inches tall, 190 pounds), with an amiable disposition—he had a warm smile and an infectious chuckle that was almost a giggle—that concealed a flaming temper that occasionally erupted. His obvious strength and that explosive temper combined to gain him added respect from the physically oriented athletes he managed. He ran the Denver club for three seasons, finishing third, second and second, and in his final year, 1957, he won the American Association postseason playoff and then the Little World Series against Rochester of the International League.

Major league teams in the market for a new manager began to eye him, but the Yankees had Houk earmarked as the aging Stengel's eventual successor. In 1958 he was brought back to the parent club as one of Casey's coaches, this time at the top of the totem pole. He had proved himself a successful manager at the highest level of the minors. He had handled with skill outstanding young players at Denver, men widely disparate in temperament and talent—retread major leaguers like Don Larsen and Ryne Duren, promising newcomers like Bobby Richardson, Tony Kubek, John Blanchard, Ralph Terry. His stature now was far above that of an obscure bullpen catcher.

The two men who shared ownership of the Yankees, Dan Topping and Del Webb, hoped to ease the 68-year-old Stengel out of the manager's job after the 1958 season, and they thought it would do Houk good to have a year of experience at Casey's right hand. Topping and Webb wanted and expected Casey to retire after the season when his latest contract with the club expired. But after Stengel rallied the Yankees to a stirring seven-game victory over Milwaukee in the 1958 World Series he was of no mind to retire and decided instead that he wanted to stay around a little longer. Topping and Webb reluctantly gave the old man one last two-year contract, with the clear implication that they expected Casey to pack it in at the end of the 1960 season.

The main reason Topping and Webb wanted to jettison the most successful manager in baseball history (at this point, Stengel had won nine pennants in ten seasons, and seven World Series) was simply his age. While he was at times as quick and sharp as ever, Stengel was getting on toward 70 and his crotchety ways were causing increasing restlessness and resentment among the players. When the Yankees slumped badly in 1959 and finished a distant third, their worst finish during Casey's tenure, there was plenty of anti-Stengel criticism, and it resurfaced in the summer of 1960 when the rejuvenated first-place Yankees were having difficulty shaking off the pursuing Baltimore Orioles. There was grumbling from the Yankee front office (though not from General Manager George Weiss, a Stengel man all the way— but then Weiss was on the hot seat, too), and even after the Yankees won 15 straight games at the very end of the season to give Stengel his tenth pennant, management felt it was time to call a halt. Casey had been great. The fans loved him. The press loved him. But he had reached his seventieth birthday in July and it was time for him to go.

A second imperative reason was the presence of Houk. He was ready to manage in the big leagues, more than ready, and with other clubs liable to approach him with offers to run their teams, the Yankees stood to lose him if Casey didn't retire. To insiders, even though the Yankee brass said nothing to the press on or off the record, it was obvious that, win or lose, 1960 was Stengel's last season. Casey seemed to know it, too, but he would not concede the fact publicly, and he adroitly kept the door open for his return for yet another season. During the 1960 World Series with Pittsburgh, stories kept popping up in the press speculating on whether or not Casey would leave, and at one point 35 baseball writers covering the Series for newspapers all across the country signed a petition that they presented to Stengel, asking him to stay on as manager—their assumption being that Casey had the choice.

Stengel knew better, and he wanted desperately to win the seventh and final game of the Series with the Pirates, hoping that a World Series victory would make it difficult, if not impossible, for the front office to go ahead with its plans to have him "retire." But Casey had backed himself into a corner. For some occult reason, he did not start Whitey Ford, still the Yankees' best pitcher even though he had had an ordinary season in 1960 because of injuries, until the third game of the Series. Ford pitched a shutout and then pitched another shutout when he started again in the sixth game. Critics pointed out that if Ford had started the first and fourth games instead of the third and sixth, he could have pitched again in the vital seventh game. As it was, Ford could not be used to start or even to come on in relief in the crucial bottom of the eighth inning in that tense game after the Yankees had taken a 7–4 lead. The Pirates rallied against lesser pitchers, scored six runs in the last two innings and won 10–9 to take the Series, four games to three, with Mazeroski's home run being the final blow.

The ancient Stengel's handling of the club against Pittsburgh was widely questioned later on (even by Casey himself, who a dozen years afterward said, in his inimitable way, "I blame myself on the whole Series. The idea was, I never pitched Ford in the first game and that's why I'm blaming myself in the Series in the long run"). The Yankees were clearly the better team, outscoring the Pirates 55 runs to 27 and outhitting them .338 to .256. They had 91 hits to the Pirates' 60, 27 extra-base hits to 15, 10 home runs to 4, and they outpitched the Pirates as well (a 3.54 team earned-run average to Pittsburgh's 7.11). Seldom had a World Series team shown such superiority, and yet the Yankees lost.

In New York on Friday, the day after Mazeroski's home run—and the day President Eisenhower, two months younger than Casey, celebrated his seventieth birthday to become the first septuagenarian president in United States history—the press confronted Dan Topping in the Yankees' office on Fifth Avenue in Manhattan and asked what was going to happen with Stengel. Was he going to retire? Or were the Yankees going to keep him on? With a straight face, Topping said he didn't know. He squelched disbelieving reporters by adding, "If anyone says he knows what's about to happen in our organization, he's strictly guessing, because right now we don't know. Nobody's more anxious to clear this up than we are, but there are still a few points that have to be settled."

The only thing that had to be settled was whether Casey would go quietly. And, of course, Houk had to agree to become manager before Casey was officially dropped. Topping may not have known whether Casey would retire gracefully or would have to be forced out, but on that Friday there was no doubt in his mind that Stengel was through, and that it had to be made official very soon. During the 1960 season the long-conjectured expansion of the major leagues from 16 teams (a number that had been fixed and unchanged for sixty years) had come to a head. After the Brooklyn Dodgers and New York Giants moved to California three years earlier, there had been concerted efforts to fill the vacuum in New York City left by the departure of those two National League teams. Coming out of retirement, Branch Rickey, the most skillful baseball executive of all time, joined others to form, on paper, an organization called the Continental League, which said it would begin play as a third major league.

Organized baseball, which owed its monopoly to a questionable United States Supreme Court decision made 40 years earlier that exempted the game from certain laws governing interstate commerce, moved quickly to undermine the Continental League before it could grow strong enough to challenge the old leagues either on the field or in court. In a dubious compromise, the two major leagues agreed to add four Continental League cities to the existing big league struc-ture, and the Continental League in turn agreed to abandon its more ambitious plans and quietly succumb. During the World Series, only three days before Topping said he didn't know what would happen with Casey, the National League announced that formal applications had been received from Continental League interests in Houston and New York for two new franchises in an expanded, ten-team circuit.

The next day the American League hurriedly announced that it, too, was ready to proceed with expansion, although it did not specify which cities it would add. No one knew how soon the new teams would spring into action, but Topping and Webb realized that with four new clubs looking for managers, along with the usual managerial changes to be expected among the existing clubs, Ralph Houk was suddenly a very hot property. The Yankee owners wanted Houk to succeed Casey, but if they didn't give him the job now it would be hard to keep him on a leash much longer.

Over the weekend after the World Series ended, they worked on Stengel. Casey, still trying to hang on to the job, was reluctant to go. But his contract had expired and it was finally made clear to him that he was not going to be offered a new one. To sweeten his departure he would receive a generous sum—$160,000—from a profit-sharing program. The Yanks were forcing him out, but they were doing it as nicely as they could. Although Topping had told reporters on Friday that he didn't know what was going to happen, by Monday—the same day that the National League officially admitted the new teams in Houston and New York and said they would begin play a year and a half later in 1962—the Yankees announced that a press conference would be held the next morning at the Savoy Plaza Hotel in midtown Manhattan to "discuss" Stengel's future. At that press conference, attended by a huge gathering of newspaper, radio and television reporters, the Yankees declared that Stengel was retiring.

As the once and future manager stood at a microphone unhappily answering questions, a reporter yelled, "Casey, were you fired?" Irritably, Stengel snapped, "Write anything you want. Quit, fired, whatever you please. I don't care."

It didn't matter. The point was: Casey was gone. It was a big story, a major item on radio and television news shows, a front-page story in the newspapers. The New York baseball writers held a sentimental farewell banquet for Stengel on Wednesday night, and there was a great backlash of criticism against Topping and the Yankees for squeezing the old man out.

The day after the banquet, on Thursday, October 20, the New York club held another press conference. At this one they introduced Ralph Houk and announced that he had been named to succeed Casey as manager of the Yankees.

2

Houk became manager two months after his forty-first birthday, but he had been with the Yankees for 18 seasons—22 if you count the four years during World War II when he was in the army. Houk had been raised on a farm near Lawrence, Kansas, where he was born on August 9, 1919. He starred in football and basketball at Lawrence High. Phog Allen, the near-legendary basketball coach at the University of Kansas, wanted Houk to come there and play for him. Several colleges—Kansas and Oklahoma among them—were after Houk as a football player. But he also played baseball, and in the summer of 1938, the year he graduated from high school, he was spotted in an amateur baseball tournament by a New York Yankee scout who offered him a $200 bonus to sign a contract. In those Depression times $200 was enough to make Houk forget about going to college. Other kids fresh out of high school were going to work for $10 a week.

RALPH HOUK:

I had a job in Lawrence in a tire shop where I was paid $45 a month. It was a different world then, in every respect. In football, for example, you played both ways. I was a linebacker on defense and a tailback on offense. I called the plays, threw the passes and I guess I ran with the ball 50 percent of the time. I was fast then. No one believes it now, but I held the high-school record for the 220 for a long time. I ran the hurdles, threw the discus and did a little bit with the shot put.

I didn't make it big in football until my senior year in high school, because I got hurt in practice in my junior year and missed the whole season. I was a guard in basketball and I was pretty good, but I was very physical. I was sort of a miserable bastard, I guess, in basketball. I was always a little too cocky, and raised on the farm like I was I was in better physical condition than most of the other kids. I hunted and trapped a lot, and I worked a lot. My brothers claimed I was playing ball all the time, but I really did work. I worked in the fields, I shucked corn, I put up hay, I got up every morning and milked cows—and every night, too. Anything you did on a farm, I did, and in those days we didn't have a tractor. We got it all done with horses. We didn't get a tractor until just about the time I got out of high school. We didn't have electricity till then either. Everything was kerosene. It's hard to believe now.

After I finished high school I had a chance to go to college, but I was playing ball in a twilight league and at the tournament in Kansas City, Bill Essick of the Yankees got hold of me. He offered me $200 cash and $75 a month as a salary, and I thought, Jesus, that's unbelievable. I had to go talk to Dad and Mom about it because I wasn't 21 yet, but they said okay, and I signed. That made a few of those college coaches mad but I thought, hey, this is the way to go.

In the spring of 1939 Houk reported to a Yankee farm team in Joplin, Missouri. It was March and it was cold, and the players had to practice indoors at the local YMCA a good part of the time. Just before opening day, Houk was sent down to a lesser Yankee farm team in Neosho, Missouri. He earned his $75 a month at Neosho, batting .286, and was named the most popular player on the team. The fans even had a "Day" for him in August, just after his twentieth birthday. He was given a shirt and a tie.

After the season the Yankees reassigned him to Joplin, but when contracts were sent out during the winter Houk discovered that his salary was still $75 a month. He refused to sign. He held out and stayed home on the farm until the early spring of 1940, when he swallowed his pride, took a bus to Joplin and reported to the manager, an old minor league catcher named Reds O'Malley. Houk told O'Malley he deserved a raise and, to his surprise, O'Malley agreed. The manager talked to people higher up, and the youngster's pay was hiked from $75 to $90 a month.

Houk hit .313 for Joplin and in 1941 advanced to Augusta, Georgia, in the Southern Atlantic League. There he played with Joe Page, who six years later became a renowned Yankee relief pitcher, and was behind the plate when Page pitched a no-hitter, the only no-hitter Houk ever caught in the minors or the majors. He batted .278, and in the normal course of events would have moved up another step in the Yankee farm system the next season.

But that December as Houk returned to the farmhouse one Sunday afternoon his brother Harold met him at the front door to tell him that the Japanese had bombed Pearl Harbor and that America was at war. Houk was 22 and single, ripe for military service. After he received his draft notice in January, he and his brother decided to enlist. They were assigned to Fort Leavenworth in Kansas where Harold, who had an accounting background, was made a clerk. When the personnel officer discovered that Ralph had played minor league ball he said, "Well, well, well. A ballplayer. Just what I've been looking for." Houk was made manager of the post baseball team and was soon promoted to sergeant.

Harold Houk decided to apply to Officer Candidates School, and Ralph followed his lead. He was sent to OCS at Fort Knox, Kentucky, was commissioned a second lieutenant and received further training as a reconnaissance officer in California and Louisiana before going overseas to England at the end of 1943. He went into France as a lieutenant with the 9th Armored Division a few days after D-Day, fought in the hedgerows of Normandy, and after the Allies broke through the German lines in July he rode across northern France in what was known as a point jeep—the lead vehicle of the reconaissance company he was part of. The point jeep was literally the point of the armed forces advancing behind it. Houk and his men went ahead to check road junctions and bridges and to find out where the enemy was. It was hazardous duty, with plenty of fighting involved, and Houk was wounded in the thigh by shrapnel. He soon returned to his outfit and in time became a company commander.

During the German counterattack in December 1944, the famous Battle of the Bulge, Houk displayed exceptional skill and courage under fire and won the Silver Star. He became a captain and, just before his discharge after the war was over, a major. Not long before the end of the fighting, as he was sitting in the jeep next to his driver, a bullet fired by a German sniper hit the rear of his helmet. Instinctively, he fell forward, and one of his men cried, "They got the captain!" The driver raced the vehicle around a corner to shelter, where Houk slowly sat up, startling the others in the jeep, who thought he'd been killed. There were two holes in his helmet, one in the left rear, where the bullet had gone in, and the other in the left front, where it had come out after passing between the outer metal shell of the helmet and the hard plastic helmet liner that was worn underneath it. Houk still has the helmet in his home in Florida.

He returned to baseball in 1946, batted .294 for Beaumont in the Texas League and in 1947 was invited to spring training with the Yankees, then managed by Bucky Harris. Houk was still a minor leaguer, but major league teams need extra catchers in spring training, and Houk played a lot. Then he had a run-in with Harris's third-base coach, Charlie Dressen, who was critical of the way Houk handled low pitches. He was demoted to the B-squad and assumed he would be sent to the minors for another year. But when the Yankees broke camp Houk was kept with the club, and just before opening day, to his surprise and delight, he was added to the Yankees' major league roster.

He got into 41 games with the Yankees in 1947, batted .272 and even got a pinch-hit single in the World Series as the Yankees beat the Dodgers. He also earned a winning World Series share of $5,830, which was considerably more than he earned in salary that season. Yet the following April, after spring training, he was sent back to the minors, and he rebelled. Almost 29, he felt he had established himself as a major leaguer. He staged a one-man strike for three days before cooling down. Then he reported to the Kansas City Blues of the American Association, at that time the Yankees' top farm club. (Kansas City did not get a major league team until 1955). He played furiously for Kansas City in 1948, batted .302, courted and married a pretty girl named Bette Porter and was recalled to the Yankees late in the year. He was sent down again in 1949, more peacefully this time, but returned in September in time to help Stengel win his first pennant with the Yankees. After that he remained with the big club as a catcher and, later, as a coach until 1955.

But he played very little. Although he was a first-rate minor league catcher (he had a lifetime average of .289 in the minors) he was a third-string reserve for all his eight seasons with New York, a bullpen catcher on a staff dominated by the brilliant and durable Yogi Berra. Houk appeared in 55 games during his first two seasons, 1947 and 1948, but in his six subsequent years with the club he was in a total of only 36 games, an average of 6 a year. He had only 37 at bats in all those years. He withered away as a ballplayer but was comforted by his major-league salary and by the largess of World Series checks won by the Yankees year after year.

He learned a great deal, had considerable influence on young players and became a sort of senior advisor. He commanded far more respect from his teammates than his inconspicuous role in the bullpen would seem to warrant. He was called "Maje," for Major Houk, and while the nickname started as a humorous putdown of his high military rank, in time it became a symbol of the regard the other players—stars and benchwarmers alike—had for him.

The Yankee management noticed, and when it was time for Casey Stengel to go, Houk was the man they wanted.

When Mazeroski hit his home run, the trigger that started the final mechanism that ousted Stengel as Yankee manager, Houk's reaction was like that of other Yankee players and coaches: shock and gloom.

RALPH HOUK:

There wasn't any criticism of Casey then, no second-guessing at all. The second-guessing came later. All I remember is that it was a sad damn day, and that the trip back to New York after the game was awful. Terrible. Bette met me and we drove home to Saddle River, New Jersey, where we were living then, and we didn't talk much.

The next day Roy Hamey phoned me. Either the next day or the day after. I know it was real quick. He said, "Can you come into the city? Mr. Webb and Mr. Topping want to see you. You know what it's about." And I signed to manage the Yankees.

I never had any idea that the Yankees were considering me as their manager until that World Series in Pittsburgh. No way. I had managed Denver for three years, from 1955 through 1957. People say that when the Yankees brought me back from Denver in 1958 to be one of Casey's coaches, I was being groomed to succeed him as manager, and maybe I was, but I sure didn't know it. After the 1957 season I fully expected to go back to Denver again. We even sold our house in Kansas City, where we'd been living. Then I got a call from George Weiss, the

Yankees' general manager, and he said, "We want you to come back to the Yankees as a coach." He said Bill Dickey, who was one of Casey's coaches, hadn't been feeling well and wanted to retire, and that Casey wanted me to be first-base coach.

Hell, I didn't know whether I was being demoted or promoted. I know Bette cried like mad when I told her because she liked it in Denver. We both did. Everything was going good there. But that's how it started. We came back to New York in 1958, and I was a coach for three years, in '58, '59 and '60. Nobody talked to me about being groomed for Casey's job, I didn't give it too much thought.

But when I was manager in Denver, Del Webb used to come there sometimes. He was a big man in the construction business, and he had some buildings going up there. Del loved baseball—he'd been a semipro pitcher—and whenever he was in town he'd come to a few ball games and I'd go visit him in the suite he kept in the Brown Palace Hotel there.

Del and I got along pretty well, although I was always kind of scared of him. After all, he was one of the owners. But I got to know him pretty well. Denver was the top Yankee farm club and naturally Del and I would sit and talk about the ball club. He'd always say, "I like the way you handle pitchers." I had a tendency to leave a pitcher in a game a lot longer than other managers in the league did, even when they were being hit pretty hard. Del really liked that, being an old pitcher himself and from the old school where pitchers stayed in there and *pitched*.

Well, I don't think Del knew it, but I had to leave the pitchers in. Denver was a hitters' ball park. It was a mile high there, the air was thin and the ball carried. Pitchers always had trouble there. You couldn't pull them too quick or you'd go right through your pitching, you'd be using everybody practically every day, and you'd overwork them and you'd ruin your staff. So I did leave pitchers in longer than other managers who weren't used to the ball park. That gave me an advantage because they'd be jerking their pitchers right and left, and after they'd leave Denver and go somewhere else to play it would take them a week to get their pitching staff straightened out.

Anyway, Del liked that, and I think he may have helped me get the Yankee job later on. I have the feeling that in talking about managers with Topping he probably said, "You know, this guy out in Denver might be pretty good." Webb and Topping were different types, but they both loved baseball and all sports, and in the meetings I was in with them they got along very well. They brought Casey in as manager in 1949 and now, evidently, they felt it was time for Casey to go, and I bet Webb put in a good word for me.

So I got to know people, and one of the people I got to know was Parke Carroll, the general manager of the Kansas City Athletics. Late in 1960, when we were about to play the Pirates in the Series, Parke got in touch with me. He said, "Ralph, what would you think about coming to Kansas City as manager?" I didn't know what to answer. It was the first time anybody had talked to me seriously about managing a big-league team. There'd been stories in the papers about me being in line for the Yankee job after Casey left, but there's always stories in the papers. The writers also had me going off to manage this club and that one. A couple of Detroit scouts did sound me out about managing the Tigers, but that was as far as that went. Nobody from the Detroit front office talked to me, except indirectly in that round-about way.

But Kansas City did talk directly. Parke Carroll asked me. So it was kind of interesting. I had no idea the Yankee job was going to be available, so I really thought about Kansas City. I told Parke, "Wait till the Series is over. I'll give you an answer then." Bette and I sat down and had a long talk about it. It was a major league managing job, but Kansas City was a bad ball club then, last or close to it every year. I kept asking myself, "Should I go there or not?"

While this was going on, Casey came to me during the Series. Well, he didn't *come* to me; we were both sitting on the bench before one of the games. It was early, and we were alone, just he and I sitting there, and all of a sudden he said, "You know, I'm thinking about retiring at the end of the year. If I do, you're the man I'm going to boost for the job." That's what he said, sitting there on the bench. Later on, I heard that he said they picked the wrong man—and maybe he did say that, I don't know—but I always felt Casey was a booster of mine. I know that day on the bench he told me he was going to push for me. I said, "That's real nice of you, Casey," but up to that time I hadn't given the Yankee job much thought. Really. I was thinking about Kansas City.

In the meantime—you know how it is at the Series: everybody's in the same hotel, and everybody's talking to everybody else all the time—Parke Carroll must have said something to Roy Hamey, who was in the Yankee front office. They were pretty good friends, and I suppose Parke just happened to say, "We're thinking of asking Ralph to manage

Kansas City." Roy was very excitable, and he got real excited then. He phoned me in my room and he said, "I gotta see you right away. Wait there." A few minutes later he came running in all excited and he said, "Goddamn now, look, I got something I want to tell you. Listen to me: don't be talking to anybody about going to manage anywhere. Don't do a thing until this Series is over. Don't go signing with Kansas City. Don't do *anything* until we talk to you in New York after the Series."

Well, you know, Weiss was still general manager but there'd been talk that Roy was going to succeed him, so now I began to get a little excited myself. Maybe there was something to all this stuff in the papers.

We got back to New York and Bette and I went home, and then Roy called me. It was like the CIA. Roy said, "Come in to town, but don't go to the office." The Yankee office was on Fifth Avenue then. He said, "Come to Del Webb's suite in the Waldorf. We don't want anybody to see you, so park your car someplace and take a cab. Get out a block from the hotel and phone, just in case any reporters are around." I drove in, parked the car, took a cab and phoned. There weren't any reporters or photographers around, and Roy said, "Come on up."

They told me Casey was retiring and that they wanted me to be manager. They offered me $35,000, for one year. Casey had been making $100,000, but they said $35,000 was the same that Casey had made in his first year as Yankee manager. There wasn't much inflation then, and pay scales stayed roughly the same, year after year. And Hamey told me if I wanted a two-year contract it could probably be worked out because "You're the man we want" and all that. But Webb and Topping said a one-year contract would be better. Webb was a pretty shrewd guy. He said you really shouldn't sign more than a one-year contract, because then if things go well you can get a real good contract the second year.

But it wasn't a question of me going in there and saying I want this and I want that. I would have signed anything they asked me to sign. I would have done it for nothing. Probably. Well, you know. The point is, there wasn't any trouble over the contract. It was so much more money that I'd ever made before, anyway. People today don't realize how much money $35,000 was in those days. The highest salary I'd had with the Yankees before that was $10,000. I'd been working like hell every winter trying to make a little extra, trying to make a living.

I worked in New Jersey for the Ballantine brewery, selling draft beer. The first year I was just a guy who went around with the regular salesman—with my baseball background I could help say hello and open doors—but later I took over a complete route myself. I opened the kegs and I ran the rats out of the cellars—oh, it was unbelievable. The company would give you something like $20 a day to spend in the bars and restaurants to create good will. There weren't too many people in those places during the day, but the old hanger-outers were always there. Always three or four of them, and they'd know when you were coming. They'd have a little beer up there on the bar but when they saw you it would be a shot and a beer. And those guys could move around. You wouldn't believe how they could maneuver. They knew your route, and they'd manage to beat you to the next place you were going. And in most of those places the bartenders had their hands out, and you'd better slip them a few bucks. A twenty didn't last very long. The people in the bar would expect you to have a beer with them, and you'd have to kind of pour it out when they weren't looking or you'd go home drunk every night.

It was a hell of a job, but I enjoyed it. I did it every winter there before I became manager, and I worked hard at it. I figured somebody might fire me as coach one of these days, and I'd better have something I could earn a living at. I'd leave the house at six o'clock in the morning to get down to the office for sales meetings, and I had to keep records. The big thing was to try to get your beer into those places, and I had an edge more than the ordinary guy because of baseball, so I did a pretty good job. They gave me a bonus, and I figured I was going to be a big beer man.

Then I got the manager's job with the Yankees and that ended that. I signed a one-year contract, there in the hotel. Afterward, they had everybody peeking out the doors, looking down the corridors for reporters, but the coast was clear, so I snuck out and got my car and drove back home to New Jersey.

I couldn't tell anyone but Bette until after the announcement because Topping and Webb didn't want the news to break while the Casey thing was still going on. We lived in a house in Saddle River, a great big old house on about three acres, which we rented quite cheaply, and I stayed there and didn't talk to anybody, didn't talk on the phone or anything. But it kept ringing, reporters kept calling and Bette kept saying I wasn't there. A lot of people assumed I'd been hired, even though they weren't real sure even on the morning of the press conference when it was officially announced.

So I hid out for a day or so. I wanted to go into the city to the dinner the baseball writers were giving for Casey, but Topping and Webb said no, to stay out of sight until Thursday. They didn't want me to go to the dinner because there'd be too many questions, and everybody would know I was the new manager, and they didn't want that yet. I guess they were right because, God, Casey was saying he didn't quit, he was fired, and all that. As far as I knew, it had been agreed he was going to retire. It hurt me when I found out later he'd been pushed out. I couldn't help thinking that Casey felt, hey, he was trying to move in on me, which wasn't true at all. Casey just never thought he was 70 years old.

With his $35,000 salary (not to mention his $5,356 World Series check) Houk was in the money for the first time in his life. It's always difficult to project the value of money from one era to another, but a quick rundown of what some things cost in 1960 may help demonstrate the extent of Houk's sudden financial improvement. He and Bette didn't need a new house—they were happy in the large place they rented in Saddle River—but if they had wanted to they could have bought a home in any one of a number of posh New York suburbs, where in the 1980's similar houses were selling for $300,000 and up, for $35,000 or so. A really elegant house in a very wealthy area, one that a quarter century later would sell for well over half a million dollars, might have cost $70,000.

In the fall of 1960 Houk could buy a high-quality suit for $85, an expensive shirt for $7.50, a pair of very good shoes for $20. (He could also buy a hat, a necessary part of a well-dressed man's wardrobe, for $15. In those days men wore hats religiously; not until President Kennedy began appearing hatless did the traditional snap-brim fedora go out of style.)

Bette Houk loved to go to the theater in New York. In 1960 she could buy a balcony ticket to a hit show for $2.90. The best seats for most Broadway shows cost $8.80, with a top of $9.90 for the most expensive musical in town. And the quality of theater in New York back then was remarkably high. In the fall of 1960 the Houks could have gone to see such musicals as *My Fair Lady*, *The Music Man*, *The Sound of Music*, *West Side Story*, *The Unsinkable Molly Brown*, *Bye Bye Birdie*, *Fiorello*, *Gypsy* and *Irma La Douce*—all on Broadway at the same time—with *Camelot* in rehearsal and on the way. The Houks could drive into New York, park their car in a garage in midtown, have dinner at an excellent restaurant, see a Broadway hit, stay the night in a hotel—and not spend $75.

While $35,000 was a lot of money and Houk was now in a position of significance—he had the best managing job in baseball—he was still an untried, all but unknown rookie stepping into the shoes of one of the most successful and most colorful managers in big league history. Houk had his three excellent years at Denver to point to, and he even had some experience running the Yankees—he handled the club for two weeks early in 1960 when Casey was ill—but he was nonetheless subject to automatic skepticism. Some critics said he would be a figurehead, a puppet manager run by the front office. Stengel himself muttered something to the effect that if he remained as manager of the Yankees he'd no longer have the authority that was his in the past. In other words, Houk would be subject to a lot of front-office interference.

When Stengel's remark was brought to Houk's attention at the press conference that introduced him as the new manager, Ralph bridled and said, bluntly, "In no shape or form am I going to be a yes man. I know there'll be pressure on me, following a great manager like Stengel, and I'll be second-guessed, I know that. But I'm not going to worry about it."

Asked if he would copy Stengel's managerial methods, he said, "I've been around Casey a long time and I learned a lot from him, but there's only one Casey Stengel. I'm Ralph Houk. I'll manage my own way."

Twenty-four hours later, as though to establish at once his independence from Stengel, Houk dismissed Casey's pitching coach, Ed Lopat, and a couple of days later hired Johnny Sain in his place. Houk won't criticize Lopat, an old teammate he still considers a friend, but he didn't see eye-to-eye with him on pitching theory. Lopat had been one of Stengel's pitching aces in the early years of Casey's reign, a "junk-ball" lefthander who relied with great success on guile rather than power. He had been brought in as pitching coach in 1959 after the Yankee management, beginning to pressure Stengel, more or less forced Jim Turner out of the job. Houk had played for Turner in the minor leagues and admired him greatly. Lopat and Stengel had made the ultimately disastrous decision to hold out Whitey Ford and start Art Ditmar in the first game of the 1960 Series.

RALPH HOUK:

It's kind of cruel of me to say this, but I'm going to say it. I think Casey lost his righthand man when he lost Turner. Turner was the best pitching coach I ever knew. The only thing you had to watch him for was that as far as Jim was concerned, the nine or ten pitchers on the roster were the whole team. But he was good. And he was gone.

I don't like to second-guess, but when Casey and Eddie started Ditmar instead of Ford in the first game, that cost us the Series. Casey liked ground-ball pitchers, and I know Lopat liked Ditmar a lot because he threw low breaking stuff. And Art did win 15 games for us that year, the most on the team. Whitey won only 12—he had some physical problems, his leg or something—but even so, he was the best.

Near the end of the season we were in Washington, staying at the big hotel there, the Shoreham. Casey had a meeting with the coaches to set up the pitching for the Series, and that's when he said Ditmar would start. I kept my mouth shut. Lopat was the pitching coach, and it wasn't my business. But I remember Frank Crosetti, who was the third-base coach, and I talking about it afterward, and we both felt it should be Whitey, Whitey, Whitey. To me, not starting Whitey—that's what cost us the Series.

So when I became manager I knew I had to make a change. I worked very closely with my coaches, especially with the pitching coach, and I've always felt a manager should have the coaches he wants. Later, in 1964 when I became general manager of the Yankees and Yogi succeeded me as manager, he didn't want Sain as his pitching coach.

Yogi and Johnny didn't get along. It was awkward for me—I'd hired Johnny—but he went, and Whitey Ford became Yogi's pitching coach.

But it's the manager who has to work close with the coaches, and he should have the people he wants. I think that's one of the problems some ball clubs have now. The front office hires the coaches and tells the manager who they'll be. That's got to cause problems.

I knew Johnny Sain, and I knew he'd done a good job as pitching coach at Minnesota, and he was available. So why wait? Doing it so quickly didn't have anything to do with me trying to make a strong impression right away, or anything like that. I've always felt if you're going to make a move, *make* it. Don't mull over decisions. Make them quick. Your first decision is usually the right one anyway. If you mull over it too long, you start to question yourself.

Besides, it wouldn't have been fair to Lopat to wait. If I'm going to make the move and I do it quick, I give him a better chance to get another job. He caught on with Kansas City, and a couple of years later he was managing them.

Lopat's replacement, Sain, was another old Yankee pitcher, who had joined Stengel's club in 1951 after years as a highly successful starter with the old Boston Braves. When Houk introduced him to the press he criticized Lopat only indirectly in his praise of Sain: "I picked Johnny because when he pitched for the Yankees I sat through lots of games with him in the bullpen, and I became familiar with his theories on pitching. They're pretty much the same as my own." Asked what those theories were, Houk grinned disarmingly and said, "I guess they're mostly concerned with getting the batter out. John?"

He deftly tossed the question to Sain, who also avoided a direct answer by saying something innocuous about different pitches for different pitchers. Even that mild reply conflicted a little with Stengel's ideas; Casey liked low-ball pitchers who threw ground balls that would lead to double plays, and he was always preaching the low-ball gospel to his pitching staff. Houk liked pitchers to go with their best stuff.

Houk named one other coach to fill the vacancy left by his own promotion. That was Wally Moses, a longtime American Leaguer who took Houk's place as first-base coach and also served as batting instructor. The other two coaches were holdovers: the veteran Crosetti, who was going into his thirtieth season with the Yankees as a player and a coach, and Jim Hegan, a once-great fielding catcher with the pennant-winning Cleveland Indians of 1954, who had Houk's old job as bullpen coach.

There was still one more change in the Yankee family. Early in November, Weiss, who had not been much in evidence during and after the World Series, "retired" as the Yankees' general manager after nearly three decades in the New York front office. Both he and Topping denied reports circulating during the Series that he'd be leaving the club after the season, Topping vehemently. Technically, they were both telling the truth. Weiss, like Stengel, had signed his final contract after the 1958 season, but his called for two more years as general manager and then five after that as an "advisor," which means that Weiss, too, knew that 1960 was going to be his last year in control.

Weiss stayed on through Casey's departure to help ease the way, and when he left he did not make the fuss that Casey did. He insisted he had not been dismissed, although it was apparent that he wasn't too happy about it despite his remarks to the contrary. When reporters pressed him, he said, "I'm not going to indulge in a lot of recriminations, so I hope you'll be charitable with your questions."

Weiss did say, rather significantly, that he felt he was leaving behind "a club good enough to win the next two or three years." After the Yankees' sudden fall from power in 1965, when after winning five straight pennants they dropped from first place to sixth, their worst finish in forty years, his prediction came to be construed as a shrewd warning that the Yankees had only a few good years left. They did win four more pennants and two World Series titles after Weiss left before collapsing, but they were swept four straight by the Dodgers in the 1963 Series and lost the Series again in 1964 before their disastrous plunge in 1965. So perhaps Weiss did see bad times ahead.

In any event, he was gone now, too, with Hamey named to succeed him at a salary of $60,000 (almost twice what Houk was being paid).

*   *   *

The changes on the Yankees and in baseball generally were in a small way echoes of the world at large. The 1960 presidential election campaign that was going on when Casey was fired and Houk hired foretold the beginning of new ways and new attitudes under John F. Kennedy after eight years under the comforting, fatherly Eisenhower, a sudden switch from an elderly chief executive to one barely in his 40s. America had not had a president under the age of 50 since Theodore Roosevelt left office in 1909, and after Kennedy's death in 1963 it would not have another—at least not until the 1990s and possibly not until well into the twenty-first century.

Along with change there was turmoil. There was the uneasy presence that fall of a newly antagonistic Cuba, long thought of by Americans as something of an adjunct to the United States—a vacation place, a land of Latin dances like the rhumba and the conga, a friendly source of sugar, cigars, strong rum and good baseball players. Now it was on the Soviet side, the enemy side. The Soviet Union and the United States had been at loggerheads since the previous May first when a high-altitude American plane called a U-2, popularly known as a spy plane, was shot down by Soviet antiaircraft fire over Sverdlovsk, a city a thousand miles inside the borders of Russia. The pilot, an American civilian named Francis Gary Powers, parachuted 70,000 feet to the ground, where he was taken prisoner by the Soviets, who published photographs of him and his wrecked plane. Until then, most Americans simply did not believe that the United States would do such things as deliberately send an airplane over Soviet territory. This was only three years after the first tiny satellites had been launched into orbit and long before such things as weather satellites and spy satellites were routinely whipping around overhead.

The U-2 incident sabotaged a summit meeting between Eisenhower, Soviet Premier Nikita Khrushchev, French President Charles de Gaulle and British Prime Minister Harold Macmillan that had been scheduled for mid-May. Eisenhower, who had been a very popular president, lost some of the warm affection and confidence the American public had in him when he said plaintively (and, it turned out, inaccurately) that he hadn't known anything about a spy plane.

As the baseball season ended, the presidential candidates, Kennedy and Richard Nixon, met in a series of highly publicized television debates, the first time candidates for the presidency had debated one another on TV. On the day Mazeroski hit his momentous home run, Kennedy and Nixon in the third of their debates argued bitterly about the islands of Quemoy and Matsu, which were held by the Nationalist Chinese (led by Chiang Kai-shek) based on Taiwan. The two small islands were only a few miles off the coast of mainland China, controlled by the Chinese Communists, who were (it was assumed) under the domination and direction of the Soviet Union. The question was how far the United States should go to defend the islands from a Red Chinese attack, and the debate was acrimonious. Quemoy and Matsu were ominous words, fighting words in 1960, an issue that was felt to be tremendously important at the time (although more than a quarter of a century later the status quo continued). Kennedy called Nixon a hawk on the subject, Nixon called Kennedy a dove. Kennedy's very narrow victory in the ensuing election was credited in good part to his giving a better performance on television than Nixon did, a factor that has greatly influenced the presidential selection process ever since. Kennedy and Nixon held their fourth and final debate on the day after Houk was named manager of the Yankees.

One added note: On the day after the third debate the playwright Moss Hart suffered a coronary attack while working in Toronto on a new musical play starring Richard Burton that was headed for New York. The musical was *Camelot,* and Hart lived to see it open triumphantly in New York before his death later in 1961. Camelot, of course, became the symbol of the Kennedy administration.

In Africa, country after country was breaking away from European domination and declaring independence. Power struggles in that vast continent began to reverberate throughout international politics. A novelty song that had gained popularity in the 1950s with an escapist refrain that used the words bingo, bango and bongo, and went on to talk about not wanting to leave the Congo, was suddenly and sadly outdated. The Belgian Congo, today called Zaire, was torn by conflict, and a volatile, popular leader named Patrice Lumumba was later murdered. Chinese Communists were said to be training native troops in Africa, and the United States and the Communist bloc seemed headed toward confrontation there.

On the Sunday after Houk was hired, the South African educator and author Alan Paton, whose bestselling *Cry the Beloved Country* had focused attention on the racial strife in his country, spoke from the pulpit of St. James's Episcopal Church on Madison Avenue in New York. "What the government of my country is trying to do," he explained to his American listeners, "is separate every racial group from every other." He said that because the word "segregation" had racially offensive overtones, the South African government had introduced the term "apartheid," but, he said, apartheid has developed "such a stench, they are now referring to 'autogenous development.' "

Paton said advocates of apartheid claimed that people were happier when the races developed separately, but he warned that was "a misapprehension that seduces many Christian people" and that the consequence of apartheid was an erosion of spiritual values among Christians who defended such policies. He warned—in the fall of 1960—that apartheid created resentment and hatred among nonwhites for all white people. That same week in Georgia the Reverend Martin Luther King was released on bail after being arrested during a sit-in protest against racial practices there—and three months later racial segregation in St. Petersburg, Florida, would cause problems for Houk's Yankees in spring training.

The currents of change upset the easy flow of Houk's managerial career in a less cosmic sense. Less than a week after he was named manager, the American League followed the National League's lead and voted officially to expand from eight to ten teams. But where the National League had dutifully followed the terms of the peace agreement with the Continental League and had accepted its owners in New York and Houston, the American League ignored the Continental and threw a couple of surprises into the pot. It put one new team in Los Angeles, where the National League Dodgers had been playing for three seasons, and the other in Washington, after letting Calvin Griffith switch his existing Washington franchise to Minneapolis–St. Paul, where the erstwhile Senators were to begin a new life as the Minnesota Twins. (A new pro football team, the Minnesota Vikings, became part of the National Football League at about the same time. The Minnesota franchises were the first to use a state name rather than that of a city.)

The American League stunned baseball by also announcing that the two new clubs would not wait until 1962 to begin play, like the new National league teams, but would start right away—that is, they would field teams at the beginning of the 1961 season. The Los Angeles and Washington clubs would be stocked with players drafted from the eight existing American League teams. Each of the old teams, including Houk's Yankees, would put 15 players into an expansion pool, and of those 15 at least seven had to come from the club's major league roster—that is, from the 25 players who were on the official roster on August 31, 1960. (On September 1, teams were allowed to increase their player rosters to 40.) The remainder of the 15 in the pool could come from any players on each team's 40-man list. No more than seven players could be taken from any one team, and the new clubs would be charged $75,000 for each player they picked. Thus, each of the old teams stood to earn more than half a million dollars for seven marginal, or only slightly better than marginal, players. That was not desirable for the Yankees, who had more quality players than the other teams, but it was a windfall for some of the lesser teams in the league, which had almost literally nothing to lose and half a million to gain. No players could be added to or dropped from the 40-man roster until after the draft was completed. No trades could be made. No one could be sold or released or otherwise disposed of. No new players could be acquired.

Thus Houk, brand new to the job, was immobilized. He could do nothing for the time being to strengthen his team where he felt it might need strengthening. Worse, he faced the loss of as many as seven players from a team that had won the pennant and come within an inning of winning the World Series. Except for hiring or firing coaches, he could do little until after the expansion draft took place.

But the draft didn't take place, at least not right away. In its precipitous haste to outdo the National League in expanding, the American League ran into problems. Rickey and William Shea, the prime movers of the Continental League, claimed the American League had ignored them and that the peace agreement between the Continentals and the major leagues had been breached. They threatened suit. Baseball Commissioner Ford Frick, who had been pretty much on the outside looking in while all this was going on, said in shaky defense of this new development that the American League expansion committee had agreed only to "recommend" that two Continental League franchises be added. The recommendations had not been followed. Then Walter O'Malley, owner of the Los Angeles Dodgers, protested the installation of another major league team in his still-new territory (the Dodgers had been in Los Angeles only since 1958). The American League expected the new team to use the Los Angeles Coliseum, where the Dodgers had been playing their home games while waiting for their new stadium in Chavez Ravine to be completed (it wasn't ready until 1962). O'Malley reacted negatively to that proposal and opposed the entire idea of a new club anywhere in Los Angeles.

Frick ruled in favor of the American League as far as O'Malley's charges of "invasion" of territory were concerned, noting that he had earlier approved a decision by baseball's executive committee to declare New York, Chicago and Los Angeles "open cities" for expansion. O'Malley argued that he deserved compensation for the intrusion of another big league team in territory that had been exclusively his and in which he had stimulated an interest in major league baseball. He continued to resist the new American League team, and with Rickey and Shea also objecting to the American League action there were strong indications that the whole squabble would land in court, always anathema to organized baseball. The arguments raged. Weeks went by, and the American League still had not announced who the new owners in Los Angeles and Washington would be. Apparently, the new owners were reluctant to take over until the dispute was settled.

Scrambling for a solution so that it could get on with its regular offseason business, such as trades and other roster changes, the American League said it would delay expansion plans for a year if the National League, the more prosperous circuit at that time, would agree to interleague play. When that proposal was rejected, the American League said if the confusion about the Los Angeles franchise was not cleared up, it would simply skip Los Angeles entirely for the 1961 season and go with a nine-team league, an awkward solution at best. Then Toronto, one of the proposed Continental League cities, was mentioned as a possible site for a tenth team in place of Los Angeles.

It was a lovely mess, and it lasted from the end of October all through November to the last day of baseball's winter meetings in early December. Then Gene Autry, the cowboy movie star who had become a multimillionaire through business investments, was revealed as the head of the group that was awarded ownership of the Los Angeles franchise. O'Malley had not succeeded in keeping the new team out of Los Angeles, but he did keep it out of the 100,000-seat Coliseum. The newcomers would have to play instead in a little, 20,000-seat minor league stadium previously used by the Chicago Cubs' farm team in the Pacific Coast League, the Los Angeles Angels, who had ceased to exist after the Dodgers' arrival in 1958. The new major league club, which adopted the old minor league club's name, agreed to televise only 11 games to avoid competing directly with O'Malley's Dodgers. It made other concessions too.

At the same time, the American League said the new Washington owners were James H. Lemon and James M. Johnston. After Johnston died, Lemon sold the club a few years later to a Minneapolis businessman named Bob Short, who in 1971 sent the new Senators down the river to Dallas–Fort Worth, where they became the Texas Rangers, leaving the nation's capital without a big league team. The American League had fouled things up beautifully.

It had taken six weeks to settle the issue, while Ralph Houk, new to his job and eager to get cracking on it, had to sit on his hands and wait. He still was not able to do anything for yet another week, until after the long-awaited expansion draft finally took place. It was scheduled for December 13 in Boston, but a big early season snowstorm blanketed the northeast (it dropped 17 inches on New York City) and delayed things another day. At last, on December 14, almost two months after Houk had been named manager and seven weeks after the American League announced it would expand, the expansion draft was held, only two months before the beginning of spring training.

Houk lost seven players. (An eighth, the veteran infielder Gil McDougald, announced his retirement from baseball four days before the draft. Houk also worried about a ninth, Bill Stafford, a young pitcher who had been an impressive rookie in 1960 but who had been called into military service after the season for six months of training.) The seven players taken from the Yankees by the new teams were pitchers Eli Grba and Bobby Shantz (the first two picked in the draft overall) and Duke Maas; first baseman–pinch-hitter Dale Long; outfielder Bob Cerv; and two minor league prospects, Ken Hunt and Bud Zipfel.

Hamey moaned that the draft had "kicked a couple of holes in our bullpen and our bench. Those three pitchers won 16 games for us." He bewailed the departure of Cerv, Long and Hunt. Houk, more optimistic, said, "As league champions, it was to be expected. At least we finally know where we stand. We're not going to waste any time repairing the damage."

RALPH HOUK:

The thing that bothered me most about expansion was that it actually happened. I really didn't expect it to. But it did, and so quickly. And then we had to sit and wait.

That was a tough time. We couldn't make any moves. We were scared. We had a lot of meetings to discuss the roster, decide which players we'd expose to the draft, which ones we'd protect. It was very difficult for me. I wanted the same team back, the one that won the pennant and should have won the World Series. We had pretty good depth on that club, pretty good ballplayers, and now we had to lose some because we could only protect 18 of the players on the regular roster. We protected Maris and Mantle and Hector Lopez, that's three outfielders; we protected our three catchers, Berra, Elston Howard and John Blanchard; we protected our infield: Bill Skowron at first, Bobby Richardson at second, Tony Kubek at short, Clete Boyer at third. That's ten. We had 11 pitchers on the staff; we protected eight of them: five starters, Ford, Ditmar, Bob Turley, Ralph Terry and Stafford, and three relievers, Luis Arroyo, Jim Coates and Ryne Duren.

We lost some good men, but we were lucky too. We were very happy that Joe DeMaestri wasn't drafted. He was our backup shortstop and he was a good man. Kubek had been hurt in the last game of the Series in Pittsburgh when a ground ball took a bad hop and hit him in the throat. He seemed all right, but we were a lot safer with DeMaestri on the bench behind him. Joe had planned to retire from baseball that winter to go into business with his father, but we gave him a raise to get him to change his mind and stay around another year. We felt we couldn't afford to lose a man as valuable as DeMaestri.

But the draft still hurt. We didn't lose any of our key men, but those guys we lost won big ball games for us. People forget that it's the three games you win here and the two games you win there that win pennants for you. Now we didn't have the depth we had before with guys like Grba and Shantz. Grba was a pretty good-looking pitcher at that time, and he and Shantz were the kind of guys you win those extra ball games with, pitchers who can get certain outs for you

And Cerv—a big powerful hitter like that on the bench means a lot to a team. It bothered me, losing those ballplayers. I hated losing all of them, and Cerv and Shantz and Grba most of all. After losing them, we definitely weren't as good a ball club.

People kept asking if I was scared or nervous taking over such a big job—you know, about following Casey, about managing the New York *Yankees*. I never was. As far as managing, hell, I knew how to do that. I'd done it in Denver for three years. I wasn't concerned about that at all. As far as stepping into Stengel's shoes, well, I respected Casey and all that—he was a great manager, and you can't get away from it—but I didn't worry about Casey or how he might do things. Casey wasn't there anymore. I didn't see him or talk to him at all during the winter—he lived out in California—and I didn't see him or talk to him until the first time we went into Los Angeles during the season.

As far as the players' reaction to me, that was the least of my worries. I knew they were just as happy that Casey was gone. I didn't call any of them during the winter because I don't think that's a smart thing to do. If you call one, you'd better be damn sure you call all of them, and you can't be sure you'll reach all of them. I did write the pitchers a letter, the same letter to all of them—just saying to be in shape and what to expect in spring training and all that kind of stuff. I ran into Ford in New York—Whitey lived on Long Island, and he was in town a lot—and I saw Mantle and Maris when they came to New York during the winter, but that's all.

I wasn't worried about the players. I didn't like losing all those guys in the draft, but I also knew there wasn't any way we weren't going to be a good ball club. I knew the team, and I knew we could win. I could hardly wait for spring training to start.

On the day after election day, when Kennedy defeated Nixon, Roger Maris was named the Most Valuable Player in the American League for 1960, edging Mickey Mantle by three votes, 225–222, in the second tightest MVP balloting ever. The close vote demonstrated the strong hold Mantle had on the imagination of the baseball writers who did the voting, because Maris had a superb season in 1960, his first with the Yankees, and was obviously the reason why the club rebounded from its dismal third-place finish in 1959 to win the pennant and nearly the world championship. Maris batted .283 to Mantle's .275, led the league in runs batted in with 112 to Mantle's 94, and let it in slugging percentage with .581 to Mantle's .558. Roger had 27 homers by the All-Star Game and was batting .320. By August 6 he had 35 home runs and was well ahead of Babe Ruth's record-setting pace in 1927. But then he badly bruised his ribs breaking up a double play, was out for almost three weeks and after his return hit only four more homers the rest of the season. He still finished with 39, only one behind Mantle's league-leading 40, even though he missed 18 games while Mickey played a full season for the only time in his injury-plagued career (he missed only one game all year). Along with his powerful slugging, Maris displayed remarkable ability as an outfielder and as a baserunner and was named to the Associated Press major league All-Star team, which consisted of one team of players from both leagues. Mantle did not even make the AP's second team. John Blanchard, the Yankees' hard-hitting reserve catcher, said, "Roger Maris in 1960 was the best baseball player I've ever seen."

But Mantle's runs-produced total for the year (an arcane but useful statistic derived by adding runs scored to teammates batted in) topped Roger's by two, and Mickey played very well during the Yankees' pennant-winning drive in September. Sportswriters tend to be inordinately impressed by what happens late in a season and that, coupled with the magnetism Mantle generated on and off the field, helps to account for Mickey's near victory in the MVP voting, even though Maris was clearly more valuable that year.

Mantle, still only 28, was in his tenth big league season in 1960. Maris, three years younger, was in his fourth. He began with the Cleveland Indians in 1957, but in 1958 he was traded in midseason to Kansas City. After a year and a half in Kansas City, he went to the Yankees in a blockbuster trade that sent Don Larsen, Hank Bauer, Norm Siebern and Marv Throneberry to Kansas City for Maris, DeMaestri and Kent Hadley. The trade didn't do much to help Kansas City—the Athletics fell into last place—but Maris's arrival in New York galvanized the Yankees, who went on to win five straight pennants.

In the fall of 1960, shortly before Maris was named Most Valuable Player, wheels began to turn that would greatly affect his career and, indeed, his life. Arthur Daley, the Pulitzer Prize–winning sports columnist of *The New York Times*, paid a visit to Baseball Commissioner Frick, an old friend of his who lived only a few blocks away from Daley's home in suburban Bronxville, New York. Frick had been a sportswriter himself and then a sports broadcaster on radio before becoming president of the National League and, eventually, commissioner of baseball.

From their conversation Daley wrote a column which noted that in all the hoopla about Stengel's dismissal by the Yankees, not a great deal of attention had been paid to the news that the National League had added Houston and New York and had expanded to ten teams. Daley's column appeared *before* the American League's hasty decision to expand to ten teams in 1961, but he wrote that the increase from eight teams to ten would require a change in the traditional 154-game schedule—in which each of the eight teams in each league played each of its seven rivals 22 times (11 games at home and 11 away). Seven times 22 equaled 154 games for the season. In order to have a similarly balanced home-and-home schedule, Daley wrote, the season would have to be stretched to 162 games, so that each of the ten teams could play each of its nine rivals 18 times (nine home and nine away). A shorter 144-game schedule (in which the teams played 16 games against one another) was not mentioned, nor did Daley and Frick apparently discuss the possibility that each team *could* play each of its rivals 17 times, which would have produced a 153-game schedule almost identical in length with the old one. The unevenness of home-and-home play in the 153-game schedule (nine at home and eight away, or vice versa) was probably disturbing to the traditional baseball mind.

In any case, it was presented in Daley's column as an accepted fact that a ten-team league would require a 162-game schedule. And then Daley raised a question that the following summer exploded into a controversy that continues to echo to this day.

"There are aspects to this revolutionary change that demand discussion," he wrote. "The owners will be able to solve the technical problems inherent in a ten-team league. But it is an intangible that disturbs many baseball men. The 154-game schedule has served as the framework for more than 60 years. Soon it will stretch to 162. Eight extra games in each season might provide just enough margin to distort and displace some time-honored marks. This theory was dropped into the lap of Commissioner Ford Frick."

The rest of the column consisted almost entirely of a long quote from Frick. He began by saying, "It's a question that has been bothering me for some time," meaning the question of whether the longer schedule might allow "cheap" records to replace some of the sacrosanct ones of the past ("the great marks we treasure," in Frick's words). "The principal records in the book seem safe," he said. Reassuringly, he talked about the impossibility of anyone even coming near Cy

Young's lifetime total of 511 pitching victories. What about Babe Ruth's home-run total of 60? "My opinion on that is almost a conviction. I don't think the Babe's record is vulnerable."

In his own words, Ruth's record was "safe," even with a longer season.

"The more I think about it," Frick went on to say, "the less inclined I am to believe that the great records are in serious jeopardy . . . [but] I intend to ask the rules committee to study this problem and try to soften the impact when necessary. My own idea is that some records might deserve to be listed in two categories—the one made during a 154-game schedule and the one made during a 162-game schedule."

At the time, late October 1960, Frick's comments attracted little attention. When they were printed in Daley's column, the American League had not yet expanded, and neither Frick nor anyone else knew that in 1961 Roger Maris and the Yankees would be playing the 162-game schedule he was concerned about. Nor that Ruth's record of 60 home runs in one season, the record that Frick, an old and close friend of Ruth's, cared about the most, would be seriously challenged in the very first year of expansion.

The American League did expand and a month or so later its new 162-game schedule, the longest in major league history, was made public. Reflecting the changes occurring in baseball was the fact that the first four teams the Yankees were scheduled to play in 1961 were from areas new to the major leagues since Mantle started in the majors—Minnesota, Kansas City, Los Angeles and Baltimore. Stengel amicably turned down an offer from Detroit to manage the Tigers in 1961. Bob Scheffing, whom Stengel always called Scheffling, got the job instead; if Casey had taken it, would he have had the Tigers head-to-head with Houk and the Yankees in the 1961 pennant race, the way, as it turned out, Scheffing did?

Earlier that fall in a crucial National Football League game between the New York Giants and the eventual NFL champions, the Philadelphia Eagles, All-Pro linebacker Chuck Bednarik of the Eagles creamed the Giants' Frank Gifford after he caught a pass over the middle.

Seldom has a man been hit as hard on a football field. Gifford was carried off the field and was hospitalized. He suffered no serious or permanent injury, but he played no more football that year, and after trying a comeback for a season or two gave up football and became a broadcaster. Clark Gable died in mid-November at the age of 59. A few weeks after the presidential election Jacqueline Kennedy, who because she was pregnant had not been much in evidence during the campaign, gave birth to John F. Kennedy, Jr., the first child born to a president or a president-elect since Grover Cleveland was in office in the 1890s.

On December 16, Houk and the Yankees, free at last to make player deals, made their first move to repair the damage caused by the expansion draft and bought lefthanded pitcher Danny McDevitt from the Dodgers. That same day a United Airlines DC-8 and a TWA Super Constellation collided over Brooklyn as both planes approached New York City airports. One plane fell onto a Brooklyn street, the other crashed on Staten Island, and 127 people died.

The United States severed diplomatic relations with Cuba, which now seemed to be completely in the Soviet camp, and major league baseball worried aloud that Fidel Castro would not let the dozen or so Cuban players on big league rosters return to the States to play ball in 1961. Among the Cuban players were outfielder Minnie Minoso of the White Sox, an American League All-Star in 1960, second baseman Tony Taylor of the Phillies, a National League All-Star, and a group of outstanding players on the reborn Minnesota Twins, including star pitchers Camilo Pascual and Pedro Ramos, shortstops Jose Valdevielso and Zoilo Versalles (later an American League MVP) and a rookie farmhand named Pedro (Tony) Oliva, who later won the American League batting title three times. But a short time later Castro said there would be no attempt to keep the Cuban players from going to the United States to play.

The new year began with President-elect Kennedy, a naval officer in World War II, going to the Orange Bowl game in Miami on Sunday afternoon, January 1. Shrugging off presidential impartiality, he rooted openly for Navy during the Midshipmen's 21–14 loss to Missouri.

Three weeks later he was inaugurated in Washington on a bitterly cold January day, after the 86-year-old American poet Robert Frost, hatless, his white hair awry in the wind, his breath showing, read with difficulty a poem appropriate to the occasion. The United States began sending combat helicopters to Laos in Indochina, near Vietnam. Norman Mailer was indicted for stabbing his wife, and another author, Yogi Berra, appeared at Macy's department store in New York to autograph copies of the autobiography, *Yogi*, he had written with Ed Fitzgerald. Some wit asked Berra, noted for his partiality to comic books, if *Yogi* was the first hardcover book he'd ever read. Berra somewhat indignantly replied that he had read his friend Joe Garagiola's book, *Baseball Is a Funny Game*, published a year earlier. Then he said he had also read *Something of Value*, a bestselling novel about tribal unrest and political upheaval in East Africa.

"Go on," scoffed his unbelieving questioner. "You never read that book."

"I did too," protested Berra. "It's all about the Mau Maus and everything."

7

Salary questions began to arise. In that era before agents and free agency, Mantle had made $72,000 in 1959. After the Yankees finished third and Mantle's batting average dropped from .304 to .285, his homers from 42 to 31, his RBIs from 97 to 75 and his runs scored from 127 to 104, the Yankees tried to cut his salary more than 20 percent to $55,000. Mantle resisted that big a cut but finally signed for $65,000, still almost a 10-percent slash in pay. After his good 1960 season everyone wondered what he'd sign for. Even though his batting average had dropped another ten points, to .275, he *had* led the league in homers and runs scored, and the Yankees had won the pennant.

Maris, meanwhile, earned $20,000 in 1960, but after winning the MVP and leading the league in RBIs, he wanted his salary doubled to $40,000. Skowron, who had led the team in hitting (.309) and had batted .298 or better in six of his seven years with the club, had made $23,000 in 1960 and also wanted a big raise. This was uncharacteristic, since the earnest, work-ethic Skowron, called Moose by his teammates, usually accepted without argument whatever the Yankees offered. Friends of his on the team told him he was a sucker, that with his stats and years of experience he deserved a lot more than he had been getting. Skowron listened and turned quietly stubborn.

RALPH HOUK:

Moose Skowron was—well, there was just one Moose, he was out of one mold. He was a quiet, hardworking guy who would do anything for anybody, and everybody on the club liked him. He didn't say much, but when he made up his mind to do something he did it. He was very sincere. I know he had a lot of trouble with his first marriage— his wife left him—and that really hurt him because he was a big family man. He took good care of his kids and they're still very close to him. He remarried and he thinks the world of the wife he has now.

Moose is still the same guy—he even looks the same, he has the same burr haircut he wore then—except that he's a little more talkative now.

He was a big strong-looking guy that never complained. He'd play hurt, he'd do anything to help the ball club. He was very, very well liked, and everybody kidded him because he took everything so serious. I mean, you could kid him and then he'd say, "Oh, I see." He was like that. The guys had a lot of fun with him, and he never minded it.

Moose was a good all-around player. He had good consistent power to right field, and he was hard to pitch to because of that—he could hit to all fields, and he hit the ball hard. He was one of those guys who when he hit a grounder the ball seemed to pick up speed as it went through the infield because of the top spin he put on it. Everybody thought of him as a hitter because of that power, but he was good all around. He was an above-average fielder, though not too many people noticed that. Some first basemen will cover tremendous ground and make spectacular plays, but Moose always seemed to be in front of the ball. He played the hitters real good. He knew what he was doing. You didn't have to be calling out, "Get over" or "Get back." He was a smart ballplayer. Maybe he's not what you'd call a brilliant man, but there are a lot of people—well, take Yogi Berra. Yogi's probably not the smartest guy in the world but he was a brilliant ballplayer. Moose was smart in baseball. If he didn't know something, if he didn't know what you wanted him to do on a play, or if he didn't know a hitter, he'd be looking into the dugout to see what you wanted him to do, and he'd do it. He'd get it done. He was always alert.

He was always in the ball game. You get some guys with great natural ability and maybe they just struck out or popped up or hit into a double play, and that's the end of them until they come to bat again. They're thinking of what they're going to do the next time they hit. Not Moose. No matter what he did at bat he knew we still had to do the defensive end of it.

Moose was a good ballplayer. He was overshadowed, being on the same team with Maris and Mantle. You know attention was going to be on them more than on the Moose. But he was a big part of the ball club.

Mantle, Maris and Skowron were not considered outright holdouts, but all three had rejected the club's first offers. Then Berra signed on January 12 for $52,000, and the logjam began to break. Someone noted that Berra needed only 54 hits to reach 2,000 for his career and asked Houk if he thought Berra could do that in 1961. Houk said, with grim humor, "If Yogi doesn't get 54 hits, we'll all be in trouble."

A few days after Berra signed, Mantle came to New York and after a brief discussion with Hamey signed for $75,000, his highest salary to that point and just about the same as Stan Musial and Warren Spahn, two veteran National League stars, were making, with Willie Mays close behind. These were the highest salaries in baseball at the time. (Mantle just about doubled his income from endorsements and personal appearances.)

Mantle had difficulties with reporters in his earlier years with the Yankees, but he was remarkably at ease talking with them at the little press conference the club called to announce his signing. He seemed older and surer of himself. Even his hair was different, considerably longer than the short, flattop burr cut that had been his hallmark for so long. The reporters bombarded him with questions about Stengel and Houk, trying to get a provocative comment—preferably a critical one—about Stengel, with whom it was known that Mantle had occasional difficulties. Mickey parried the questions easily.

Asked how he thought a rookie like Houk would do managing an important club like the Yankees, he said, "A manager who has the respect of his players can win, and Ralph has it."

Didn't Casey have the respect of his players? he was asked.

"Sure," Mantle said. "Casey had it too."

When one of the reporters asked sharply, "Didn't you and Casey have differences?" Mantle didn't bristle, as he might have done in earlier years. Instead, he grinned and said, "Only those that were printed."

When other questions quickly followed, mentioning criticism Stengel had directed at Mantle, Mickey grinned again and said, "Whatever Casey said about me was right."

He was diplomatic, poised, relaxed. It might have been the normal accretion of poise that came with age. It might have been the psychological load off his shoulders with the departure of Stengel. Whatever caused it, he was a new, more gracious Mantle.

When the reporters finished with him Mantle waved and left, and Houk took over. He was asked about the 162-game schedule and whether he thought Mantle's chronically damaged legs would hold up through the longer season. Houk said routinely that he hoped so and then made a remarkably prescient comment.

"I hope he plays 162 games, and if he hits 60 homers and Maris hits 59, they'll make me a hell of a manager," he said. This was on January 15, and it was the first time in the great Maris–Mantle home-run year of 1961 that anyone had mentioned 60 home runs.

Before Mantle left New York, Houk talked to him about becoming "leader" of the team. He made it clear to Mantle that he was the big man on the club, the one the others would look to. It seems obvious in retrospect that Mantle *was* the leader of the club, but at the time Houk suggested it, the notion came as a surprise to Mickey. He had been a young, raw kid when he first joined the team, growing up in the shadow of dominant players like DiMaggio and Berra and the veteran pitchers Allie Reynolds, Vic Raschi and Ed Lopat, who did so much to set the tone of the club through Mantle's early seasons.

Now, except for Berra, they were all gone, and Yogi, fading as a player, was no longer a dominant factor. Casey was gone, too, so that Mantle was shorn of the nagging sense of guilt, the failure to measure up to Stengel's insistence that he become not just a very good ballplayer but the best of all time. Under Houk, Mantle felt free, relaxed, grown up. Ralph didn't think of him as an irresponsible kid but as the big man, the leader of the team, and Mantle found he liked the idea of that.

"I didn't think about it much," Mantle said, "until Ralph kept saying I was going to be the leader and that as Mantle goes, so go the Yankees, and things like that. He told me he was going to put me hitting cleanup instead of third. I'd always hit third, and I never cared much about hitting fourth, but Ralph told me it was better for the team that way. And it was. It made a lot better hitter out of Roger, and it didn't hurt me any. So it *was* best for the team. And it made me feel that Ralph was depending on me. Casey always talked about me, what I could do and all, but I never felt he had quite the confidence in me that Houk did. Ralph really made me feel like a major league ballplayer."

Maris, meantime, had not yet signed his contract. Because of his outstanding play in 1960 he was in great demand on the dinner circuit that is so much a part of baseball's winter, and he was making extra money from commercial endorsements, too. In January he was in New York to attend the sporting goods fair as "a member of the staff" of the Spalding sporting goods company. He conceded that he was asking for a big raise from the Yankees but said, "I don't expect any trouble." He also said, with the flat practicality so characteristic of him, that the fans might be expecting more, maybe too much more, in 1961. "I just hope I can do the job," he said. "I'd like to see the club win the pennant again."

Maris, still only 26, was married and had two children. He and his wife, Pat, were expecting a third (it was a boy, born that summer) and would have three more children later on. He talked a lot about his family and his house in Raytown, Missouri, a suburb of Kansas City. He called it a "ranch home" in proper real estate style, and said he'd been fixing up the basement during the offseason. "I'm a sort of do-it-yourself guy," he said, "but I've had outside help this winter. We're building a spare bedroom, a laundry and a playroom for the kids." He was a small-town man, a family man.

He left New York after the sporting goods fair but was in the city again later in January for a B'nai B'rith dinner. The next night he was in Rochester, New York, for the Hickcock Award dinner, and the night after that in Jamestown, New York, for yet another dinner. He was back in New York the next day for a salary conference with Hamey but still did not sign a contract. There were no agents; he handled the negotiations himself. Then he left for Boston and another dinner.

While Maris was traveling around, Ford, who had been with the Yankees since 1950, signed for $35,000 and Elston Howard, who was gradually moving ahead of Berra as the team's number-one catcher, signed for $28,000. While $35,000 seems a modest salary for a pitcher of Ford's stature, even for those days, it should be remembered, first, that $35,000 was a big salary in baseball then and, second, that Ford, for all his ability, had not yet made a really big splash as a pitcher. Although he was noted, ironically, as a "money pitcher" who won the tough games, and though his career winning percentage at that point was an extraordinarily high .693, Ford had never won 20 games in a season, that mystical hallmark of high pitching prowess. At 32 he was generally thought of as a good—maybe a very good—pitcher, but not yet a great one.

That was to change in 1961. Ford, who had had some physical problems in previous seasons, said after signing his contract, "I really feel great. I'm still hopeful of winning 20 games in a season. Houk promised to work me more often this year, and that should help."

Houk had run into Ford at a basketball game in Madison Square Garden and in the course of conversation asked Whitey if he felt he could start every fourth day—or nearly 40 times during the season—something he had never done under Stengel, for whom he had started more than 30 games only once. In the last three years he had started 29 games each season. Under Houk that would jump to 39 games, and Ford would respond with the best season of his career.

Maris returned from Boston and again conferred with Hamey. He still wanted $40,000, but Hamey and the Yankee owners would not go that high. Not only had Ford and Howard signed for considerably less, but now Art Ditmar, who had made $20,000 in 1960, the same as Maris, signed for $25,000. With his fifteen victories, Ditmar, despite his poor performance in the World Series, was still at least technically the ace of the staff.

Maris finally yielded to pressure and signed for about $38,000. He wouldn't reveal the exact figure but said he was happy with the contract and that the club had come close to what he had asked for. A reporter asked again what the exact amount was. Maris fixed his eyes on the questioner and said, "I don't think it's really anybody's business."

When the subject turned to hitting, Maris was more relaxed. He said he was confident he could improve at the plate and become a .300 hitter. Batting averages were very important then. Nobody even thought to ask him if he felt he could hit more home runs.

"I was a better hitter on the road than I was at home," Maris said, expanding on the batting-average theme, "because I swung with the pitch. I was just trying to get hits. At the Stadium I was trying to pull the ball toward the right-field seats all the time. I'm going to change that." Add that to your list of famous predictions gone awry.

Someone mentioned to Maris that he seemed to be in pretty good shape despite all the banquets he had been to. He smiled his little smile and nodded. "I've been to a dozen dinners," he said, "but I eat only the meat, no trimmings, no dessert." Then, vehemently, he added, "But I've had it. Next year there'll be no banquet circuit for me, not even if I hit .380."

Put that one on the list, too. And notice again that Maris felt a high batting average was more apt to focus attention on him than, say, hitting home runs. He simply had no idea.

By the end of January everyone had signed except Skowron and the shortstop–second baseman combination of Tony Kubek and Bobby Richardson. After Hamey met with Skowron late in January the general manager said, "We're still far apart." Skowron, in a typical Skowron remark, denied that he was a holdout—that was a bad word—but said he wanted a raise.

Richardson had established himself as the club's regular second baseman in 1959, and in 1960 he'd been named the outstanding player in the World Series—he batted .367, drove in 12 runs, a Series record, and even hit a grand-slam home run. He was 25 and had been with the Yankees for all or part of six seasons. Short, chunky, highly intelligent and deeply religious, he was uncomfortable holding out for more money, even though he felt morally certain that he deserved a substantial raise. Disliking the haggling and bickering that went on in contract disputes, he disengaged himself by saying he would wait and bring his unsigned contract to spring training and work out a solution there.

But even that left him uneasy. He wanted to get it settled. He wrote a letter to Hamey in which he said he would sign for a certain amount—$21,000, apparently—which, he declared, "is exactly what I think I'm worth and is a very fair figure, both to the organization and myself." It was a carefully worked out compromise. Hamey said, "That's the first time I ever had a player write a letter like that," and immediately sent Richardson a contract for the amount Bobby had specified.

Skowron finally signed, getting the big raise he more than deserved, but not until mid-February. A week or so later Kubek, a quiet but very stubborn bargainer, also agreed to terms, and with that Houk had everyone in hand just as spring training began.

When Houk headed south to the Yankees' training camp in St. Petersburg, Florida, change was in the air everywhere. In Florida heavyweight champion Floyd Patterson and ex–heavyweight champion Ingemar Johansson were in training for their third fight. Patterson had lost his title to Johansson in the first one by a knockout, and regained it (the first heavyweight ever to do so) by knocking out Johansson in the second fight. Before the rubber match Johansson, the last white to hold the heavyweight crown, sharpened his speed by working out with an 18-year-old youngster from Louisville, Kentucky, named Cassius Clay, who had won the Olympic light-heavyweight championship in Rome the previous summer. After sparring ten rounds with Clay, Johansson marveled at the youngster's skill and quickness in the ring. In their fight Patterson knocked out Johansson. Three years later in Miami, Clay (who had not yet changed his name to Muhammad Ali) won the heavyweight championship himself by beating Sonny Liston—who had dethroned Patterson in 1962—and began his long dominance of the championship.

There were many beginnings. The Minnesota Vikings drafted their first players in January. American tennis authorities said they would vote for open tennis, a radical departure from the nominally amateur atmosphere of big-time tennis. In St. Louis, the baseball Cardinals disclosed plans for a new $25-million stadium to be built in a downtown area the city was rehabilitating, close by the new 630-foot Gateway Arch that was rising from the banks of the Mississippi. In New York it was announced that a new Madison Square Garden would be built on top of Penn Station. At the same time Mayor Wagner of New York prodded the state legislature to approve the issuance of bonds for the construction of a stadium on Long Island for the new and still unnamed National League expansion team.

Branch Rickey was approached about becoming president and general manager of the new team, but when Joan Whitney Payson, the wealthy owner, learned that Rickey wanted both a sizable percentage of the club and carte blanche control of its operation, she backed away—the Whitneys hadn't made their money by letting other people control it—and Rickey was out of the picture. There was a strong rumor that Leo Durocher, who had been gone from baseball for five years, would be named manager of the new club. Then the Dodgers signed Durocher to serve as a coach under Walter Alston, amid speculation that Durocher would soon succeed Alston as manager—which proved to have little validity, since Alston continued to manage the Dodgers for another 15 years. The Chicago Cubs introduced a startling new concept in managing: instead of having one man direct the team, a staff of coaches would take turns running it. For the next two seasons Vedie Himsl, Harry Craft (who had managed Houk in the minor leagues), Elvin Tappe, Lou Klein and Charlie Metro alternated as "head coach" before the Cubs abandoned the method as a bad idea. By 1966 the ubiquitous Durocher, dismissed by the Dodgers, was managing the Cubs, and in 1969 he made a strong bid for the National League pennant before his Cubs folded under the onslaught of the team he and Rickey had not become part of in 1961—the New York Mets.

The Yankees revealed that their venerated hero, Joe DiMaggio, would be going to spring training as a "coach" under Houk. DiMaggio's duties involved little more than showing up in camp for a week or two, putting on a uniform, posing for pictures and signing autographs, but his willingness to be present at spring training camp was significant. It was the first time since his retirement almost a decade earlier that

DiMaggio had joined the Yankees in an official capacity, and it was more than a coincidence that his return came in the first spring training after the departure of Stengel, whom DiMaggio didn't care for. Having him come to camp was a good omen for Houk.

RALPH HOUK:

It was pretty much a P.R. thing. We thought it would be a nice addition for spring training, having DiMaggio there, and it would be a plus for me just to have Joe come down and let people know that maybe he approved of the situation. It was good public relations for me and for the Yankees.

Mel Allen, the Yankee broadcaster, foretold an aspect of the future when he said he was going to do his telecast of a spring training game from a position next to the Yankee dugout, where he would be cheek by jowl with the players on the bench. Frick quickly vetoed the idea as much too radical. He said it might set a bad precedent; newspaper reporters, magazine writers and all sorts of media people might demand equal time, he said. Dugout cameras were still a long way in the future.

A more profound change began to take shape at the end of January, shortly before Houk was to open his first spring training camp. Dr. Ralph Wimbish, a black physician in St. Petersburg, Florida, where the Yankees had trained since 1926, had for several years helped the Yankees and the St. Louis Cardinals, who also trained in St. Petersburg, to find living quarters for their black players in that racially segregated city. Jackie Robinson had broken the color line in baseball 14 years earlier, but segregation was still in command in Florida. Elston Howard, the first black to play for the Yankees, had been with the Yankees for six seasons but for six springs he had lived apart from his white teammates because of the "whites only" policy of St. Petersburg hotels.

Now Dr. Wimbish declared he would no longer help the baseball clubs solve their housing problems. "It's time the management of the clubs take a hand," he said. He suggested that the hotels the Yankees and Cardinals used (the Soreno for the Yankees, the Vinoy Park for the Cardinals) be persuaded to house and feed their black players too. Howard had lived with the Wimbish family during previous springs but, Wimbish said, "This business contradicts my active fight against discrimination, and I can no longer participate in it."

RALPH HOUK:

The change started that year, the real change. They were beginning to have trouble in the minor leagues and all over at that particular time. That was a problem, it sure was. And it wasn't just a problem in St. Pete. It was that way in a lot of places on the road too. We had a road secretary—well, he was an old guy and he was old-fashioned, and there were a lot of problems with that. I remember talking with Ellie Howard about it.

I wasn't involved in the talks about the St. Petersburg thing, but I remember Bob Fishel working like a dog on all the problems involved with it, the contracts and all. It was too late, I guess, to get anything done about it that spring. We still stayed at the Soreno and Ellie stayed with that doctor's family he lived with.

But that year was when it started to change. And the next year, when we moved to Fort Lauderdale, everybody stayed together at the Yankee Clipper.

The Yankee management responded immediately to Dr. Wimbish's remarks. Topping said that Howard, Lopez, Jesse Gonder and Pedro Gonzalez, the black players on the team's spring training roster, meant as much to the club as any other players. "We would like very much to have the whole team under one roof," Topping said. Fishel, the astute public relations director, tried to work out a solution with the Soreno Hotel, where the Yankees had stayed for so many years, but before he could accomplish anything, the assistant manager of the hotel, Norville H. Smith, issued a public statement saying, "We have always enjoyed having the New York Yankees with us. We hope to have them with us for many more years to come on the same basis." Asked what "same basis" meant, Smith said, "I mean on the same basis as we've always had them—by making arrangements for some of the players outside."

Smith's boss, hotel manager Martin McNeil, was in Tulsa, and when he was tracked down there he echoed his assistant's remarks: "We expect to continue on the same basis. We expect to have them back. I understand arrangements already have been made."

McNeil was substanially correct. The Yankees had made arrangements to stay at the Soreno, and it was much too late in the busy Florida winter season to find other accommodations, assuming that another hotel could be found in the area that would accept the black players. Obviously, the club should have been sensitive to the problem a lot sooner, but Topping had been busy working out a switch of the Yankee training site from the west coast of Florida (where St. Petersburg was) to Fort Lauderdale on the east coast, near where Topping had a winter home.

The Yankees had a long-range contract with St. Petersburg, and Topping's plan to switch to Fort Lauderdale had been kept secret. Further, the Yankees had not yet had complaints from their black players. Howard, a hardworking man who kept his troubles to himself, was not thought of as a militant black. Black militancy, for that matter, despite Robinson's breakthrough and his well-publicized criticism of segregation and discrimination, was still only beginning to make itself felt in baseball.

So it came as something of a surprise when the quiet Howard, asked about the St. Petersburg/Soreno Hotel flap, said, "I'm extremely concerned. I feel that all players should be given the same treatment. We get it on the field but not off the field."

Birdie Tebbetts, the former major league catcher and manager who was then executive vice-president of the Milwaukee Braves, said that black members of the Braves were satisfied with spring-training housing arrangements in Bradenton, Florida, where the Braves had their camp. But Henry Aaron and Wes Covington of the Braves and Bill Bruton, who had been traded from the Braves to the Detroit Tigers the previous December, disputed Tebbetts' remarks. The three black players said they hadn't complained previously about the Milwaukee club's spring-training arrangements but had decided to speak out now because of the widespread discussion of Florida segregation practices caused by the Yankee dispute.

Bing Devine, general manager of the Cardinals (who later was president of the Mets for a time), excused himself and the Cardinals from the segregation problem by saying, "We recognize it as highly desirable for all players to stay together, but we don't make the rules and regulations for the various localities." Warren Giles, president of the National League (who was later elected to the Hall of Fame), similarly hid his head in the sand. "I never heard one word of complaint on this subject from any ballplayer, colored or white," Giles said. "I do not want to comment further on a problem I do not know exists."

On the other hand, Bill Veeck of the White Sox, whose squad included six black players, took a more positive approach to the problem by publicizing the fact that the White Sox had booked the entire squad, including the black players, into the Biscayne Terrace Hotel in Miami for April exhibition games with the Baltimore Orioles. The Yankees quickly followed suit. Fishel, an old friend of Veeck's, said that when the Yankees went to Miami in March for exhibition games, they would not stay at the McAllister Hotel, where they had originally booked rooms, because it was segregated. Instead, the Yankees—all of them, including the black players—would stay under one roof at the Biscayne Terrace.

Thus spurred, Yankee management continued the effort. Early in March the club insisted that Howard be included in the handful of Yankee stars invited to a chamber of commerce breakfast at a St. Petersburg yacht club. Howard didn't particularly want to go to the breakfast—like all ballplayers, he would have preferred to sleep in a little longer in the morning—but the Yankees persuaded him to attend. Howard was the only black at the breakfast, but at least the barrier had been broken.

But the Yankees couldn't change the attitude at the Soreno. C. H. Alberding of Tulsa, president of the firm that ran both the Soreno and the Vinoy Park, said he was happy to have both clubs at his hotels "but when either the Yankees or the Cardinals or both feel the situation has developed so that they insist on housing all their personnel in the same hotel, then the Yankees and the Cardinals should look elsewhere."

Fishel said, "We are under contract to stay at the Soreno this spring. We hope eventually to break down the segregation which exists in spring training, but it's apparent that we will not be able to accomplish that this year—although we feel the Yankees have made more of an effort than any other club.

"Neither the hotel manager nor city officials," he said, "care to risk jeopardizing the existing social structure at a time when the tourist business is at the height of the season. The Yankees feel that the problem will be solved through more discussion at a more leisurely pace."

Then he broke the startling news that the Yankees would transfer their spring training site to the east coast of Florida in the near future. The Yankees had three more years to go on their St. Petersburg contract, but there was an escape clause. Topping explained that if the Yankees could provide a substitute major league club to replace them, they could vacate St. Petersburg after the 1962 spring training period. He also talked about the proposed move to Fort Lauderdale and warned that there could be segregation problems there, too.

The story settled down. Segregation was under attack, but it persisted. Howard continued for one more spring to live with Dr. Wimbish and his family. And the Yankees finally began spring training.

PART TWO

Snags in Spring Training

On February 13 Houk and his staff started working with rookies at early camp, what Stengel used to call the "instructual school." He paid particular attention to those he thought had a chance to make the big club (infielder Pedro Gonzalez, for example, who didn't make it, and pitcher Rollie Sheldon, an impressive 15–1 in a low minor league in 1960, who did), as well as prospects for the future from the Yankees' minor league system (such as Tom Tresh, Joe Pepitone and Jim Bouton, who were still a year or so away from big league status). Also at the early camp were several regulars Houk felt could benefit from extra work: pitchers Ditmar, Coates and Duren; catchers Blanchard and Gonder; infielders Boyer and Deron Johnson (Houk talked about alternating the slick-fielding Boyer and the hard-hitting Johnson at third base). Other pitchers in camp included Johnny James and Bill Short and an ex–Cincinnati Red with an impressive name: Franklin Delano Roosevelt Wieand, who had been born one month to the day after FDR began the first of his four presidential terms in 1933. For some perverse reason, Wieand's nickname was Ted, possibly after President Theodore Roosevelt. Whatever, he didn't stick and never pitched a regular-season inning for the club.

The second stage of training began a week later when the rest of the pitchers and catchers came to camp, and the third stage on March 1 when the remainder of the squad—the Mantles, the Marises, the

Skowrons—arrived and spring began in earnest. Houk made some changes in the routine. For one thing, he altered the players' diet, or at any rate the food available to them in the clubhouse at lunchtime during training sessions. Instead of the usual run of bologna and tuna-fish sandwiches, Houk ordered light food to be served: soup, celery, carrots, apples, cottage cheese, things like that.

He divided the squad into groups of rookies and regulars instead of mixing them together, in order to give the young players the undivided attention of the coaches when they were on the field or at bat. And instead of playing ordinary intrasquad games between teams bearing names like the "Crosettis" and the "Sains" or the "regulars" and the "yannigans," in the time-honored tradition of spring training, Houk introduced a novel system in which he had three squads playing at the same time: a pitching squad, a fielding squad and a hitting squad. The same defensive lineup would stay in the field for six outs or more, while the same group of batters continued to hit against a succession of pitchers, each of whom stayed on the mound for a certain number of pitches, no matter how many outs he got. If a pitcher was retiring batters one after the other, Houk would put a runner or two on the bases just to stir things up. After a while, the hitters would become fielders and the fielders would become the hitting squad.

RALPH HOUK:

What we did in those three-squad practices was set up a simulated game. It wasn't a regular game. If you play an ordinary intrasquad game and you have a couple of pitchers who are really in control of it, nobody gets on base and nothing happens.

This way, you send a pitcher to the mound and he's going to stay out there until he gets so many outs or he throws so many pitches. If a batter makes out but you want to see him on the bases, you put him on first base. Now the pitcher has to work with a man on. You can have the man steal, you can put on a hit-and-run, you can bunt. You can do things continually where *something's* going to happen. What might ordinarily be a third out doesn't end things. You keep the runners on the bases and see what the next batter can do. In a regular intrasquad game there may never be a play where you'd need a cutoff man. This way you're going to have plays like that all the time.

You keep the same men in the field for six outs or so, and then send another group out, and all of them get action because there's always something going on. You might have fifteen hitters coming to the plate, and all of them can be in a situation where they've got men on base that they have to move around. Everybody has a chance to do something.

It worked good. I used it in spring training all through my managing career.

As for the food, I never thought heavy sandwiches were a good idea in a spring-training clubhouse. At one time under Casey we'd have two workouts a day and we'd come in to the clubhouse after the morning session—which usually had a lot of baserunning and pickoff plays, things like that—and you'd go in and gorge yourself on those sandwiches. Then you'd go back on the field, and you were half asleep. You just didn't feel like working out much. So I decided on a very light lunch, and I tried to cut things down to one workout a day as much as I could. I think most clubs do that now.

Despite Houk's changes, the first period of training before the exhibition-game season began on March 10 was fairly routine. The last holdouts had signed, although one or two players reported a day late. Before Luis Arroyo, the great little relief pitcher, arrived tardily from Puerto Rico there was an extravagant rumor that he had been quarantined because of "exposure to bubonic plague" in Venezuela, where he had played winter ball. Arroyo arrived the day after the rumor did, looking plague-free and amused by the story.

Writers clustered around certain players—Bob Turley, for instance. Turley had won the Cy Young Award as the best pitcher in baseball in 1958 (there was only one award then, given to the man considered the best in both leagues), but in 1959 and 1960 he had two disappointing seasons in a row. He won nine and lost three in 1960, but he completed only four of his 24 starts and his strikeouts (Turley was a power pitcher), which had dropped from 168 in 1958 to 111 in 1959, fell even farther to 87 in 1960—even though he pitched more innings in 1960 than he had the year before.

Turley blamed his decline on lack of work and said sardonically, "Ask number 37 about that." Stengel wore number 37. But, except for his Cy Young year, Turley started more games in 1960 than he had in any season since 1955, and while he complained about Stengel removing him from games too quickly, his 9–3 record in 1960 indicates that perhaps Stengel had taken him out at precisely the right time.

The unhappy truth was that Turley, only 30, was just about finished as a pitcher. But he had been so imposing on the mound in the past that Houk stuck with him, hoping he'd regain his touch, counting on him as one of his four principal starters along with Ford, Ditmar and Ralph Terry.

Houk said he might platoon Boyer and Johnson at third base, but he made it clear that Kubek, who in his four seasons under Stengel had platooned back and forth between shortstop and the outfield, would be the full-time shortstop now. Talking with the baseball writers in camp, Houk said cautiously, "I don't want to sound critical of the way Tony was handled in the past. There were reasons why Casey maneuvered him in and out and played him so often in the outfield. But if everything goes the way we expect, we won't have to do that anymore. Hector Lopez will be the left fielder and Tony will be the shortstop. The only way Kubek will play in the outfield is if there's an emergency—if Mantle or Maris got seriously hurt and was out for a long time."

Kubek had obviously disliked his late-inning shifts to the outfield under Stengel's platooning. "I don't blame him for feeling that way," Houk said. "He never played much outfield, and it's not easy to move to a strange position, especially late in a game. And it isn't easy for a man to come off the bench to take his place at shortstop, even for someone as experienced as Joe DeMaestri. So we won't be moving Tony around this year. He's the shortstop."

The writers began to zero in on Houk. For years, they'd been used to the rich copy that flowed effortlessly out of Stengel, and while Ralph was accessible and open to questions it wasn't the same. So they probed and probed, trying to get answers from him that could by hyped into a story—particularly anything that could be tied to Stengel. For the most part, Houk handled them well.

RALPH HOUK:

I think probably the biggest lesson I learned from Casey was in handling the press, the media. That's a big job for a manager, one of the toughest jobs he has. Casey was great at it. People laughed at the way he talked, but he always knew what he was doing.

He told me once, "Never admit to the press that you're wrong. You know more about the game than they do, so always have a reason for what you did, even if you don't have one. Not too many of them can second-guess you, because they don't know enough. Just be sure to give them a reason why you did something."

I've never forgotten that. And he sure could do it. One time in Yankee Stadium there was a righthanded pitcher going against us, and it was one of those situations—tie score, men on base in the last of the ninth, two out. Casey wanted a lefthanded hitter to bat against the righthander, but by mistake he sent Ellie Howard up to pinch-hit. Howard batted righthanded. As Ellie walked into the batter's box Casey realized his mistake. He said, "No, no, no," but it was too late. Ellie was already in there.

Well, Howard hit a pitch off that righthander into the seats and we won the game. I can't remember now who the pitcher was but my locker was just outside Casey's office, and I could hear him in there after the game talking with the writers.

"How come you sent up a righthanded batter to hit?" they asked him.

"Well," Casey says, "I guess you don't know that boy wears that fella out."

One of the writers said he didn't remember Howard getting many hits off that pitcher.

"Yeah," Casey said, "but you should have seen some of the *shots* he hit off him."

That took care of that. They didn't keep as many records then as they do now, with the computers and all, and you could get away with something like that then. Today you probably couldn't. Anyway, I thought it was pretty shrewd, and I used it a little bit myself a few times when writers asked me why I did this or why I didn't do that. I'd say, "You probably don't remember some of the hits that guy got . . ."

Not that I tried to copy Stengel. There's no way you could copy him. And never mind the writers, some of the things he said and did I couldn't understand myself. In spring training once, at the early practice, the instructional school, Casey had an idea. It had to do with teaching a whole bunch of young players how to handle the rundown play between third and home, and he must have laid awake all night figuring this one out. He had it worked out where each time a player handled the ball on the rundown he'd go past the runner and then handle the ball there at that end. He explained it to us coaches, and we're trying to explain it to the players, and Frank Crosetti said, "My God, Ralph, there's no way this is going to work."

Now Frank was a great coach, a manager's coach. He was early to bed and early to rise; you could set your watch by him. He was the kind of coach a manager loves. He did his job. So Frank worked on this play, and I worked—he was with the infielders and I was with the catchers—and we must have spent 45 minutes a day on this drill. We finally got it down to where, you know, at least we were *doing* it the way Stengel wanted. Casey's watching all the time, and finally one day he comes wandering out and he stands there for a while, and then he says, "This ain't gonna work, is it?"

He was something. Back when I was a young coach, just off the roster, the older coaches—Crosetti, Dickey, Jim Turner—would get hold of me on the train when we were traveling someplace. We almost always went by train back in those days, and the coaches would sit with Casey and talk. That is, Casey would talk. He'd sit there and drink and talk damn near all night sometimes. The other coaches didn't like to stay up with him because he'd never let them leave, not all of them.

So the other coaches would corner me and say, "Now, somebody has to stay here and talk with Casey." And I was the newest guy, so I was always elected. I sat with Casey a lot of nights. Sometimes it was fun, sometimes it got a little crazy. Like, one night he said to me, "What do you think of the hit-and-run?"

I said, "Well, you know, if the situation is right and you've got the right hitter facing the right pitcher with the right man on base, I think it's a pretty good play at times."

He tipped his head back and half closed his eyes and looked down his nose at me, and he said, slowly, "It ain't worth a *damn.*"

Then he took off and told me all about why the hit-and-run was no good, how it took the bat out of the hitter's hands, and all that stuff. We must have sat there for two hours while he told me why the hit-and-run wasn't any damn good.

Now, it's maybe a month later and we're on the train again, going somewhere, and it's late, and I'm sitting with him again, and I guess Casey forgot we ever talked about the hit-and-run, because he turns to me and he says, "What do you think of the hit-and-run?"

I'm ready this time. I say, "I don't like it."

He says, "It's a *great* play!" and he spends the next two hours telling me why it's great.

I loved the guy though. You had to love him. I remember a time in Detroit when I was a player, and I got in a fight in a bar. The fight didn't make the papers, but it was a bad fight, and Casey heard about it. I could have been in a lot of trouble. He called me in, and he said, "Where was you?" I told him and I told him what happened. No sense trying to lie to him.

He said, "Well, you know, that's pretty serious. That's pretty late to be out and getting into all that trouble."

I said, yes, it was, and I said it was all my fault. I'd been out with Gene Woodling and Hank Bauer, but I was going to protect them.

"Well," he says, "that's real bad."

I said, "I know it is, Case. But I'll tell you, maybe if you played me more I wouldn't be doing these things."

He just looked at me, and then he said, "You're probably right," and that was the end of it.

I'd talk with him a lot in the mornings before an afternoon game and in the afternoons before a night game. I've always been one of those guys who get to the park real early, and my locker was close to his office. He'd come in and I'd be sitting there putting on my uniform, and he'd growl, "Hey, come in here," and I'd go into his office, and we'd sit and talk, and it was almost always baseball.

But I didn't pattern myself after him. He was out of one mold, and there's no way anyone could copy him because he was so different. There'll never be another Casey.

10

Nonetheless, the baseball writers kept pressing the comparison, Houk versus Stengel, as though Houk were on trial—which in a very real sense he was. Some were quite favorable to Houk. John Drebinger of *The New York Times,* who was in his seventies, had been writing baseball for nearly 40 years and had been a friend of Stengel's when Casey played outfield for John McGraw in the 1920s. Yet he wrote approvingly of Houk and said perceptively that Houk's presence and the departure of Stengel might prove a boon for Mantle. He mentioned an incident that had occurred the previous season in Chicago when Mantle, after popping up, put his head down in disgust and barely trotted to first base. Casey angrily yanked him out of the game, which went fifteen innings before the Yankees lost. Drebinger said he could not imagine Houk exploding publicly at a ballplayer the way Stengel had. Under the younger, more understanding Houk, Drebinger argued, Mantle might emerge at last as the towering player the Yankees had not really had since DiMaggio retired.

Old Drebinger enjoyed sitting and talking baseball with young Houk. One day Houk and Drebby, as he was called, kicked around the subject of "ten-man baseball." This was the term used then for what later came to be called the DH, the designated hitter, which did not become part of the game until more than a decade later. Drebinger told Houk that McGraw had talked about adding a tenth player back in the twenties. Houk in 1961 said he was against the idea, but after the American League adopted the DH in 1973 he grew to like it.

RALPH HOUK:

I was against it back then, but not now. I like it, and I can't understand why the National League hasn't adopted it. I've been told that a majority of the National League clubs are for it, but they need a three-quarters majority to pass it, and there are just enough against it to keep it from passing. But they'll come around. They're going to get tired of seeing those star National League hitters leaving the league and coming over to the American in their last years. Those old stars have drawing power. Imagine if a Stan Musial was still around, and he couldn't play in the field anymore, and he came over to the American League. Imagine what his appearance in a lineup would have meant.

I like the DH. I disagree with people who say it takes strategy away from the game. I think it adds strategy. It was much easier to manage when you didn't have the DH, though I hear just the opposite from National League managers. But when you don't have the DH there are practically automatic bunt situations, almost automatic times to take a pitcher out. If you're behind two runs in the sixth or seventh, you're going to use a pinch-hitter for your pitcher, even if you'd like to leave him in. On the other hand, suppose you have a star pitcher in there and he's not going well and you'd kind of like to get him out of there without causing a fuss or a lot of second-guessing. In the National League, you say, "Hey, sorry, gotta pinch hit for you. Gotta take you out." In the American, it's a little more difficult. It's not an automatic situation anymore. It's a decision.

With the DH, every inning is a run-potential inning. You don't have those innings where you know the pitcher is going to be hitting second or third, which means you can feel pretty safe trying to squeeze another inning out of your pitcher. With the pitcher batting in a game, you know he's going to come up at least three times, and maybe four, and that means most of the time you're playing with three or four dead innings. You know the pitcher is going to bat, and you know he's going to be an out. You can work around a hitter to set it up so that the pitcher leads off an inning, which is easy to do. That leaves them with only one other out to work with before the third out ends the inning. With the DH, you face an offensive inning every time you walk out there. You have to make every move with your pitchers knowing that. There are no more innings when you can manage without really thinking about it, when it's more or less automatic.

On the other hand, sometimes a pitcher is going pretty good but he's hurt by errors and now he's behind and you need runs, so you have to take him out for a pinch-hitter. You can't leave him in, even though he's pitching good. The move is forced on you. With the DH, you don't take him out until you want to.

I think the manager has more decisions to make with the DH. And it keeps players in the game who attract fans. The one thing I don't like about it is that it can hurt some good all-around athletes who maybe aren't all that great at the plate. They're signing kids now who can't really field, just hoping they'll become a good DH.

The media's critical interest in Houk continued but even so, spring training went serenely enough until the Yankees began playing exhibition games. The first one, Houk's first formal game as manager of the Yankees, was against their crosstown St. Petersburg rivals, the Cardinals, in Al Lang Field down near the waterfront. The Yankees lost 6–1. That meant nothing, of course; it was just a spring exhibition game. But the Yankees lost to the Cardinals again the next day, and the day after that they lost to Minnesota when Earl Battey, the Twins' catcher, hit a grand-slam home run in the last half of the ninth inning.

Three straight losses at the beginning of a season, any season, even an exhibition season, are as glaringly obvious as a bandaged nose. People were beginning to make little remarks. Then the Yankees lost a fourth straight and, to make that defeat even more grievous, Luis Arroyo, pitching batting practice, was hit on the left forearm, his pitching arm, by a line drive off the bat of Jesse Gonder. He was led off the field and taken to a hospital, where X-rays disclosed a fracture of the ulna.

RALPH HOUK:

That scared me half to death. I saw it happen. I was watching from behind the batting cage. It was a bad situation, because I was counting heavily on Louie. When I got to him there was a big knot on his arm where the ball hit. It looked awful bad, but Louie said, "Skip, don't worry. I'll be all right." I made some kind of a joke, like "With that stuff you throw, we don't have to worry too much," but I was scared. Here we'd lost four in a row, and now my best relief pitcher was gone.

I was very fond of Arroyo. I had known him since I managed in San Juan in the winter league in Puerto Rico in the 1950s. We became pretty good friends and he was a great help to me there, and not just pitching. We had a lot of players and only five of them could be from the States. Otherwise a team could have as many players as it wanted, and I'll never forget opening night when we lined up along the third-base line before the game. I swear, our line of players went right down the foul line to the fence. And you never saw so many different uniforms on one team in your life.

The baseball players down there in the Caribbean knew English better than we did Spanish, but I tried to learn a little Spanish anyway just to know what was going on. I've forgotten it all now, but it was mostly baseball talk, just enough to get by. I had a coach named Luis Olmo, an old Dodger outfielder, and he'd interpret what I'd say in meetings, and so on. One day Arroyo came to me and said, "Skip, watch out. That guy might be trying to get your job." I still don't know whether he was or not. I always got along great with Luis Olmo. But evidently he was saying some things in there that I didn't know about.

Louie looked different from the rest of the players. If you met him on the street you'd never have known he was a ballplayer. He looked like a businessman. He was short and a little roly-poly, and he smoked big Havana cigars. He was a good-looking guy, with wavy dark hair that was getting a little gray. He always wore good suits, and he was smooth. He looked like a guy that might own a bank somewhere.

He pitched in the winter leagues and he played in the minors for a long time and he was in the National League for a while before we got him in 1960. He had gone back down to the minors then, and I think it was Bill Skiff, the Yankee scout, who saw him in the International League and recommended him to Weiss. He came up to the Yankees in the middle of the season in 1960 and did a real good job for us. He had learned how to control the screwball, and he was great with it. The other clubs didn't seem to realize it but even though Louie was lefthanded, he was very effective against righthanded hitters. I expected him to be a big help to me in 1961 because I think I'd rather have an outstanding short reliever like Arroyo than a starting pitcher. It's not just the games he wins or saves for you, it's what he gives to the club. He helps you win in other ways. Let's say you're losing a ball game and in the eighth inning you rally and go ahead. Now you bring in your relief pitcher. If you don't have that good end man and you can't stop the other club and they come back and score and beat you, that hurts your whole club, the morale of the players. The fact that you came back and were winning made everybody happy, and now you blow it and, hell, everybody goes into the clubhouse down. If that happens three or four times it affects the whole team. Nobody plays well. They start getting on each other. But if you have the good short man you can use in those tight situations at the end of a game, and you *know* this guy is going to come in and shut the other club down, the whole team just plays better ball. You know you're a better club.

One of the reasons we didn't win much in spring training that year was that we weren't bringing in the good short man in the eighth inning when we had a two- or three-run lead. That's what a guy like Arroyo can do for you.

So when Louie got hurt it seemed awfully bad, but the scare only lasted two or three days. It was a hairline fracture, and the swelling started to go down, and the doctors said he'd be ready by the time the season began. He was throwing again before the end of March.

And then we won the next day. Boy, that was a big win. We were beginning to wonder whether we'd ever win a ball game. I had to cover up the fact that I was concerned, but you got to be concerned. Normally, you're never really concerned about winning or losing in spring training because you have a set way to play the games. In other words, you want to win but you don't set up your club to win. You're giving your players work, you're letting your pitchers stay in to get the innings they need, you're not pinch-hitting the way you might, you're not worrying about who's in the field in the late innings. But when you lose four straight, especially at the beginning, you have to be concerned.

After that lone victory, the Yankees lost four more in a row to send their spring-training record to a depressing 1–8. After two infield errors in the eleventh inning cost the Yankees one game, a reporter who knew about Houk's temper wrote, "The good manager is still maintaining his even disposition, but a blow-up can't be too far away." That afternoon the Yankees played the Orioles, who themselves had lost six in a row, and lost again. Houk, still outwardly calm, claimed there'd been three or four games the Yankees could have won if he'd been going all out for victory. "There are things you've got to find out about your players," he argued, "and spring training is the time to find them out."

To reporters his explanation rang a bit hollow, and the critics began to sharpen their knives. The implication was clear: maybe Houk wasn't up to the job. Maybe Stengel's shoes really were too big for this unknown rookie manager to fill. Even the gentlemanly Al Lopez, manager of the Chicago White Sox, had a comment. "We all lost seven players in the draft," Lopez said "but the Yankees were hit the hardest. And they no longer have Stengel. Don't get me wrong. Houk could very well prove to be a fine manager. But any club that loses a Casey Stengel is losing a great manager."

The Stengel–Houk thing grew as the Yankees kept losing. Some people wondered aloud if Houk was calling Casey for advice. Jimmy Cannon, the renowned *New York Post* columnist, assumed that he was, despite Houk's repeated insistence that he was doing his own thing.

"I'm not another Casey," Houk protested. "I worked for him most of my baseball life, and no man ever had a better teacher. I'm grateful to him for all the help he gave me, but I'm not Casey. I won't talk like him or act like him."

That wasn't enough. Arthur Daley, who in the spring of 1949 had expressed doubts about Stengel's ability after he succeeded Bucky Harris as Yankee manager, now had similar doubts about Houk succeeding Stengel.

RALPH HOUK:

Arthur didn't like me much at first. He got to like me later, but that first year he was still a Casey man. I think I was too young for Arthur to like me as a manager. And, of course, he didn't come to the ball park much. In Florida I didn't see his columns that often, but you can tell what's being written about you by the letters you get. When the club goes bad, your mail does, too, and a lot of it said, "I agree with Arthur Daley." That spring I certainly was not a Casey Stengel in Arthur Daley's mind.

Hamey was more nervous about the Yankees' spring-training performance than Houk was. Hamey was a new boy on the block, too, and he was getting just a bit edgy, but losing eight of the first nine games didn't sit well with anyone. In one game against Baltimore, Houk kept his regulars in the lineup all the way in an effort to break the losing spell, but a rousing Yankee rally in the ninth inning was snuffed out when Oriole first baseman Jim Gentile made a sensational play on a hard drive by Mantle for the final out. It was that kind of spring.

Mantle was playing very well, going all out in every exhibition game as though to justify Houk's faith in him. He was hitting beautifully. The day after Gentile robbed him of that ninth-inning hit, he had a homer, a double and a single as the Yankees beat the Dodgers for their second victory of the spring. But the Yankee pitching was becoming a question mark. In one game, Houk let Ditmar go six innings and he gave up six runs.

Still, it was early.

RALPH HOUK:

I wasn't all that worried. It's true our pitching didn't look good, but in a lot of games that was because I was bringing in people who weren't ready to throw hard yet. Most managers do that in spring training; you're giving your players work, and you end up losing about as many as you win. And that's okay in spring training. I don't like to have a real outstanding spring because when you're winning all the time in the spring you tend to overlook the things you're doing wrong. But you don't like to lose all the time either. A .500 spring is ideal. You're not hurting the confidence of your players and you're also seeing the mistakes that have to be corrected if you're going to have a good season.

But, jeez, that spring we couldn't win a damn game. Mickey and Yogi would come by and say, "Don't worry, Ralph, we'll start winning," and Hamey would say, "Don't worry, don't worry." But I knew Roy was getting concerned. He tried not to act like it—he'd say, "Oh, don't worry, Ralph"—but shit, boy, I could tell. He was getting *nervous.* We'd lose another and he couldn't help it, he'd say, "My God, Ralph." Hey, we were both new in our jobs. And we lost *eight* of the first nine.

We were getting to the point in spring training where I was beginning to play the regulars all nine innings every other day, or almost every other day. My theory ordinarily was not to play the regulars more than two or three at bats in a game until the last week or so of spring training. This was a little early, but I was getting anxious, no question about that. I needed to win a ball game or two to get the press off the subject. After that one and eight start we played about .500 ball the rest of the spring, but our overall won-lost record still looked bad, and the mail was starting to pick up.

One of the writers who had been particularly critical of Houk was a feisty little red-mustached reporter from the *New York World-Telegram and Sun* named Joe King. King was a bright man and a good writer, but he had a somewhat bristly personality, and he and Houk didn't get along too well. Bob Fishel, seeking to mend public relations fences, arranged a small dinner party at which Hamey, Houk and King could get together and talk things over.

RALPH HOUK:

There was a little restaurant out by the dog track, and we all went there to have dinner. I guess we were still losing at the time, and I was thinking about the game we'd dropped that day and the one coming up tomorrow, and figuring what I'm going to do with this player and that one, and now I have to go to dinner with this writer and worry about getting him on my side. I wasn't in the greatest mood, that's for sure.

We sat down, and we're going to have a nice quiet evening, a drink or two, a good dinner and a little talk. I think Joe may have had a couple of snorts before he got there, because I know he started getting on me about the team right away. He just kept at it, giving me a kind of rough time.

Finally, he said, "Have you asked Casey what to do?"

I said, "No, I haven't."

"Why not?"

"I'm managing the team."

He said, "Well, when was the last time you called him?"

I said, "I haven't called him."

He said, "Don't tell me you haven't called him."

I was getting madder and madder, and I said, "Are you saying I'm a liar?"

He didn't say anything and I blew my top. "Piss on you," I said. "I don't need you."

Then *he* got mad, and he got up and stomped out of the restaurant. Some peace conference. Poor Hamey was saying, "Oh, my god. Oh, my god."

And we never did get our food.

11

A truce was worked out with Joe King, but Houk faced another crisis that spring. Ryne Duren, one of the Yankee relief pitchers, was an alcoholic. He later stopped drinking and today works extensively at counseling and helping other alcoholics. Ordinarily an amiable, intelligent man, Duren became obstreperous and physically aggressive when he drank. He had been behaving fairly well that spring but one night he got royally drunk, threw a chair out of a hotel window and at four in the morning banged loudly on Houk's hotel-room door, yelling for him to come out.

Duren liked Houk. He had pitched for him in Denver after failing to make it in the major leagues with Baltimore and Kansas City, and he had done well, moving up to the Yankees in 1958 as a relief pitcher. He had an amazing fastball and erratic control, which made batters uneasy, particularly since Duren didn't see too well (he wore thick eyeglasses). He pitched very well in relief in 1958 and 1959, but in 1960 he was much too wild and didn't do as well. During the winter Houk had talked about changing Duren into a starting pitcher in 1961. The big pitcher was one of the first players to praise Houk openly after he succeeded Stengel. "We all liked Casey," Duren said, "and there's no denying he was a great manager. But I think the other players feel the way I do. We can win with Ralph."

Now he was pounding on Houk's door at four in the morning. Houk quieted him down and got him to bed and said nothing about the incident to anyone but Hamey. None of the baseball writers were aware of the disturbance, nor did they know that Houk called a chastened Duren on the carpet the next day, gave him a bawling out and fined him $200. Duren's salary at the time was $17,000, which means that the $200 fine was equivalent to at least a $2,000 fine for a ballplayer today.

A week or two later when the Yankees were playing exhibition games on the east coast of Florida, Duren was chatting with some old friends on the Kansas City Athletics and told them about getting drunk and being fined. Some time later a press-association reporter covering the Athletics heard Kansas City players talking about Duren and ended up writing a big story about Duren's fling and the big fine imposed on him by Houk.

Back in St. Petersburg on the other side of Florida, the writers covering the Yankees were miffed that they had been beaten on the most sensational story of the spring by a writer who wasn't even with the club. When they confronted Houk, he admitted, "Yeah, I did fine Duren. He stayed out late a couple of times. But this all happened a couple of weeks ago. He's behaved good ever since." The Yankee writers were still annoyed that they hadn't been told.

RALPH HOUK:

That was bad, not telling the press. That was a mistake. But I was trying to protect the player, and I didn't think about the writers getting chewed out by their papers for not having the story. I always tried to protect my ballplayers. I think you get more out of them if you protect them rather than ridicule them in public.

Ryne had gotten drunk several times that spring. I had him in Denver and he was drinking back then, too. This night in St. Pete, when he was making all the noise, I told him, "I'll talk to you in the morning," and I got him out of there. Next day, I said, "Ryne, all the players know what you're doing, and you know we have rules. This has been going on too long. I can't let you get away with it anymore. It's not fair to the other players. I'm going to fine you." He was apologetic, all sorry and everything, and I said, "I'm not going to tell the writers." That was a mistake. But I was thinking of him and his family and all the bad publicity that would come out. A couple of years before that, when we won the 1958 pennant, we were coming home on the train and Ryne got drunk. He came roaring through the car, raising hell. I was sitting there with a big cigar in my mouth that I was about to light. He said, "I've always wanted to push a cigar into your face," and he did. I got up and grabbed him. I didn't hit him, but I got him by the throat and pushed him down, and that was the end of it. Except that Leonard Schecter of the *New York Post* wrote the story and it was splashed all over the place. I thought that was bad.

So I didn't say anything about this incident, except to Roy Hamey. But now the Yankee writers, they're all madder than hell at me because they're down here covering the ball club and their papers are asking them, What is this? This other guy breaks a story like that, and you don't even know what's going on? I learned a lesson from that one. The Yankee writers should have had the story.

But you see, Ryne and I were close. He'd done a great job for me at Denver as a starter, and you'll keep the devil if he can win for you. I recommended him to Casey, and Casey brought him up and made him a reliever. He was pretty good for a while. Damn, nobody threw a ball harder—he could throw a ball as fast as anybody I've ever seen— but he couldn't see. He wore these thick glasses, and he never knew where the ball was going. He was the only person I ever saw who wore his glasses to take a shower, that's how bad his eyes were. Batters didn't like to hit against him.

He could be funny, too. We'd have these meetings to go over the hitters on the team we're about to play. We'd be discussing how to pitch to this hitter and that one, and Ryne would say, very seriously, "You have to mix it up with this guy. Keep the ball in here and move it out there." Hell, Ryne had only one way to pitch to a hitter. He reared back and fired the damn ball, and we'd just pray he'd get it over. And here he's saying you got to put it in here and out there. It got to be a big joke with the other pitchers. We'd be having a serious meeting, going over the hitters, and Whitey or somebody would say, "Ryne, how would *you* pitch this guy?" and they'd all break up laughing.

But he was a fine fellow. He'd never show up at the ball park loaded. You might smell it on his breath once in a while, but I can't say I ever saw him pitch drunk, like maybe an Ellis Kinder used to. It would happen quick afterward—real quick. The odd thing is, and he'll tell you this himself now that he doesn't drink any more, I honestly believe he could get drunk on two martinis, just like that. It was unbelievable. Two drinks and he was just terrible. It got to the point where the other players didn't want to be around him.

It was too bad. He pitched pretty good that spring, but he was still drinking, and in time he ruined his career, his first marriage, everything. But sober, he was great, one of the nicest people you'd ever meet, give you the shirt off his back, do anything for you. That's the way he is now. He hasn't had a drink for years. He's married again, and he does a lot of valuable work with alcoholics now.

At that point Duren was still a long way from recognizing alcohol as his problem (as Houk said, "After I fined him I imagine he didn't drink again for, oh, maybe four or five hours"), and he took exception to assumptions that he had been fined for heavy drinking. "Houk made no reference to drinking when he chewed me out," he said, defensively. He did concede that his chances of being shifted from relief pitching to a starting role weren't as good as they had been when Houk mentioned the possibility during the offseason. "But not because of this," Duren protested. "It's because of the changes on our staff." He was thinking of the excellent pitching of young Sheldon, who won the James P. Dawson Award as the outstanding Yankee rookie that spring, and of Arroyo's broken arm, which meant that Houk needed Duren in the bullpen at least until Arroyo was fit again.

The continuing pressure on Houk eased a little when another controversial Yankee-related event occurred back in New York. A little more than four months after he had retired from the Yankees with a five-year contract as a "consultant," George Weiss was named president of the new National League club in New York. Under his contract with the Yankees he was not supposed to take a general manager's job with another big league team for five years. Technically, he was not becoming the new team's general manager; he was to be its president. But it was obvious that his duties would be all but identical with those he had when he was general manager of the Yankees.

Topping and Webb were annoyed but they did not challenge Weiss's right to take the new job. Topping, keeping perfect—or nearly perfect—control over his feelings, said, "Our contract with Weiss calls for him to act in an advisory capacity for us through 1965. He is not eligible to become general manager of any other team, but the contract does not prevent him from holding some other office. As far as we're concerned, he's in the clear." Then, throwing a little jab at his former employee, Topping added, "Whether he's in the clear under the rules of baseball will be something for the commissioner to decide."

Weiss reacted by quoting from the agreement: ". . . may accept employment in any office or capacity other than full-time general manager with another baseball club." Under that agreement, according to Weiss, if he took such employment the Yankees agreed not to call on him for any service that would conflict with his duties in his new job. "This makes it very clear," Weiss said, "that if there is any conflict it would have to be created by the Yankees."

The ill-feeling between Weiss and the Yankees was also evident in his reversal of attitude toward New York's plans to build a stadium for the new team. When he was with the Yankees he had vigorously opposed the idea. Now Weiss said, his phlegmatic face expressionless, "I have a different picture now. With the additional information I have received, I think the new stadium is a good deal for both the city and the club."

A city official had suggested earlier that the new team might play its home games in Yankee Stadium until its new park was ready. Webb said, "I'd be surprised if Weiss asked to be allowed to play in the Stadium after the way he attacked the idea of a new team playing there when he was our general manager." Topping suggested that the old Polo Grounds, empty for three years since the Giants left for San Francisco after the 1957 season, would be a better temporary home for the new club. When asked again if the Yankees would make an issue of Weiss receiving $35,000 a year from them (his "consultant" fee) while at the same time acting as president of the new club, Topping said, "Absolutely not. The Yankees couldn't care less." Again he slid in a dig. "If there's a question about Weiss receiving payment from us while also drawing salary on his new job," he said, "that's something for Commissioner Frick to decide. We have no further interest in the matter."

But Weiss had stuck it to them and there was nothing Topping or Webb could do about it, and they knew it. Besides, they had a reason for not antagonizing the new club. Fort Lauderdale, which was building a new spring-training stadium, said it would be ready for the Yankees the following year, in the spring of 1962. But the Yankees could not leave their old base in St. Petersburg with impunity unless another big league team could be found to take over the training site there. The antagonism between the Yankees and Weiss was submerged under a mutually satisfying solution: the new team said it would take over the Yankee training base in 1962, and the Yankees were free to go to Fort Lauderdale long before their contract with St. Petersburg actually expired.

Now, suddenly, it was a fact. The Yankees, who had begun training in St. Petersburg in Babe Ruth's day, were leaving. On Wednesday, April 5, they beat the Cardinals 5–4 in eleven innings in their last exhibition game in Florida in 1961, their last home game ever in St. Petersburg. Fred Lieb, an ancient sportswriter who had written baseball for New York newspapers before World War I, threw out the first ball in the game that "ended their long link to St. Petersburg." One more change for 1961.

Houk was optimistic in talking about his team as the Yankees broke camp to head for St. Louis and three last exhibition games there with the Cardinals before returning to New York for the opening day of the season. Mantle had hit the ball hard and consistently throughout the spring. Ford, beginning his tenth season with the Yankees, had thrown with strength and consistency, and a day or two earlier had pitched a shutout against the Cincinnati Reds, the first complete game by a Yankee pitcher in spring training in three years. Howard, doing much of the catching as Berra slowly worked himself into shape, had been extremely impressive; seven baserunners had tried to steal on him, and Howard had thrown out all seven.

Houk's infield—Skowron at first, Richardson at second, Kubek at short and probably Boyer at third—was solid. Mantle looked great, and while Maris had not hit well in the exhibition games, Roger seldom hit impressively in the spring. Hector Lopez was considered a solid fixture in left field. Ditmar and Turley had not looked good on the mound, but Terry and Coates had; so had Sheldon and the even younger Stafford, who rejoined the club in March after six months of Army service. Arroyo was over his hairline fracture and was throwing again and his arm seemed strong. Even the attendance at the spring exhibition games was up nearly 20 percent despite the team's poor record.

Forgetting his earlier complaints that the club had been badly hurt by expansion, Houk said flatly that the Yankees would win the pennant again. He had almost exactly the same starting team as the one that had begun the 1960 season, the same catching, the same infield, the same outfield. The bench looked thinner, and so did the pitching, although Houk disagreed with the latter appraisal.

"The pitching staff is better," Houk said. "We're in much better shape than a year ago. Ford's arm hasn't looked this good in I don't know how many years. We have Arroyo now [who didn't join the 1960 team until midseason] and he's coming along nicely. We have Stafford now [who also joined the club during the 1960 season]. We have Sheldon, who has definitely won a spot. The rest of the staff is set, and so is the rest of the team. I'm ready to go with what we have. I don't expect any trades."

He had indicated earlier that Berra would alternate with Howard behind the plate. And while he had toyed with the idea of platooning Boyer and Johnson at third base, it now appeared that he was leaning toward Boyer, since Johnson, who couldn't compare with Boyer in the field, hadn't hit well in spring training. To fill gaps on the roster caused by the expansion draft, Houk replaced Dale Long with rookie Lee Thomas, a big young lefthanded-hitting outfielder–first baseman, and Bob Cerv with rookie Jack Reed, a slick-fielding outfielder who couldn't hit with anything like Cerv's power. In place of Shantz and Grba were Danny McDevitt and young Sheldon. To replace Duke

Maas he had looked at Billy Short and Johnny James, who had been with the Yankees off and on for two or three seasons, as well as Ted Wieand. Then just before the season began he got Maas back in a trade that sent reserve shortstop Fritz Brickell to the Angels.

Brickell's was a sad story. Only five feet, five and a half inches tall and 157 pounds, he played briefly with the Yankees in 1958 and 1959 but spent most of his time in the minor leagues. In spring training in 1961 he played very well but never figured seriously in Houk's plans. The Yankees' reserve shortstop was the veteran DeMaestri, an excellent fielder who had been a regular with Kansas City for seven years before coming to the Yankees in the Maris trade after the 1959 season. DeMaestri played very little for the Yanks in 1960 (he came to bat only 35 times all season) but Houk thought highly of him and had persuaded Hamey to give DeMaestri the raise that kept him with the team for another year.

So Brickell had no chance to stick with the Yankees, and a week before opening day he was traded to the Angels for Maas, whom the Angels had picked in the expansion draft. Maas had a sore arm, but he had been 5–1 in relief in 1960, and the Yankees felt he was a better bet than the 26-year-old Brickell, a perennial rookie whom everyone liked but who no one thought was ever going to make it big in the majors.

Poor Brickell. His father Fred, who had been a National League outfielder in the late 1920s and early 1930s, died one week after his son was traded away from the Yankees. Fritz opened the season as the Angels' regular shortstop but he played in only 27 games, batted only .122 and was sent to the minors. He never played major league ball again. Four years later, on the day after the 1965 World Series ended, Brickell died of cancer at the untimely age of 30.

In St. Louis, away from the Florida sun, the weather turned cold and wet and the weekend was miserable. On Friday night the Cardinals beat the Yanks, 8–6. Mantle hit a homer and Arroyo pitched an inning or so in his first appearance of the year, but it wasn't much of a game for the Yanks. Saturday was worse, a cold, windblown, frostbitten, drizzling day. Mantle hit another home run, his seventh of the spring, but the Cardinals won 16–12 to put Houk's spring-training record at 9–19. The weather was so bad on Sunday that the teams did not even try to play this final game of the exhibition schedule. The Yankees climbed into a plane and flew back to New York to await the opening of the season.

PART THREE

The Tough Pennant Race

12

On Tuesday, April 11, six months after he was named manager of the Yankees, Houk took his team onto the field at Yankee Stadium to begin the regular season. He got up at seven that morning, ate breakfast at his home in Saddle River, left the house at 8:30—game time was 1:30 P.M.—drove over the George Washington Bridge and reached the Stadium by 9:15. The toll taker at the bridge recognized Houk and wished him luck. "But he took my fifty cents, just as he always did," Houk said.

RALPH HOUK:

I was nervous, oh yeah, yeah. There were so many things going through my mind, lots of things. You're that way usually on opening day but this one—this was the first day I was going in to manage the club. That was a tremendous, unbelievable feeling. I could hardly wait to get there.

I don't know how to explain it. It was just a feeling that you wanted the game to *start*, right now, right away. And it seemed like five weeks before it did.

Then I wanted to get it over with. I wanted to win it—I wanted to win it so bad.

Reaching the stadium four hours before game time was standard procedure for Houk, who as a coach under Stengel had always come in early. Now when he arrived in the all-but-empty clubhouse he found that Casey's old office had been completely redecorated. Gone were the pictures and mementoes from Casey's reign. The room had been done over in gray paneling, and a modern desk stood in place of the old rolltop that had served Yankee managers since the Stadium first opened its doors in April 1923, when Miller Huggins was in command. Since then, Bob Shawkey, Joe McCarthy, Bill Dickey, Johnny Neun, Bucky Harris and Stengel had all used the rolltop desk. With Houk, it was gone.

The redecorating had not been his idea. Pete Sheehy, the old clubhouse man who served the Yankees from the 1920s until his death in 1985, grinned like a kid showing off a surprise and led Houk into his new quarters. "I think Pete was responsible for the whole thing," Houk said.

Opening day was windy and very cold, and the crowd was a meager 14,607. The players' hands stung during batting practice, and there were a lot of "ouches" and shaking of fingers and blowing on hands. But the Yankees were relaxed, seemingly unconcerned about the up-coming game and the pennant race. A good part of the pregame conversation dwelt on the finish of the Masters golf tournament the day before, when Arnold Palmer had taken a double-bogie six on the last hole to lose to Gary Player by a stroke ("I thought sixes only happened to other people," Palmer said afterward).

There was a lot of ceremony before the game. Commissioner Frick and American League president Joe Cronin gave rings and watches to the Yankee players for winning the American League championship in 1960. Two pennants were raised on the flagpole in center field: one for 1960, the Yankees' twenty-fifth championship, and one for their first, the 1921 flag they had won 40 years earlier. Dick Young of the *New York Daily News*, chairman of the local chapter of the Baseball Writers Association, presented Maris with his Most Valuable Player award. Mrs. John McGraw, Mrs. Babe Ruth and Mrs. Lou Gehrig, three baseball widows, sat together in a box next to the Yankee dugout. Frank Kridel, a hotel executive, formally welcomed Houk as new manager and presented him with a floral piece. Borough President James Lyons of the Bronx threw out the first ball, and the great, explosive 1961 season began.

Very quietly.

Pedro Ramos of the Twins pitched a three-hit shutout and beat Ford and the Yankees 6–0. Ford himself had a two-hit shutout through six innings, but in the seventh he gave up a homer, a double, a walk, a single and three runs. Terry relieved him and gave up two more runs in the eighth. Coates relieved Terry and gave up another run in the ninth. The Yankee bats were quiescent. Berra singled in the first inning and Skowron in the fourth (after Mantle and Maris, batting fourth and fifth, both struck out). Ford had an infield hit in the fifth, and that was all. The only Yankee threat came in the second inning after a Minnesota outfielder dropped an easy fly ball hit by Maris. Kubek walked then and Boyer hit an outfield fly that moved Maris to third base, but Ford grounded out to end the inning, and that was that. Arthur Daley wrote, "The Yankees behaved as ineffectually in the chilly North as they had during spring training in the broiling South."

That night the Boston Celtics defeated the St. Louis Hawks 121–112 to win the National Basketball Association championship, the fifth straight NBA title for the near-legendary Celtics. This was the team of Bill Russell, Bob Cousy, Tom Heinsohn, K. C. Jones, Sam Jones, Jim Loscutoff, Bill Sharman, Frank Ramsey, Gene Conley. Yet there was far less attention paid to the Celtics' victory than to the opening day of the baseball season. *The New York Times* didn't even send a reporter to the NBA championship; instead, it used a wire service report that ran for little more than half a column on a back page of the sports section.

But if the Yankees and baseball upstaged the Celtics and basketball, both sports were upstaged by a major world event. Just as the baseball season began, a Russian cosmonaut named Yuri Gagarin orbited the earth three times in a space capsule, the first human being ever to circle the globe in a spacecraft. The media were filled with stories about it. One headline said, "New Era in War May Be Opened, with Space Ships Used in Battle." Star Wars was on people's minds even then. The Russians were circling the earth, and the United States had yet to put a man in space.

Adolf Eichmann went on trial in Israel for crimes committed under Hitler during the Holocaust. He said at the trial that he "just took orders" and would have killed his own father if he had been told to do so. On the night of opening day, Jacqueline Kennedy, hitherto almost an unknown quantity, made her first extended appearance on television. Her husband had gone to the first game of the season in Washington and had rooted shamelessly for the expansion Senators as they lost to the White Sox, 4–3. He patiently signed autographs, too, leading a baseball writer to comment, "Mickey Mantle ought to take notice."

Mrs. Kennedy was part of an hour-long TV show during which the president led a guided tour of the White House, primarily to show how he and his staff functioned. No president had ever done that before. Mrs. Kennedy appeared on camera during the last part of the show, and TV critics praised her "voice of haunting delicacy" and described her as "a lady of captivating graciousness and charm." Thus, another new element, Jackie Kennedy, entered the American consciousness.

The Yankees, who had no game scheduled on Wednesday, held a two-hour workout at the Stadium and hit ball after ball over the fence. A sportswriter named Robert Teague mentioned this to Houk, who replied, "They always hit them in the seats in batting practice. We're waiting for them to start doing it in a game." Teague (who later went into broadcasting) was black. The next day Charlie Sifford became the first black golfer to play in a PGA event in the South. He shot a 68 to take the first-round lead in the Greensboro Open in North Carolina. A black sportswriter and a black golfer in the same week— what was the world coming to?

On that Wednesday, President Kennedy replied to rumors that American forces were preparing to invade Cuba to unseat Fidel Castro by declaring that United States armed forces would not intervene in Cuba "under any circumstances." He was just as emphatic when asked if the United States would approve an attempt by Cuban exiles in Florida to mount an offensive against Castro. Kennedy said, "I would be opposed to mounting such an offensive." He was splitting hairs. "Such an offensive" could mean an offensive from a point within the United States. As he spoke, Cuban exiles were preparing an offensive with CIA help at a staging area in the Caribbean. But Kennedy's remarks were reassuring to those who didn't want America involved in a military action.

The Yankees' slow drift into the 1961 season continued on hold Thursday when their scheduled game with the Twins was rained out. On Friday, with no game scheduled, they traveled up the Hudson River to West Point to play an exhibition game against Army. The high point for the West Pointers came in the first inning when a Cadet pitcher struck out Mantle and Maris in succession. The euphoria didn't last. The Yankees won 14–0, and a sardonic headline said, "Cadets Hold Rivals to 18 Hits." Houk used Maas, Arroyo and Sheldon against Army, and the three gave up only two hits.

The Yanks played in their second game of the season, on Saturday against Kansas City. Bud Daley, a lefthander, started for the Athletics. In the second inning Skowron singled and Maris, now batting sixth, walked. Daley successfully picked Skowron off second, but when Moose broke for third base the Kansas City shortstop's throw to third was dropped, and Skowron was safe. Daley then hit Howard to fill the bases and walked Boyer to force in a run. Bob Turley hit a sacrifice fly for a second run. Daley walked Kubek to load the bases again, and Richardson drove in two more runs with a single, knocking Daley out of the game. Turley, who started for the Yankees, led 5–0 on a two-hitter after seven innings, but with one out in the eighth he walked one batter and hit Dick Howser, Kansas City's "sensational young shortstop," with a fastball that richocheted off Howser's batting helmet. Howser shrugged off the beaning, which was obviously accidental, and trotted down to first base, but Turley seemed unnerved. He gave up two doubles and three runs before Houk relieved him with the score now 5–3. Stafford got the third out in the inning and held Kansas City down in the ninth, and Ralph Houk had his first regular-season victory as manager of the Yankees.

"Oh, jeez, that was a good one to win," Houk said with relief, but the weather stayed bad and again everything stalled. The season just wouldn't get moving. On Sunday a doubleheader with Kansas City was rained out, and Houk's carefully prepared pitching rotation—he had planned to use Ford, Turley, Ditmar and Terry in order during the first weeks of the season—was all fouled up.

On Monday, six days after Opening Day, the Yankees squeezed in their third game of the season. It was bitterly cold, and only 1,947 spectators were in the vast, chilly Stadium. News bulletins that morning had carried the unsettling news that anti-Castro forces had invaded Cuba. Even so, it was a heartening day for Houk's ball club as Ford pitched a complete game and shut out the Athletics 3–0 for his first win. Mantle, burning with frustration after going hitless in the first two games of the season, blasted a two-run homer in the first inning and batted in another run with a single to account for all three Yankee runs.

That night the cold weather turned wet and Tuesday's game was canceled. It was still cold and wet on Wednesday, and that day's game was postponed, too. Nine days into the season now, and the Yankees had played only three games. It was a damp, dreary, dismal week, with the war news from Cuba casting a pall over everything.

As the news broke on radio and television and in glaring headlines in the newspapers, international antagonisms flared up. The Cuban representative at the United Nations charged that the United States had armed the invading forces, which was dismissed at first as Communist propaganda. The Soviet Union repeated the charges, criticized the United States, said it would help Castro and warned that war might come to America. Kennedy warned the Soviets to stay out of it, and Secretary of State Dean Rusk declared that America would not intervene in Cuba, although he said the "sympathy of the nation" was with Castro's foes. Editorials began defending America's apparent role in the invasion, declaring that the United States stand had its roots in the Monroe Doctrine, which was designed to keep Western Hemisphere countries free from European intrusion. Kennedy said the United States would "not allow Communism to take over Cuba."

The editorials and Kennedy's declaration quickly became academic as news that the rebels had suffered a devastating defeat at the Bay of Pigs began to come out of Cuba. At first, Castro's claim that the attack had been crushed was dismissed as more propaganda, but by Thursday it was obvious that he was telling the truth. The Cuban dictator called the failure of the rebels "a damaging blow to the United States," and as the extent of the disaster became known, even political experts in Washington agreed it was a major setback to American foreign policy. (Prime Minister Nehru of India, whose collarless jacket became an "in" fashion for American men in the sixties, said the United States had encouraged the invasion.)

Survivors of the anti-Castro forces bitterly accused the CIA of what they called "monumental mismanagement," saying the CIA failed dismally to coordinate plans among different segments of the invading forces and that it had ignored warnings from knowledgeable anti-Castro people against attempting the invasion at that point.

By this time the Bay of Pigs affair was being called a "debacle," and the United States made no further overt efforts to undercut Castro. The Soviet Union, for the time being, stayed away from the Caribbean, and the threat of war shifted to Algeria, then a French possession, where Charles de Gaulle crushed an attempt by rebel French officers to take control of the colonial government. Algeria soon went independent, along with other African areas that had been controlled by European powers.

It was quite a week, and during it, on Thursday, April 20, the 1961 season really began for Houk and the Yankees. Until then, it had been mostly just frustrated waiting. In sunny Florida they had played 26 games in 26 days. In the gloomy North, Houk's team had been idle nine times in fourteen days.

RALPH HOUK:

That was awful. It was terrible. We were beginning to play real good at the end there in Florida, and the press was starting to get off us. Then came all those rainouts, and all our pitchers needed work again, and we didn't have a place to throw underneath the stands in the old Stadium.

When we left Florida we were in better shape physically and mentally than we'd been the year before, and I felt there was no way we wouldn't take the pennant. And then we couldn't play at all, just sit around and wait. It was only natural that sportswriters looking for something to write about on a rainy day would come around and ask me about the club, but now some of them were saying this guy Houk isn't going to get the job done. The Bay of Pigs stuff took a lot of attention off us—nobody was talking much about baseball—but the sportswriters were still after me. They kept asking: What are you gonna do? What are you going to change?

There was nothing to do, nothing to change. Nothing to do but wait.

It was still cold on Thursday, but clear and sunny, and the Yanks got in a doubleheader with the new Los Angeles Angels at the Stadium. A modest crowd of 7,000 was on hand, but half of them left the chilly ball park long before the end of the second game. In the first inning of the first game Mantle rammed his second home run of the season 12 rows deep in right field to give the Yanks a 2–0 lead. The Angels tied the score, but in the fifth inning Mantle hit another homer to put the Yankees ahead 5–2. They went on to win 7–5, with Mantle driving in five of the seven runs, and they won the second game, too. Ditmar pitched seven innings in the first game and got credit for the win, with Stafford pitching well in relief. Turley started the second game and while he gave up six hits and nine walks he lasted seven and two thirds innings, struck out eight and gave up only two runs. But he was in and out of trouble all afternoon. Arroyo relieved him and saved Turley's win by retiring the last four batters in order. Berra caught the first game, Howard the second, as Yogi sat that one out.

Mantle hit another home run the next day in Baltimore, his fourth in four games, and the Yankees won again. The excitement Mantle generated with his dramatic hitting, especially after his slow start, was simply astonishing. Among the Yankee players there was a widespread assumption that Mantle would have a great season.

"I don't think I've ever seen him more determined to come through with a big year," Houk said. "I could almost feel him burning up inside when he failed to hit in those first two games." After the home run in Baltimore a newspaper wrote that Mantle was "now 18 games ahead of his 1960 pace and eight games ahead of the pace set by Babe Ruth when he hit 60 in 1927." That was on April 21, when the season was only six games old.

The sweep of the Los Angeles doubleheader and the win over Baltimore gave the Yankees five victories in a row after their opening-day defeat and moved them into a tie for first place with the Tigers. The bad weather was over, the unnerving war news had quieted down, and everything seemed just fine. . . .

13

Everything *seemed* just fine, but it wasn't to be that easy. The Yankees played another doubleheader, their second in three days, in Baltimore on Saturday, which meant that after playing only three games during the first nine days of the season the Yanks played five in the next three, which put a strain on Houk's pitching. It was a day-night doubleheader, not a twi-nighter, but two separate games, one in the afternoon, the other several hours later at night. Houk sent Terry to the mound in the afternoon game for his first start of the season.

Terry, born in Oklahoma, had first joined the Yankees in 1956, when in spring training he impressed Berra and others with his ability. He was a very promising young pitcher but in June 1957, still only 21, he was included in the famous deal that sent Billy Martin away from the Yankees. Martin had celebrated his twenty-ninth birthday at the Copacabana nightclub in New York with a group of teammates, including Berra, Mantle and Hank Bauer. There had been an argument at the Copa and Bauer was charged with punching another customer. The charge was dismissed, but George Weiss, then the Yankee general manager, did not like Martin, blamed him for the trouble and decided it was time to get rid of him. Weiss worked out a trade with Kansas City that sent Martin, Terry and a couple of lesser lights to the Athletics for Duren, and three other players who didn't do very much for New York. For that matter, Martin didn't do much for Kansas

City, either. But Terry became a regular starting pitcher for the A's, and after the 1958 season the Yankees got him back. He started and relieved for New York in 1959 and 1960 without remarkable success. He started one game in the 1960 Series with Pittsburgh and relieved in another (the fateful seventh game) and was the losing pitcher in both—he gave up the home run to Mazeroski. At 25 and in his sixth season, Terry was still in the category of "promising," but Houk had him in the starting rotation with Ford, Ditmar and Turley and obviously expected him to come through. He *needed* him to come through, particularly since Ditmar and Turley had looked less than overwhelming thus far.

Terry was a tall, hard-throwing righthander with a fastball, a curve and a slider he threw more frequently than Houk thought wise. (It was a slider that he'd thrown to Mazeroski.) Houk was trying to get Terry to simplify, to throw his good hard stuff and not try to be too fine.

RALPH HOUK:

Ralph was a real good-looking fellow then, big and tall, kind of slow and drawly. He did everything sort of slowly. He looked slender, but he wasn't slender. He was big. He was fairly quiet at that time. Later on he became a little more talkative.

Ralph had all the pitches. He had a good fastball, maybe not a Bob Feller fastball or even a Whitey Ford fastball, but a good one, and he had a real good breaking ball that helped make his fastball better. He had that slider, and he had the change.

He was a real good pitcher but I felt at times that maybe he thought a little too much out there on the mound. He might be getting them out real good pitching one way, and the next thing you knew he might shift and go into something else. There were times when I thought he was too dedicated to trying to mix his pitches.

And I thought he was paying too much attention to the slider and was losing his curveball, which was his best pitch when I had him in Denver. I had the feeling—Jim Turner felt the same way, I think—that some of the kids in trying to learn to throw the slider were taking something away from their curveball. The curve, you know, you really snap when you throw it while the slider, it kind of slides out of your hand. Terry got to the point where neither pitch was all that effective.

Ralph was a very finicky kind of guy, very conscientious. You didn't have to worry about him off the field. He was a hard worker. But everything had to be just right when he was on the mound. He wanted things this way or that way. He paid attention to details, and everything had to be just right. He was a very good golfer, you know. Used to win players' tournaments and that sort of thing. He loved golf and wanted to be a pro. Well, he did become a club pro out in the middle of Kansas after he stopped playing ball, but what he really wanted, I think, was to go on the pro tour.

When he was a ballplayer he got to thinking so much about golf there at the end that I think it bothered his pitching a little. He couldn't concentrate enough on it, and he was the kind of guy who had to concentrate on things. When he got that slider he worked hard on it, trying to get it right, and he spent all his time working on it and there goes his curveball. So I said to him, "Let's forget the slider for a while and get the curveball back." I wanted him to concentrate on it and the fastball. I didn't tell him to stop throwing the slider altogether. I just didn't want him to stop throwing his curve, which was a better pitch for him than the slider.

But ballplayers are funny. They get ideas into their heads. When he was at Denver, Terry came to me one time and said, "I can't pitch in this ball park." He meant the altitude, the thin, light air. And Denver *was* known as a hitters' park. I said, "Gee, Ralph, I can't set the pitching up so that you only pitch on the road." He said, "Well, I just can't pitch in this park." We talked for a while and then I said, "I'll bet you don't even know what your record is here." He didn't. It was something like seven and one. It was much better there than it was on the road, so that stopped that stuff.

And the slider, pitchers fall in love with it, but I don't know. I've seen some pitchers—Mark Clear, when he was with the Red Sox, for example—what he called his slider was the damnedest curve you ever saw. A slider is—well, Dizzy Dean called it a halfbaked curve, and the real oldtimers say it was a nickel curve, a ball that breaks only this much. But it's a nickel curve thrown *hard*. A slider has to be thrown hard to be effective. It doesn't have to break much as long as it breaks quick. The advantage of a slider for most pitchers is that it's easier to control than a curve, and they can throw it on a three–two pitch and get it over. Johnny Sain was a great slider guy—he called it a cut curve, but it was a slider—and I give him credit because he could show his pitchers how to throw that pitch and get it over better than most of them could get a curveball over.

For a righthanded pitcher the slider usually breaks away from a righthanded batter. Some people think it works good off a fastball because a fastball tails in and a slider tails out, but that's not necessarily so. Some pitchers have fastballs that go down and away a little, or down and in. That movement is important. People talk all the time about 90-mile-an-hour fastballs, 95-mile-an-hour fastballs. To me, that has nothing to do with how good your fastball is. It's the way it moves. Some pitchers have an 88-mile-an-hour fastball that's better than one that's 95 miles an hour because of the movement of the ball.

Like Frank Shea, who was so good with the 1947 Yankees, my first year with the club. Frank was a rookie, and he goes 14 and 5 and wins two games in the World Series. He was righthanded and he had little hands for a pitcher, and the way he threw the fastball it always kind of sailed in on a lefthanded hitter. Even Ted Williams will tell you he had a little trouble hitting Shea. Well, he might not agree now, but at one time he did have trouble hitting Shea. It was nothing but a fastball and it wasn't that fast, but it came in on you and Ted had trouble with it.

God, that reminds me of a day back then. This is when Bucky Harris was managing the Yankees, and we were playing Ted and the Red Sox in Fenway Park and for some reason I was catching Shea. Rudy York, a big home-run hitter, was batting behind Williams. Shea pitches a real good ball game and we're one run ahead in the last of the ninth with two out and the bases empty. Ted is the hitter. We get two strikes and a ball on him off that fastball in, and then I see Ted moving back in the box, getting away from the plate. He's gonna get that damned pitch that's coming in on him. I don't know what in God's world entered my mind, but I decided that if he was looking for the fastball that much I was going to call for a changeup. Shea, I don't know how well he's remembered now, but Frank was a cocky individual. I called for the change, and old Shea, he just kind of grinned. You could see he just loved the idea—he was going to slop that change in and fool Ted. Well, he threw it, and Ted hit a shot back through the box about three feet off the ground. If it had hit Shea it would have killed him. You couldn't fool Williams. He just waited on the pitch and *whack!* it went clear out to the center-field corner in Fenway, and he winds up on second with a double. York is the next batter and he hits one into the left-field screen for a two-run homer, and we get beat. And after we were leading with two out and the bases empty in the last of the ninth.

We walk back into the clubhouse and I sit down on my stool and Bucky Harris comes in. He stops by my locker and he says, very slowly, "What was that pitch you threw Williams?" I said, "It was a change of pace." He said, "He sure changed the pace of it, didn't he?"

Williams was the most amazing hitter I ever saw. He could hardly wait to get up to the plate; you could actually hear him. They didn't use batting gloves then, they used resin on their hands, and you could hear him twisting his hands on the bat getting ready to hit. The sticky resin would creak, and I'd hear *crick, crick,* and I'd think, "Oh, God, here he comes."

Of all the hitters I ever saw he was the best at waiting and hitting the ball almost out of your glove. He could wait that long and still have the strength to snap his wrists and really hit the ball. It was just unbelievable.

Of course, as the years went on—he *wouldn't* admit to this—but as the years went on the umpires—well, it used to get me so damned mad. The umpires wouldn't call strikes on him. If he took a pitch, they'd call it a ball. You'd be there behind the plate and here's a three–one pitch you *know* is in there and, shit, ball four. The old umpires praise Williams because they say he never complained. Well, why would he?

But that was smart. The umpires loved him. I used to tell my players, don't go up there and yell at the umpire on every pitch. An umpire is like anybody else; he doesn't like to be criticized. You show him up, and he remembers. Wait till the right time to tell an umpire he missed a call.

Terry did well enough in Baltimore for four innings as the Yankees took a 2–0 lead, but in the fifth the Orioles' Marv Breeding hit a home run. It was the only home run Breeding hit all year; his batting average that season was .209. Careless pitching, in other words, which was Terry's habit. Then with two out in the same inning Jackie Brandt singled, and Whitey Herzog, the same "white rat" who later managed the Kansas City Royals and St. Louis Cardinals, hit a long drive to left center. There was no warning track where the chainlink outfield fence cut across the grass of the field, and Mantle ran against the fence trying to catch the ball. He recovered and threw to Kubek, the cutoff man, but Brandt scored to tie the game, and when Kubek threw wildly on the relay, Herzog kept running and he scored too to put the Orioles ahead. Stafford replaced Terry and pitched creditably, but Houk had to pinch-hit for him in the seventh when the Yankees rallied to tie the score. Duren came in, and in the eighth inning he gave up a walk and a game-winning homer.

That unpleasant defeat fit the day, gloomy and heavy with the threat of rain, which began falling during the evening, delaying the start of the night game almost an hour. When it began Houk tried Coates as a starter. Coates was a very tall, rangy Virginia country boy, who looked and acted like a hillbilly. He had been 13–3 in 1960, starting and relieving, and he started out well this night. With the scored tied 1–1 the Yankees filled the bases in the fourth inning, and Baltimore manager Paul Richards, a noted baseball thinker, took out his starting pitcher and brought in a reliever to face Bill Skowron. Skowron hit the first pitch for a grand-slam home run.

Coates thus had a 5–1 lead and things looked good, but he gave up a couple of homers and Stafford, relieving for the second time that day, gave up another and the score was tied. By this time rain was falling again, and after another long delay the game was called. Not suspended, to be completed at a later date, but called, ended. It went into the record as a 5–5 tie. It was a long, fruitless day for the Yankees, who fell from first place to third, behind Detroit and Minnesota.

The next day Houk, still rummaging around in the bottom of his pitching barrel, started McDevitt, the retread obtained from the Dodgers during the winter. McDevitt fell behind early, 1–0, but Mantle tied the game with another home run, his fifth of the season. The Orioles rallied, got three straight singles off McDevitt, regained the lead, 2–1, and had men on first and third with Breeding, the demon home-run hitter of the day before, at bat. Boyer, playing third base, remembered Breeding's batting average and anticipated not another homer but a bunt. He edged forward. Breeding swung away and hit a hard grounder that got past Boyer and bounced off the Baltimore baserunner, who was called out by the umpire for being hit by a batted ball.

But the lean, hawk-visaged Richards came angrily and elegantly out of the Baltimore dugout to protest the call, pointing out that the ball had gone past the fielder before it hit the runner, which under the rules meant that the runner was not out even though the ball had hit him. The umpire reversed the call, and that brought Houk out, fuming, in his first display of temper that season. It was frustration and irritation more than a justified gripe that had him arguing, and after yelling and stomping a bit he returned to the dugout.

McDevitt got out of the inning without any more damage, but Houk replaced him the next inning with young Sheldon, who was making his major league debut. He did well for two innings before leaving for a pinch-hitter, but that was the last bright spot of the day. Maas, also making his first appearance of the year, went to the mound in the seventh inning but had nothing. He gave up a single, a sacrifice bunt and a triple that put the Orioles ahead 3–1 and Houk brought in Arroyo. It was not just Maas's first appearance of the season, it was also his last. In fact, it was his last major league game. He was only 32, with six good big-league seasons behind him, but suddenly his arm was gone and he was all through, making Houk's once impressive-looking pitching staff seem patchier than ever.

"We thought Maas was going to help us when we got him back," Houk said, "but Duke had the sore arm. He wasn't real big—he was built more or less like me, maybe not quite as big—but we really thought he was going to help us. We figured he'd be a backup in the bullpen, and be a middle reliever and maybe spot start now and then. But Duke just couldn't throw. He'd lost it all."

Maas had been a versatile pitcher for Detroit, Kansas City and New York, starting and relieving both. Two seasons earlier he had won 14 games for the Yankees. In 1960, used almost exclusively as a reliever, he had won five and saved four games. The Yankees let him go in the expansion draft and although they got him back in the trade for Brickell before the season began it was as though the Yankees' giving up on him had taken something out of Maas. In any event, his arm was gone and so, soon, was he. His life, like his career, ended early. He died in Mount Clemens, Michigan, near Detroit, in 1976 at the age of 47.

Arroyo gave up another run, and the Yankees lost 4–1. Worse, Mantle had to leave the game in the eighth inning with a badly swollen knee, the result of his encounter with the fence the day before. It was a glum party of Yankees who flew on to Detroit to play the league-leading Tigers.

They were met in Detroit by Hamey, who had flown out from New York to see what was wrong. Just about everything was. In Detroit the Yankees fell to fourth place after losing to Frank Lary, who was called "Taters" by his teammates but "Yankee Killer" by the sportswriters because of his mastery of the New Yorkers. This was Lary's twenty-fifth career win over the Yankees against only eight defeats. Turley, who at this point had started as many games as Ford, again pitched poorly and left the game in the fifth inning.

Ford started the next day and was given a quick 6–0 lead as Maris hit his first homer of the year, but then he too was routed as the Tigers roared back to take the lead. Ford, who didn't finish the game, was saved from defeat when Mantle tied the game with a homer in the eighth and then won it (for Arroyo) with yet another homer in the tenth, his seventh home run in eight games. The wild come-from-behind victory was the Yankees' first in five games, ended a Detroit winning streak at eight and kept Houk's club above .500.

Back in New York the Yankees beat Cleveland 4–3 behind Ditmar, who pitched a complete game, his only complete game of the season and, as it turned out, the last complete game of his career. Ditmar had trouble but he was courageous on the mound and never quite lost control of the game. With the score tied in the seventh, Mantle came to bat with two out and a runner on second base. Cleveland manager Jimmy Dykes, an engaging raconteur who with his baseball knickers and impressive stomach looked something like the portly overseer of an English estate, walked to the mound in his stately way to confer with his pitcher. The question was whether to walk Mantle purposely, since first base was open. Because there were two out Dykes decided after some discussion to have his man pitch to Mantle. He turned and walked with slow dignity back to the dugout. He had hardly settled himself on the bench when Mantle boomed a triple to left center that scored what proved to be the winning run. Ditmar held on to the lead—but just barely. In the ninth inning the Indians had a man on first base with two out when Bubba Phillips hit a line drive to right center. The tying run was headed for the plate when Mantle made a great sliding, skidding catch to end the game and give Ditmar his victory, his last in the major leagues.

All this heroic work at bat and in the field was swinging the affection of the fickle Yankee Stadium crowds Mantle's way. During his first ten years with the club, the fans tended to dismiss his remarkable accomplishments at bat, in the field and on the bases. Instead, they focused their booing attention on his failures, which really weren't that extensive. Why he was so unpopular then is difficult to understand or explain. Perhaps it was because so much more was expected of him than he was able to achieve. Perhaps Stengel's obvious disappointment in Mantle had contributed to the fans' antagonism. But so had other factors: Mantle's curtness with the press, a product of shyness that came out in the form of indifference, short answers or utter silence; his awkwardness with fans, which led him to push his way rudely past people gathered to see him and sometimes refuse to sign autographs; the fact that he had succeeded DiMaggio as the big player on the team and hadn't filled his shoes adequately. DiMaggio himself had suffered similar unpopularity in his first five seasons after he had succeeded Babe Ruth and then Lou Gehrig. Not until he caught the imagination of the country with his 56-game hitting streak in the summer of 1941 did Joe gain widespread affection. Up to then he had been routinely booed. When the 1961 season began Mantle too was booed almost automatically when his name was announced over the PA system.

But now, with Stengel gone and the openly admiring Houk praising him almost daily, the spectacular things Mantle was doing at bat and in the field finally began to capture the crowd. The day after the game-winning triple and the game-saving catch, the Yankees had a night game scheduled with the Indians. It was a wet, threatening evening, but there was a fairly good crowd on hand and the club hoped to get the game in. They even had the lineups announced before rain forced a postponement, and as the PA announcer intoned, "Batting fourth, playing center field, number 7, Mickey Mantle . . ." the few boos that sounded were drowned out by cheers, a novel enough event to be noted and reported in the newspapers. "As nearly everyone knows," said one account, "Mantle has been the favorite target of the boobirds for years." But times had changed, and Mantle was emerging as the well-loved hero he was to be for the rest of his career and after his retirement at Oldtimers Games and other gatherings.

The reclamation of Mantle started long before Maris came to the center of the home-run stage. At this point in the season Maris simply was not a factor. He had a poor spring training and through the first dozen games of the season (while Mantle was hitting all those homers and batting .340 and leading the league in runs batted in) Roger was floundering along under .200, with one home run and exactly two RBIs. Houk had put him as low as seventh in the batting order.

The great Yankee team of 1961 had not yet jelled, and it was Mantle who was holding the shaky club together. There was a brief flurry of achievement at the end of April and the beginning of May when the club won eight of nine and regained a momentary tie for the lead, but that didn't last. Howard was the only regular other than Mantle batting over .300, and he was platooning with Berra. A big disappointment was Lopez, whom Houk had counted on to hold up his end in left field; Hector was in an inexplicable slump. Maris wasn't hitting. The pitching was erratic.

Houk was not pleased with things when the club left New York at the end of April on its first long road trip of the season. The first stop was Washington, where the Yanks split a Sunday doubleheader with the Senators before being rained out the next day, their eighth postponement in 19 days. They left Washington to fly to Minneapolis and on to Los Angeles. The season was beginning to get serious, and they hadn't even settled in yet.

There was a great disruption of the pattern of travel in the American League that season. For decades under the old schedule the league had been arbitrarily divided into four "eastern" and four "western" teams. The east consisted of Boston, New York, Philadelphia and Washington, the west of Cleveland, Detroit, Chicago and St. Louis. When in the mid-1950s the St. Louis Browns moved to Baltimore (to become the Orioles) and the Philadelphia Athletics to Kansas City, the two traded places as "west" and "east" clubs and the schedule continued to follow the same rhythmic pattern. The four eastern clubs played one another for a couple of weeks while the four western clubs did the same thing, each group staying near home, so to speak.

Then the four eastern clubs traveled west and took turns playing in the four western cities, after which the western clubs would travel east and tour the eastern cities. "Western trips" and "eastern trips" were part of the lingo of baseball; the American League schedule meshed with that of the National League, which followed a similar procedure—or did before the transfer of the New York Giants and the Brooklyn Dodgers to San Francisco and Los Angeles in 1958, which distorted the system. Until then, when the American League east played in the west, the National League west played in the east. This reciprocal arrangement had developed because until the mid-1950s five of the eight cities in each league had a rival club from the other league in the same city. This was so in Boston, New York, Philadelphia, Chicago and St. Louis, and the schedules were drawn up to avoid direct conflict. If the Cubs were playing the Giants in New York, say, a Chicago fan knew the White Sox were playing at home, and a New York fan knew the Yankees were on the road. And so on.

This neat pattern began to fray with the shift of franchises in the 1950s. The old clockwork movement didn't function the same way, and in 1961, when expansion began, the east–west pattern went out the window completely and road trips became erratic and irregular. A minor thing, perhaps, but more evidence of the changes that took place in baseball in 1961.

In New York Governor Nelson Rockefeller signed the bill that cleared the way for the stadium to be built in Queens for the new New York team. Bill Shea said there was a good chance the new stadium would be ready for the 1962 season—he was two years too optimistic—and he said it might eventually have a retractable roof, another overoptimistic appraisal. He also displayed a model of a completely round stadium that didn't look much like the Shea Stadium that opened three years later.

At about the same time, the new club officially adopted the archaic nickname "Mets," a name last used by a New York team in the 1880s. The club's official corporate name was The Metropolitan Baseball Club of New York, and sportswriters had gotten into the habit of calling them the Metropolitans and, jokingly, the Mets. To promote interest in the new team, New York fans were asked to choose an official nickname and the club received 2,653 pieces of mail with 9,613 suggestions that made use in one way or another of 644 different names, including Continentals (for the Continental League), Burros (for the five boroughs of New York City), Skyliners, Skyscrapers, Bees, Rebels, Avengers, Jets (which was adopted a few years later by the local American Football League franchise, the Titans, when they moved from the old Polo Grounds into Shea Stadium) and so on. The name Mets finished first, the choice of 69 voters, with 47 preferring Empires and 45 liking Islanders (which became the nickname of the new NHL hockey team on Long Island some years later). Other voters picked Mets as a second or third choice, with 287 of the 2,653 ballots listing it in one form or another (Metropolitans, Mets, Metro Dodgers, Metro Giants, and the like). Thus, by the wishes of 287 people, or fewer than 1/100 of 1 percent of the population of New York City, one of the most popular nicknames in baseball history came into being. The Mets were now officially alive, although when you said that in May 1961 you'd said about everything. The Mets were breathing, and that was about all. They had no players, no manager, no coaches, no stadium—nothing but a name and an astonishing future.

Gene Conley, who only a couple of weeks earlier had helped the Boston Celtics win the NBA championship, was now pitching for the Boston Red Sox (he won 11 games in 1961 and had two shutouts, including one over the Tigers, who were leading the league at the time). Pumpsie Green, the first black ever to play for the Red Sox, was at shortstop. A year or so later Pumpsie and Conley got a little squiffed together and in one of the more memorable examples of baseball truancy decided to jump the club and fly to Israel. They got as far as the airport.

Marv Throneberry, not yet Marvelous Marv and not yet thought of as a comic figure, drove in all of Kansas City's runs in a big win for the Athletics over Minnesota. Bill Veeck sold the White Sox, who had won the pennant two years earlier, to Arthur Allyn (Veeck, who was ill in 1961, repurchased the club many years later). An Ohio State undergraduate named Jack Nicklaus won the NCAA golf championship and then the United States amateur golf title for the second time before turning professional. Art Mahaffey of the Phils struck out 17 men, one short of the major league record set by Bob Feller in 1938 and equaled in 1959 by an erratic Dodger lefthander named Sandy Koufax. That was the first real hint of Koufax's greatness, which came to fruition in 1961 when he won 18 games and struck out 269 batters (a figure Feller exceeded only once in his career and Walter Johnson only twice. Koufax bettered it three times in the next five seasons). The Cubs continued to shift their coaching staff around.

Harry Craft took the head-coach reins from Vedie Himsl for a while, and then Vedie took them back again.

Gabe Paul, who after years with the Cincinnati Reds had left that club the previous November to become Houston's first general manager, now quit the state of Texas to return to Ohio as general manager of Cleveland, replacing the colorful Frank Lane, who had left Cleveland to run (he thought) the Kansas City Athletics, which had just been purchased by an insurance man from Chicago named Charles O. Finley. Finley, in his first season as a club owner, quickly took matters into his own hands, overriding Lane, occasionally firing him and frequently selling and trading players on his own, without consulting his general manager. Two years later Finley upset old-line baseball people by abandoning the traditional white and gray uniforms and outfitting his A's in green and gold from head to foot.

During the first two weeks of the season the Los Angeles Angels played all their games on the road, punitive scheduling that was apparently part of the agreement in which O'Malley dropped his objections to the club's invasion of his previously exclusive Los Angeles territory. The Angels' absence from California at the beginning of the season kept them from drawing opening week attention away from the Dodgers. It also served to take the bloom off the rose, since the new club lost eight of its first nine games and returned home to Los Angeles in last place. Only 11,931 people showed up to watch them play on opening day.

President Kennedy, back in the ring after the Cuban knockout, cut his weekend short—the first weekend of the Yankees' long western road trip—for a crisis talk with advisors on the situation in Laos and Vietnam. Southeast Asia was very troubled, with civil war in Laos threatening peace in the entire area. The French, who for a century had been the occupying power in Vietnam, Laos and Cambodia (jointly called French Indochina), had suffered severe military setbacks and had pulled out of the country. The United States began moving into the political and military vacuum left by the French withdrawal. An abortive coup the previous fall had failed to force South Vietnamese president Ngo Dinh Diem out of office. Now Kennedy sent Vice-President Lyndon Johnson to Saigon to talk with Diem, who two years later was ousted by an American-supported military revolt. While he was there, Johnson spoke to the South Vietnamese legislature and promised it that the United States would help South Vietnam with weapons and advisors in its struggle against the Viet Cong and the North Vietnamese. A former Marine lieutenant named Tom Rosandich, who was working with sports groups in Southeast Asia, wrote with remarkable prescience to a friend back home that the trouble in Laos and Vietnam could develop into a second Korean War, and that if we weren't careful America would find itself involved in another Asian conflict that we couldn't win.

On May 1, at about the time the Yankees were flying from Washington to Minneapolis, several hundred miles to the south a passenger on a twin-engine Convair belonging to a local Florida airline put a knife to the throat of the pilot and ordered him to change course and fly the plane and its dozen or so passengers to Havana.

This was the first hijacking of a commercial airliner—although the term was not used at that time. At first it was widely assumed that the takeover was a Cuban plot, a bit of Castro revenge for the Bay of Pigs, which had occurred only two weeks earlier. Castro had declared in one of his long speeches that Cuba was now a "socialist" country and that there would be no more elections for the time being, which convinced just about everyone that Cuba was firmly in Soviet hands. The assumption was that the Cubans would hold the plane and its passengers to force concessions of one sort or another from Washington. But Cuban authorities at the Havana airport seemed surprised by the plane's arrival and after a short time the Convair and all its passengers (except for the "bandit," as he was called, who was taken into custody by Cuban police) were sent back to Florida.

The hijacker had told the pilot that General Rafael Trujillo, the dictator of the Dominican Republic, had offered him $100,000 to assassinate Castro but that he decided to warn Castro instead. (Before the end of May, it was Trujillo who was assassinated. His son briefly took over control of the country. Later in the decade, President Johnson sent American troops into the Dominican Republic to restore order.)

Black activists in the American South staged sit-ins at bus depots in an effort to end racial segregation in transportation and by September nearly 70,000 black and white students had taken part in the protests. Four hundred Federal marshals were sent into Alabama after conflicts there erupted into riots. The Freedom Riders, as they were called, moved from city to city in the South, and in May two dozen of them were jailed in Jackson, Mississippi, five minutes after arriving there from Montgomery, Alabama. Dr. Martin Luther King was arrested and jailed, but the protests continued.

Late in May President Kennedy asked Congress for more money for space research. He urged a "moon trip," sending manned spaceships to the moon, an ambition fulfilled eight summers later when Neil Armstrong took that first great step for mankind. But in 1961, America's space program was still puttering along, trying to catch up to the Soviets, who had been ahead since the 1957 World Series. That year, between the second and third games of the Series being played by the Yankees and the Milwaukee Braves, Russia sent the first sputnik, a small, basketball-sized sphere, into orbit around the earth. The third game was the first World Series game ever played in Milwaukee, and it inspired a local paper to run a banner headline across the top of its front page saying TODAY WE MAKE HISTORY, while consigning the story of the first space satellite in history to the third page.

After that America geared up its Mercury space program and assigned seven astronauts to prepare for flights into space. On May 5, as the Yankees arrived in Los Angeles for their first game on the West Coast, America's Alan Shepard, riding in a Mercury capsule, soared 115 miles up and 302 miles out from Florida's Cape Canaveral in our first manned space shot. Shepard's flight was over in fifteen minutes, but it was big news. During it Shepard could be heard saying everything was "A-OK" when he was asked how the spacecraft was functioning. It was explained to a rapt public watching on television that "A-OK" was rocket-engineer patois for perfection, and the term quickly entered the language.

At the end of May, Great Britain announced that the British West Indies would be given their independence the following year, and at the same time Kennedy left for a summit meeting with Khrushchev in Vienna—a year after the Eisenhower–Khrushchev summit had been canceled because of the U-2 flight. On his way to Vienna, Kennedy stopped in Paris to consult de Gaulle, and the two announced that they had agreed to defend West Berlin against any Soviet attack there—a possibility that seemed increasingly real in 1961.

All in all, it was an uneasy year, which may explain why the Mantle–Maris assault on Babe Ruth's record later in the season so caught the American imagination. Here was something Americans could do better than anyone else: hit home runs. Kennedy had become president with high hopes, but the Bay of Pigs was a disaster, the crisis that was developing over Berlin was frightening, and despite the president's optimistic talk about putting a man on the moon in ten years, the space program in 1961 seemed helplessly behind the Russians. Who knew the future then? There was a strong undercurrent of resentment and restlessness, and changes were eagerly welcomed. An ordinary little bar in mid-Manhattan called the Peppermint Lounge became internationally famous when it introduced a revolutionary new dance called the twist. Despite his setbacks Kennedy remained popular, a strong, welcome symbol of youth and change after the dull years under Eisenhower. The first wave of baby boomers, who were not yet called that, were in their early teens when JFK became president, and they went on to take over the decade. Jack Kerouac, the beat novelist, was more their hero than Jack Kennedy, but Kennedy gave the youth movement a certain legitimacy. His hatlessness, his hair (thick and brushed almost carelessly compared to the slicked-down fashion of the past), his casual vacation clothes, his great-looking young wife, his small children and his flip, humorous personality helped set the tone for the vigorous, restless young who during the sixties embraced not only the twist but the Beatles, long hair, Bob Dylan, changes in racial attitudes, smoking marijuana, far-out clothes, Woodstock and antiwar protests that changed the nation.

15

Struggling out of wet cold April into May, the Yankees found bright warm sun in Minnesota for their first game in that state. Metropolitan Stadium in suburban Bloomington—the first major league park located outside a big city—was packed, and the game was superb, still tied at the end of the ninth, 2–2. In the tenth Kubek doubled and both Lopez and Maris walked to fill the bases. Mantle, who had driven in the Yankees' first run, came to bat and, in the lyric words of a contemporary sportswriter, "hit a ball through the dazzling sunlight and over the 402-foot marker into the centerfield bleachers" for a grand-slam home run. The Yankees won again the next day when Maris hit a homer, and completed a sweep of the series the day after that when Mantle hit another one, his ninth, and extended his batting streak to 16 games—every game the Yankees had played since Mickey went hitless in the first two of the season. He was now 11 games ahead of Ruth's record pace, the newspapers noted. Maris was not mentioned. Turley pitched a complete game in Minnesota, and Ford won his fourth victory of the season there. Things were looking up as the club flew on to Los Angeles.

The Yankees' first game in California attracted a near-capacity crowd—all of 18,000 people—which was very big attendance for the Angels that year. Capacity in minor league Wrigley Field, a smaller version of Chicago's Wrigley Field, was supposed to be 20,500, but you had to work hard to squeeze that many into the park. (That O'Malley! The Coliseum, where the Dodgers were playing their games and out of which Walter had kept the Angels, could seat 90,000 for a baseball game.)

Mantle put on a show in batting practice by belting ball after ball over the fence, but in the game he went oh for four, ending his hitting streak, although he did score a run in the Yanks' 5–4 victory. Casey Stengel came to the game from his home in Glendale, the first time the Yankee players had seen him since his dismissal, and the question can be raised: Did Casey's presence affect Mantle? In the first two games of the season in New York, Mickey pressed so hard that he went hitless. Did he do the same with Stengel on hand? He didn't get a hit in any of the three games in Los Angeles.

But Yankee power up and down the batting order, which had been rather quiet so far, was beginning to show. The slick-fielding Boyer had been batting only .179 (and his alternate, the supposedly hard-hitting Johnson, only .133), but against the Angels Boyer drove in the tying run in the seventh inning and won the game in the ninth with a two-run homer off Tex Clevenger. (The Angels had picked Clevenger from the old Senators in the expansion draft, and so far in the 1960 season he'd been one of the most effective relievers in the league.)

Maris was still batting under .200, but like a long-dormant volcano he was beginning to rumble. Although the Yankees lost the next day, he hit a long home run, his third of the season and the 100th of his career. A couple of months later Mantle hit the 350th of his career, which is mentioned here only to show that although Maris and Mantle are linked in baseball history as home-run twins, it should be remembered that Mantle was a star of long standing at this time, Maris a comparatively new one. At the time Mantle hit his 350th home run, only six players in baseball history had hit as many as 400. (Today, in contrast, fourteen are past 500.) In 1960 Mantle was a lifetime .307 hitter, with more than 1,500 base hits. Roger didn't even have 500 hits yet, and his lifetime average was .257.

To understand the antagonistic pressures that fell on Maris later in the year, it's necessary to recognize the different status each was accorded at the time. Maris was a splendid ballplayer, voted the Most Valuable Player in the league the year before, but he was a newcomer, a Johnny-come-lately. He was in his second year with the Yankees (Mantle was in his eleventh) and it was the first time in his brief career that Roger had played two successive full seasons with the same club. Further, he was quiet and reserved and in no sense colorful; baseball writers didn't seek him out for quotations, and he didn't buddy up to the media, as many players do. His personality on the field reflected his personality off it; he was strong, capable and matter-of-fact. He was a powerful hitter, a superb fielder with a fine arm, an excellent baserunner (although he did not steal bases; with Mantle usually coming to bat when Maris was on base there was little reason to). Roger played with great skill but quiet efficiency. Before his home-run splurge, fans and sportswriters tended not to notice him the way they would a Willie Mays or a Mantle.

Even the way he ran was markedly different from Mantle. When Mickey slowed to a trot he moved in an odd, cramped way, as though his feet hurt, but when he shifted into top speed he was like a rapidly spinning wheel, a rhythmic, dynamic blur. Maris was fast, too, though not as fast as Mantle—nobody was—but he ran almost methodically, and when he slowed to a trot he moved in the same steady, unruffled manner, his impassive face showing no strain or emotion. He was by no means ungraceful, but neither was there anything beautiful or striking about the way he did things.

He had a friendly little smile, but he didn't use it much. His face seldom showed much emotion, and he had what many writers called "cold blue eyes." He had a small mouth for such a big man, and in repose it tended to turn down at the corners, which made him look disdainful and disapproving. He was well liked by other players and he made strong friendships, but to those who didn't know him he seemed almost to be sneering. Maris did have a tendency to complain, to bellyache about things that annoyed him. When Ford was made player representative that season he said jokingly that he was going to form a cabinet, like President Kennedy's, and he assigned various players to mock positions. In that fanciful cabinet Maris was Secretary of Grievances.

Even the way he spoke was deflating. Mantle had been a difficult interview, but when he did talk he had an engaging charm, a pleasant voice with an appealing southwestern "cowboy" accent. Maris's flat, almost monotonous manner of speaking was as noncommittal as he was, and his voice was not noticeably deep or warm or resonant in tone. He tended in all ways to blend into the background, which he preferred. Then all those home runs he hit in 1961 forced him into the spotlight, a place he abhorred.

Mantle was a much better-looking man, particularly as he grew older and after he abandoned his flattop crew cut (a style Maris kept for most of his life). Mickey had an engaging grin and a warm smile, and despite his reputation for having a sulky, sometimes explosive temper, he was actually good at keeping his feelings under control most of the time. He had been strongly influenced by his courageous father, who died the winter after Mickey broke into major league ball. Elvin (Mutt) Mantle came from a world where you kept your troubles to yourself, where you did your best no matter how bad things went, and where you showed respect for older people and for those in authority. Inside himself, Mickey certainly resented people, notably Stengel, but his resentment came out in anger at himself or at umpires (who don't count) or at inanimate objects—he'd throw a batting helmet, punch a water cooler. He might show anger but usually he kept his opinions to himself.

Maris came from a different background. His father, Rudy (Roger's brother was also called Rudy), who worked for railroads in the upper Midwest for years, is a well-liked man with a tendency to be cantankerous, much like Roger. Generally, Rudy is amiable, but tread on the elder Maris's toes and he'll let you know it, by word of mouth or angry letter. He doesn't hide his feelings. And he's slow to forget a grudge, as Roger was.

16

The Yankees lost the third game in Los Angeles—lost two out of three to a last-place expansion team—as Mantle's slump continued. Hitless through the entire series, he struck out three times in the final game, his last whiff coming with the tying and winning runs on second and third. Tied for first place when they arrived in L.A., the Yanks were two and a half games behind the Tigers when they left town.

As Mantle stopped hitting, some of the others began. Maris went 6 for 11 against the Angels, and Boyer was on a tear. However, Lopez was still not hitting. Houk had expected to use Lopez in left field most of the time, but Hector was unable to shake off his inexplicable slump. Baseball writers talk about "career" seasons—a year in which a player does everything right and plays well above his normal form. For instance, first-baseman Norm Cash of the Tigers had a "career" season in 1961 by hitting a league leading .361, the only time in his 17 years in the major leagues that he batted over .300. That same year, Lopez had a career slump, finishing at .222, almost 50 points *below* his lifetime batting average, which was only two points lower than Cash's. Lopez was usually a solid, dependable hitter and a valuable all-around player during his dozen years in the majors, but not in 1961, and by mid-May Houk felt he had to find someone to do the job Hector wasn't doing. Elston Howard meantime was hitting .371 and would continue to hit steadily and occasionally spectacularly all season long, finishing with a .348 average, second in the league behind Cash. He was also catching splendidly, but he'd been sharing catching duties with Berra and playing only about half the time. When Yogi was out briefly with a minor injury, Houk used the lefthanded-hitting Blanchard in Berra's place in the catching platoon. Now he decided to make Howard his full-time catcher, with Blanchard as backup, and shift Yogi to left field in place of Lopez. Berra accepted the reassignment to left field without complaint. He had played the outfield before—he'd been in left field when Mazeroski's homer sailed over the wall—and he did well out there, occasionally sharing the position with the righthanded-hitting Lopez and, later, Bob Cerv.

RALPH HOUK:

Yogi was slowing down but he was still a heck of a ballplayer and I wanted his bat in the lineup. I think Yogi could wake up on Christmas morning and hit, even today. I saw more of him as a ballplayer than anyone else on the team because we came up together in 1947. He'd been in a few games in 1946, but 1947 was his first full year, same as me. He just amazed me then the way he could hit. He was always a great hitter but it impressed me the way he could start right off quick hitting in the spring. So many hitters with the power he had, it takes them a lot of time to get going in the spring. They have to see a lot of breaking balls and different speed pitches. Not Yogi. He was always ready.

He was known as a bad-ball hitter. That is, he'd swing at anything near the plate. Pitchers didn't give Yogi many good balls to hit, but even so he still didn't walk as much as other hitters. I don't know what he might have batted if he'd laid off the bad pitches. Or maybe if he swung at more bad pitches, he might have hit even better. Who knows? It was just that Yogi could hit. He could get around on an inside high fastball better than anyone I've ever seen and just whack it down the right-field line.

He looked kind of funny on the ball field, kind of short and lumpy, but he was a great athlete. One thing that always impressed me about him was how fast he could run. He didn't look fast but Yogi ran better than anyone realized. He was quick behind the plate, too. He was great. But he'd been around fifteen years, and now we had Howard.

Elston was a high-class guy and a very versatile ballplayer. Catching was naturally his best position, but he could play first base and the outfield too. He might not have been the greatest outfielder in the world, but if the ball was hit in his area he'd catch it, and the same thing was true at first base. And Ellie could hit. He could hit. The ball jumped off his bat. His ground balls would go through the infield like a shot. When you have protection like that on a ball club . . . well, you're just not going to find anybody else who can hit like that and still get you by in three positions.

Ellie was a ballplayer I just had to have in the lineup every day, too, so we put Yogi in the outfield, even though I'd say Yogi was a better catcher than Howard. Ellie might have had a stronger arm, but all around Yogi was better. This isn't putting Howard down. Ellie was a *very* good ballplayer, but Yogi was a bona fide Hall of Famer.

And in the outfield, Yogi was faster. He could run, and he could throw. He made a great play in the outfield against Detroit in September that year when he threw Kaline out at second base on a ball hit down the left-field line. Kaline still talks about that. It shut off a rally in a very important ball game. God, he made a hell of a play— backhanded the ball down the line and threw a perfect strike to second base. Yogi was good.

So he went to the outfield and Howard took over as catcher. He couldn't move around back there as quick as Yogi—he was a lot bigger, he was six inches taller than Berra—but he had a good active arm and he knew what he was doing. He loved to talk baseball. I used to like to sit with him discussing things. Like, with this guy pitching we better make them beat us with this pitch and not that one. Ellie was smart. Just because a batter couldn't hit a curveball, say, Ellie wouldn't sit back there and call for the curve all the time. He knew how to mix the pitches. Some catchers take a long time to learn that, and you're almost afraid to say anything to them because they're liable to— Well, you say to them, "Goddamn, how did you let him hit a *fastball?*" Then that catcher may go out there and call 15 straight curveballs and you're sorry you said anything.

Ellie wouldn't do that. He listened and he understood. He noticed things on the field. He was well liked by players on the other clubs, so that once in a while he'd get pretty good information that way— you know, maybe this guy's got a little bad leg, or something like that. You're always looking for that type of information, which sometimes is a lot bigger help than what the scouts give you.

Bob Cerv, who had been drafted by the Angels in December, was traded back to the Yankees in May just as the club was leaving Los Angeles. He was a 35-year-old veteran of 11 big league seasons, and he was sitting on the Angels' bench with a pulled muscle, but he was also a righthanded power hitter who could help beef up Houk's uncertain bench. With Lopez not producing, Houk wanted Cerv, so Hamey worked out a trade with the Angels, giving them Duren, Lee Thomas and Johnny James for Cerv and Tex Clevenger. Houk was losing his patience with Duren, who was still drinking; Ralph needed to have confidence in his players, and he could no longer depend on Ryne. Duren had given up three home runs in four relief appearances for New York, but he was still capable of being an overpowering pitcher. He turned in three hitless innings of relief against the Angels just before the trade, and he did well with the Angels. He started 14 games, relieved 30 times and showed flashes of his former brilliance (he was even named to the American League All-Star team).

But Houk was disenchanted with Duren; James was a spearcarrier (he'd appeared in only one game for the Yankees, did not pitch particularly well for Los Angeles and was gone from the majors after 1961); and Thomas was an untried rookie outfielder who had pinch-hit twice for the Yankees but otherwise had not been in a game. With the Angels Thomas was an impressive hitter for two years, batting .285 with 24 homers and 70 RBIs in 1961 and .290 with 26 homers and 104 RBIs in 1962. After that he went into a decline and except for a fair season or two later on with the Red Sox he deteriorated as a hitter and didn't last out the decade.

RALPH HOUK:

Lee Thomas was a lefthanded hitter, a big kid from Missouri. He hit good in the minors and he became a real good hitter for a while with Los Angeles, but he came to the Yankees at a bad time. There wasn't any place for him. They played him at first base later, but he was mostly an outfielder and just a fair outfielder. He came along when we had Mantle and Maris and those guys, and there just wasn't a place for him. Johnny James was kind of small, probably smaller than most pitchers. He was a good fielding pitcher who moved around a lot, a sort of pepper-pot guy, but we didn't use him much. Ryne was still drinking, but he wasn't causing any trouble. We weren't really trying to get rid of him. We were just looking for Cerv. We needed more protection on our bench, and that's why we wanted Cerv.

Cerv had solid credentials as a power hitter who could both pinch-hit and help out in left field. Although repeatedly hobbled by injuries (he lasted only one more season in the majors) Cerv was the piece Houk needed to complete the jigsaw puzzle of Yankee power. His home-run bat was always a threat and frequently a reality. He had been let go in the expansion draft the previous December only because Houk thought the younger, spryer Lopez was a better bet in left field. Now he was hedging that bet by reclaiming Cerv at the price of giving up Duren.

To take Duren's place in the bullpen the Yankees insisted on getting Clevenger, who in Los Angeles' first 19 games had relieved 12 times and had a fine 1.69 earned run average. Houk hoped Clevenger would be a righthanded counterpart to the lefthanded Arroyo, which would spring Stafford for starting assignments. Clevenger didn't really fill the bill, but he was better than James in the bullpen. Tex was a cheerful man with dark eyes and heavy black eyebrows, and he'd been a useful starter and reliever for six seasons in the American League.

RALPH HOUK:

Clevenger might have come out of Texas. They called him that anyway. He looked kind of like an Indian. Tex was smart. I think he got into the oil business later on. He was kind of an unnoticed fellow on the ball club, really a middle-line pitcher. He'd battle them good, but you weren't sure what was going to happen when you brought Tex in. He had some good games for us and some bad games. He had a good fastball that moved at times but was not real consistent. He never had a great curve, and that hurt him, and he didn't have outstanding control. But considering that he was not an Arroyo—not the kind of pitcher that you could say, "This is the guy I'm going to have ready in the bullpen"—I think Tex had a pretty good year. I wouldn't say he was great, but he filled a role.

Bob Cerv, he was a pretty good ballplayer. It was good to get him back. He could be pitched to, but he was a tough hitter and he could hit a ball a long way. He was a great big guy that looked like a football player, but he played basketball at the University of Nebraska and he could run pretty good—until he hurt his knee. He was a good base-runner. Nobody seemed to realize that, but when Casey managed the club, Bob did a lot of pinch-running for him. Not that he'd steal, but he was good on the bases. He'd slide in there hard. When Casey wanted to break up a double play, Cerv was the best we had at it. He'd go down there and used that rollover block and nobody would stay near second base. He couldn't get away with that now because they've changed the rules, but, jeez, he was tough then. He was a pretty good outfielder, too, pretty good all around in everything. He was an underrated player.

He talked an awful lot, too. Oh, lord, he could talk. He never stopped, just constant. He was an intelligent person that, you know, liked to talk. The players got a big kick out of him. They'd kid him about knowing a little bit about everything, but Bob was pretty well read. He was a good family man with quite a few kids [ten, in fact—six daughters and four sons]. He was a good guy and well liked on the club, but he was just one of those people who liked to talk on any subject you wanted to bring up.

Cerv signed for a lot of money with the Angels after they picked him in the draft—$50,000, I think. I know that when we got him back he was making more than Maris. Everybody was shocked that the Angels were paying that kind of money. But Gene Autry was pretty free with his money right then, and he had Bobby Reynolds in there with him and Bobby was a nice guy.

Roy Hamey (with an em) worked out the trade with Los Angeles general manager Fred Haney (with an en). The Yankees were also supposed to send the Angels a player "to be named later," but the player to be named later turned out to be $50,000. That became evident a week or so after the trade when a Yankee check in that amount, made out to the Angels, was found on a floor in the Los

Angeles Coliseum, where Haney or some other Angel official had accidentally dropped it. The check had a notation saying it was part of the "Cerv–Duren" trade. The embarrassed Angels explained it away by saying the deal with the Yankees was a complex one requiring both clubs to "purchase" players from each other for the same amounts, but they didn't say why—or who the other "purchased" player was.

17

The Yankee slump held over from California into Kansas City where Ford, leading 4–1 in the eighth, gave up a double and a run-scoring single and hit a batter. Houk brought Arroyo in, but he gave up a walk to load the bases, a two-run single that tied the score and another walk to load the bases again—still with nobody out. Haywood Sullivan, Kansas City's catcher then, the president of the Red Sox now, lined to Skowron for the first out, but Bill Tuttle, a righthanded hitter facing the lefthanded Arroyo, hit an infield chopper that drove in what proved to be the winning run. Despite Arroyo's prowess with righthanded batters Houk might have preferred to use the righthanded Clevenger against the righthanded Tuttle at that moment, but Clevenger had been given permission to take an extra day to straighten his affairs in Los Angeles before reporting to the Yankees in Kansas City. Cerv, on the other hand, joined the club immediately, and Houk hurried him in to bat for Arroyo in the ninth. Alas, Cerv made an out, and so did the Yankees, and the club had lost three in a row. Mantle, by now mired in a terrible slump, went hitless for the fourth straight game.

There was a temporary improvement the next day in Kansas City (the last day of the long road trip from New York to Washington to Minneapolis to Los Angeles to Kansas City to New York, the first regular-season transcontinental trip the club had ever taken). When

Terry was touched for four runs, the newly arrived Clevenger relieved him and shut out the Athletics with only one hit through the last four innings. With the score tied in the seventh, Boyer singled, Mantle singled (he had gone oh for 18), Howard singled, Maris singled and Clevenger (of all people) doubled.

The Yankees won, but Clevenger had hit his peak as a Yankee in his first game with them. Tex was the winning pitcher, and it was his only win with the Yankees all season. The double was his only hit. He pitched 28 innings the rest of the season, saved no games and lost one. His earned run average after that auspicious debut was 5.46, high for any pitcher and especially so for a reliever. Clevenger played a similar minor role the next season and then was finished in the majors. His failure to become a righthanded counterpart to Arroyo didn't do much to ease Houk's worries about his in-and-out ball club. Neither did the fact that Mantle pulled a muscle in his right calf in that game.

RALPH HOUK:

The Cerv trade was a three-for-two deal, and that got us down to one man above the player limit, but we still had to cut one more, so we sent Jack Reed down to Richmond on recall. He was a great kid. If your daughter brought a Jack Reed home, you'd want him for a son-in-law. He should have become a manager. I talked to him once about managing in the minors, and he would have been a good one. But his daddy died and Jack cut his career short because of that. His family had a big farm or plantation down in Mississippi, lots of acres, and after his father died Jack had to run it, so he gave up baseball. Jack was smart, and he had a good education. He graduated from the University of Mississippi.

As a ballplayer he had good speed and he was an outstanding outfielder, but he couldn't hit, though he won a 22-inning game for us in Detroit a year later with a home run. Mostly, he was a fielder. If you wanted a ball caught you'd just as soon it was Reed going for it as anybody. He could go get 'em, both ways, left and right. I could put him at any outfield position and know I had a good man out there. And I could use him as a pinch-runner because he was fast. He was a good young man, and he fit in nice on the club. Everybody liked him, and he was happy to be there.

It was a luxury to be able to have a player like Reed around. Of course, when I had to make room on the roster for someone, he was the easiest one to send out. He understood that, and I'd always tell him I'd bring him back as soon as I could, and I would. After the Cerv trade I sent Jack down. Then the very next day Mantle got hurt. I wanted Reed back but when you sent a guy out like that you couldn't bring him back right away. You had to wait ten days. So Reed was gone, and just when I needed him. Maris played center when Mickey was out.

The victory in Kansas City salvaged the erratic road trip, which was a good thing because Detroit was coming into New York for a four-game series—one game Friday night, another Saturday afternoon and a doubleheader Sunday. It was the first real showdown of the season, and with the Tigers two and a half games ahead, the Yankees had to gain some ground. If they could win three of the four games, they'd be only half a game behind. If they could sweep all four, they'd be in first place by themselves for the first time all season.

In the first game Friday night Houk started Ditmar against Lary, the Yankee Killer, who won 23 games that year. Ditmar lasted only five innings. When he weakened Houk turned to Arroyo, who pitched through the eighth before leaving for a pinch-hitter. Lary gave up 11 hits but still had a 3–3 tie when Coates came in to pitch for the Yankees in the ninth. Lary then hit a home run off Coates to put the Tigers ahead, 4–3. Mantle did not start the game—he was still bothered by the muscle pull in his calf—but in the last of the ninth he pinch-hit. Losing by a run, the Yankees rallied and had the tying and winning runs on base with two out when Houk called on Mantle to bat. Lary, pitching cautiously, walked Mickey to load the bases and then got Boyer to ground out to end it. Instead of gaining ground, the Yankees were now three and a half games behind.

During the game the father of Tiger outfielder Rocky Colavito, sitting eight rows behind the Detroit dugout, got in a dispute with a fan who had been riding the Tigers. The rancorous argument attracted the attention of the players, and when Colavito saw that his father was involved he charged into the stands to help. It took four team-mates, four policemen, three ushers and an umpire to separate Rocky and his father's antagonist. Colavito and the fan were both ejected from the game.

The next afternoon, as though in retaliation for his father's dis-comfort, Colavito unloaded on the Yankees, going four for five with two home runs and batting in half of Detroit's eight runs. Turley pitched precariously, giving up ten hits, but he still held a 3–3 tie into the eighth inning before the roof caved in. The Tigers scored five times in the last two innings, won again and shoved the Yankees four and a half games behind, the farthest back they'd been all season. Mantle played but went hitless, as did Maris. It was a low point for Houk. Mickey had stopped hitting, Roger hadn't started and, except for Ford, the starting pitching was terrible. Detroit, with 20 victories against 7 defeats, was threatening to tear the pennant race apart in May.

A big crowd turned out on a warm sunny Sunday afternoon to see the wrapup of the series, the doubleheader. Houk turned to Ford, who pitched shakily in the first inning, giving up a run. Then he settled down and allowed the Tigers only two hits from the second inning through the eighth. Cerv and Skowron hit home runs and the Yankees had a 4–1 lead going into the ninth inning. But Al Kaline, Detroit's great right fielder, tripled to lead off the ninth and with Colavito the next batter, Houk didn't hesitate. Ford had a track record of tiring in late innings, and a sudden winning rally by the Tigers now would drop the Yankees five and a half games back. It would also leave Detroit with the chance of sweeping the doubleheader and the series, a demoralizing prospect. Houk needed this game badly. He brought in Clevenger, who had pitched so well a few days earlier in Kansas City in his debut with the Yankees. Tex got the dangerous Colavito to ground out as Kaline scored to make the score 4–2, and he retired the next batter, too. The Yankees were only one out away from a very big victory.

Then Clevenger, pitching carefully, too carefully, walked the next two batters, Steve Boros and Charlie Maxwell, which brought a big lefthanded pinch-hitter named Larry (Bobo) Osborne to the plate. That didn't seem too much to worry about. There were two out already, and Osborne had been with the Tigers off and on for three or four seasons without ever hitting much above .200. But now, against Clevenger, he sent a drive down the right-field line that bounced around in the corner as Boros scored from second base and Maxwell all the way from first to tie the game.

Maris and Berra (who was sitting out the game in the Yankee bullpen in right field) yelled to the umpires that the ball had bounced over the low right-field fence and then back onto the field. Under the rules, such a hit is a ground-rule double, and the runners are allowed to advance only two bases. Maxwell, who had scored from first, would have to return to third. The Yankees argued this point strenuously, but in vain. The umpires ruled that the ball had not gone over the fence but had bounced off the top of it, and that it therefore remained in play. Maxwell's run was good. The score was tied. After losing the argument Houk, angry and upset, yanked Clevenger and brought Arroyo in. Luis walked the first two men he faced to load the bases before getting the final out to end the disastrous inning.

The Yankees were unable to score in the last of the ninth, and neither team scored in the tenth. Arroyo left for a pinch-hitter and Coates relieved him. Coates had lost the game Friday night after he relieved Arroyo, but this time he pitched well and got rid of the Tigers without difficulty in the eleventh inning. In the bottom of the eleventh Mantle, still in pain but apparently out of his slump, led off with his third hit of the game, a single, and moved around to third as the Yankees filled the bases. Houk called Berra in from the bullpen to pinch-hit, and Yogi hit a clean single to drive in Mantle with the winning run.

It was a tremendous victory for the Yankees, particularly after blowing the 4–1 lead in the ninth. Revived, they started quickly in the second game and jumped ahead, 7–0, but once again Houk saw his pitching falter. Terry gave up five runs before Coates, making his second appearance of the afternoon, relieved him. Coates stopped the

Tigers cold through the last four innings, and the Yankees won 7–5 to sweep the doubleheader, with Coates getting credit for both victories. The club had fought back from the edge of the cliff and trailed the Tigers now by two and a half games instead of the six and a half it would have been if they had lost both ends of that Sunday doubleheader.

Despite his bad leg Mantle had five hits in the two games and scored five runs. His batting average, which had plummeted during his slump, was back up over .300, but the Orioles' Jim Gentile had moved ahead of him in the home-run race, 11 to 9. Babe Ruth's name wasn't being heard as much. As for Maris, he had only two hits in nine at bats in the doubleheader, a disappointing afternoon but one that actually improved his batting average, which was now .217.

That doubleheader sweep may well have been the most significant moment of the year for the Yankees because after it they continued to stumble, losing four straight to Washington and Cleveland to fall into fourth place, five games behind Detroit. They had lost 9 of their last 12 games, and if they had blown the doubleheader to Detroit it would have been 11 of 12. Instead of being five games behind they would have been nine games out, a discouraging margin to overcome. Confidence in Houk would have been shaken, and the entire season could have collapsed—especially since their defeats in the week after the Detroit doubleheader were so disheartening. Washington was an expansion team, a club made up of culls and castoffs, and Cleveland had lost 11 games in a row to the Yankees before their two victories that week. Ditmar and Turley failed in successive starts for the third straight time, and even the relief pitching looked bad. "Everything disappeared," a sportswriter wrote after the Cleveland series, "including Arroyo and Clevenger."

18

Still, in that bad week the future began to unfold. Ditmar and Turley had pitched badly but Stafford and Sheldon each appeared twice, Sheldon starting, Stafford relieving, and while they didn't win both impressed Houk with their ability. And, although no one paid a great deal of attention to it at the time, Maris began hitting home runs.

The Yankees played another Sunday doubleheader in the Stadium a week after the Detroit series, this one with the Baltimore Orioles, their closest pursuers in the pennant race a year earlier. A crowd of almost 50,000 was on hand, the largest American League crowd of the season to that point and, as an alert statistician noted, the largest number of fans in Yankee Stadium before Memorial Day in five years. They saw Ford beat the Orioles 4–2 to stop the four-game losing streak, and then the Yankees lost another heartbreaking game in the nightcap. Sheldon started, only the fifth time in six weeks that Houk had used a starter other than one of his supposed big four of Ford, Ditmar, Turley and Terry, and in the third inning plate umpire John Rice called a Sheldon pitch a ball.

Howard, as catchers will, said to the umpire, "What did you call that?"

"Don't turn around," Rice said. "You know what I called it."

Umpires will tolerate mild arguments from catchers or hitters as long as it is not evident to the fans that the umpire's call is being disputed. But when a catcher or a batter turns toward the umpire, the protest becomes obvious, and umpires object because then they become targets of abuse from the crowd.

Howard turned around anyway and said, "I still want to know what you called it," and with that, Rice tossed him out of the game.

Houk came running from the dugout, protesting, asking what had happened. Rice said he'd ejected Howard because he was "delaying" the game. That inane remark infuriated Houk. His temper, which he'd kept pretty well under control through the frustrations and defeats of the past weeks, came pouring out, and he argued louder and longer with the umpire than the mild-mannered Howard had. Managers cannot come from the dugout to argue strike-and-ball calls but Houk was complaining only about the ejection of Howard. In any case, Rice, perhaps abashed by his own abruptness in banishing Howard, let the angry Houk have his say, and finally the game went on, with Howard out of the game and Blanchard catching in his place.

With the score tied in the seventh inning, one Oriole runner on base and two men out, Blanchard, who was noted more for his hitting than his deftness behind the plate, dropped an easy foul fly that should have ended the inning. Sheldon, who had pitched well up to then, walked the batter, yielded an infield hit that loaded the bases and allowed a two-run single by the Baltimore pitcher that gave the Orioles a 3–1 lead and the ball game.

It was a sour ending, and it meant that since the victory in the first game in Los Angeles early in May, the Yankees had lost 10 of 14 and were now six behind the Tigers, their lowest point of the season. The press critics and the letter writers were all over Houk. There was an outspoken school of thought that felt the Yankees had made a serious mistake in dropping Stengel and a worse one in hiring the inexperienced Houk.

Yet things were changing for the Yankees. In losing to the Senators earlier that week, they had rallied from an 8–1 deficit to score five times in the eighth and once again in the ninth and had the tying run on second base when the game ended. That was a harbinger of explosive rallies to come. So was the fact that in that five-run eighth,

Maris hit a two-run homer, his fourth of the year. He hit another homer in the Yankees' next game (another loss), one more the next day in another defeat and another, his fourth in four games, in Ford's victory over the Orioles in the first game of the Sunday doubleheader.

Maris did not hit one in the nightcap, and in a game with the Orioles the next day he had no chance to hit one. Troubled by an eye irritation during batting practice, he put drops in his eyes just before the game and had an allergic reaction. He played right field in the top of the first inning as the Orioles batted and, luckily, had no fielding chances, for when he came into the dugout after the inning he told Houk he couldn't see—at least not clearly. Houk took him out of the game and sent Blanchard up to bat for him in the bottom of the first inning. There's one for you, trivia fans: Who was the only man to bat for Roger Maris during his 61-homer season? Berra had started catching that game with Howard at first base in place of Skowron, who was in a bit of a slump. Now Berra moved to right field in Maris's place, with Blanchard remaining in the game behind the plate. Thus, all three of Houk's hard-hitting catchers were in the game at the same time, evidence of the versatility and depth of his bench strength.

It also serves to puncture one of the pleasant myths about the 1961 Yankees: that the Yankee catchers as a unit hit over 60 home runs that season. The three did hit 64 homers (Berra 22, Howard 21, Blanchard 21) but not all of them were hit when they were catching. The three also played in the outfield and at first base, and pinch-hit frequently. Berra caught only fifteen games all year; Blanchard played fifteen games in the outfield and Howard played nine at first base. The trio pinch-hit 59 times (Blanchard 26 times, Howard 14 times, Berra 19 times). The myth is fun to think about—that a kind of mass Yankee catcher broke Babe Ruth's record—but it's misleading.

Maris, his eyes okay, was back in the lineup when the Yankees played again two days later and hit another home run, his eighth of the season and his fifth in six games (not including the eyedrop game in which he appeared for only half an inning). Playing center field in place of Mantle, who was still bothered by the muscle pull, Maris also made a fine running catch. Houk started Terry, who so far had won only one game and had been almost as disappointing as Ditmar and Turley, and he responded with a three-hitter. Unfortunately, the third and last hit drove in the tying run in the eighth. When the Yankees came back to fill the bases with one out in the last half of the ninth, Houk sent the limping Mantle up to pinch-hit. The crowd yelled in anticipation. The count on Mantle went to three and two. Mickey backed away from the next pitch, which was well inside and should have given him a base on balls that would have forced in the winning run. But in backing away Mantle accidentally tipped the ball with his bat. Instead of a game-winning walk, it was only a foul tip, and the crowd groaned. On the next pitch Mantle struck out, and the crowd groaned again. But Kubek followed with a two-out single that drove in the run and the Yankees won after all.

Mantle was still unable to play the next day, and after that there were a couple of days of rain. The Yankees won, split a doubleheader, lost again. They were still marking time. It was nearly the end of May, and they were dawdling along in third place, behind both the Tigers and the rather startling Indians, who had won 11 of 13 games. Almost defiantly, Houk said he was still counting on Ditmar and Turley, but when he started them against Chicago in a Sunday doubleheader in the Stadium on May 28 it was really a final test—and they both failed. Turley was hit hard early in the opener, giving up a grand-slam homer and falling behind 6–0. The Yankees rallied to tie the score, the big blow another grand-slam homer, this one by Cerv, that carried all the way into an exit gate in the distant left-field bleachers. They went ahead on homers by Berra and Skowron, but Clevenger was blasted and the Sox scored eight late runs to win 14–9. Mantle started the game but left for a pinch-runner in the seventh inning when the Yankees went ahead.

In the second game Ditmar gave up three runs in the third inning and was relieved by Coates, who pitched shutout ball the rest of the way and won 5–3. Maris hit another homer, his ninth, and the Yankees left for Boston where Ford lost to the Red Sox 2–1 in a game played in a cold drizzle. (After that game Whitey didn't lose again until Maris had 46 home runs.) Mantle got the Yankees' only run in Ford's game with a home run in the second inning, his first homer in two weeks, and in the ninth he almost tied the score with another one when he sent a long drive toward the bullpen in distant right field that was caught at the fence for the final out of the game.

The Yankees were still in third place, still five games back, still only four games over .500, but the situation was changing. Things were falling into place. Maris was hitting. Mantle's leg was okay at last. Moving Berra to the outfield and playing Howard regularly behind the plate strengthened the offense. And now Houk dropped Ditmar and Turley as starting pitchers. "I don't know what's wrong with Art," he said at the end of May, "but he's not pitching the way he should be. He'll work out of the bullpen for a while." He said nothing at the time about Turley, but a few days later, after Bob started and failed again, he too was taken out of the rotation.

Houk replaced the two veterans with Sheldon, the rookie, and Stafford, who had not started a game all season. It was a gamble, really a bold gamble for a rookie manager. He was benching the team's biggest winner from the year before, and a Cy Young winner who was still only 30. It isn't easy to tell pitchers like that to sit down. If Stafford and Sheldon failed he'd be open to all sorts of abuse from his critics.

But Houk knew he had gone as far as he could—maybe too far—with his fading stars. Turley simply was no longer the pitcher who had been the best in baseball in 1958, when he won the Cy Young Award. A bright, perceptive, intelligent man who derived great pleasure from watching an opposing team closely in order to steal their signs (which he did with almost miraculous ease), Turley was slow to recognize his own deterioration as a pitcher. He had blamed Stengel for not working him often enough in 1960 but Houk gave him full opportunity in 1961—starting him regularly through April and May (he had more starts by June 1 than anyone but Ford)—but he couldn't cut it. Later in the season, when Terry was out for a time with a stiff shoulder, Houk started Turley three more times, again without success.

He was put on the disabled list in July, returned in time to be eligible for the World Series but didn't pitch in the Series. The Yanks kept him on the roster mostly as a gesture of appreciation for his past work and maybe with the faint hope that he might still regain his old form. But, sadly, Turley, not yet 31, was washed up. He persisted for two more seasons with the Yankees, the Angels and the Red Sox, but in his last 35 starts as a major leaguer he won only three games. He did some good work in relief but not much, and at 33 he packed it in.

RALPH HOUK:

Turley was having a tough time. He wasn't throwing the ball good at all. He had some tenderness in his arm but not enough to bother him. We put him on the disabled list for a while, but it didn't make any difference. His arm was gone. He'd lost his great fastball, and Turley was strictly a fastball pitcher. He never had great breaking stuff. He was amazing at stealing signs and at reading other pitchers, getting what pitch a guy was going to throw from the way he held the ball and stood on the mound. He must have had eyes like a telescope.

I went with Bob an awful long time that year, I didn't just take him out of there and say, "That's it." I had a lot of talks with him. He was an intelligent man, a high-class guy. He's done very well in business since he left baseball. I just happened to get him when his arm was going the other way. We'd talk and I'd say, "I'm gonna have to do something." He'd say, "Don't worry, I'm going to be all right. I'll be all right."

So many times when a power pitcher loses it, he still thinks he's got it. But the ball doesn't do the same thing it was doing before. I went as far as I could, but I finally had to sit him down. I said, "We'll bring you back by using you in the middle and get you to where you're going to be all right again." When we finally made the decision he never complained or went to the press or made a big issue out of it. He didn't like it, but I think he understood.

But he never did come back. He just couldn't throw the ball like he did before, and I had to make the change. It was a tough thing for me to do, and it was tough on him. Later, I did spot-start him in a couple of games I thought he could win just to build his confidence back, but it didn't work. He was a power pitcher, and he'd lost it and it never did come back.

Ditmar didn't have it anymore either. He was a tall, kind of lean fellow, well dressed, well spoken. The main thing he threw was a sinking fastball, and it wasn't sinking. He had to have pretty good speed on it and he had to have good control—he had to keep the ball low. When he lost something off that pitch, he wasn't tough to hit. The ball wasn't moving, and I think everybody in the league got on to it. People began laying off the ball down, and when he came up they'd hit him hard. Art was basically a ground-ball pitcher and the balls they hit off him they were hitting harder, and they were going through the infield. That's what happened in Pittsburgh in the Series, and again the next spring.

Art was a good battler and all of that, but he wasn't that great a pitcher to begin with. He never had a real good breaking ball—just a little slider.

That was when I told Roy Hamey we were going to have to give some thought to changing the pitching staff. I said, "The hell with it. I'm going to go with the young pitchers. We can score runs. We can win with them." And I gave the ball to Stafford and Sheldon.

Stafford had pretty good natural all-around ability. He was big and he was fairly strong and he had a good curveball, a good fastball, a fair change. Those are the three basic pitches and he had them. He had the kind of stuff that opened your eyes. I thought Bill had a chance to be a great pitcher. He did pitch pretty good that year and the next, but a lot of times he seemed to get in trouble during a game. He'd be going along, pitching as great a game as you ever saw, and two innings later he'd start making bad pitches, hang breaking balls. He was only 21 and on certain days he looked like a worldbeater, but I could never get the complete consistency out of him that I thought I should be getting. He never reached the potential I thought he should have reached.

His career ended too early. He had some shoulder problems. I don't believe he was 28 when he was through. I think a lot of things began happening to Billy in his life outside of baseball—things that just didn't work out real well for him. I don't think he handled his off-the-field activities as well as he should have. He's doing all right now, though. He lives near Detroit and he has something to do with one of those places where you go for exercise and to lose weight and all that stuff.

Bill was a funny kid. I'm not sure I ever really figured him out. I don't think he really had confidence in himself, not even when he pitched so well there those first few years. He looked confident, and he acted confident outwardly, but I don't believe he was.

Sheldon didn't have as much ability as Stafford but he had an exceptional year for us in 1961. He was a big, tall, kind of slender kid, and everything went right for him that year. That can happen, but basically Rollie was just a low-ball, fastball pitcher with more of a slider than a curve. He's another one who after a while lost just a little off his fastball and that was the end of it. He never had quite the right delivery, and we couldn't seem to correct that. Everybody says, well, you can teach a guy to do this and you can teach him to do that but, hey, if you could do that every time, there'd be a million great pitchers.

Sheldon was a real solid person, took good care of himself, the kind of a fellow you'd like to have for a son. A good solid kid. He was a rookie but he was 24, and his attitude, everything about him, was much more mature than rookies usually are. He had good composure. He was the kind of pitcher that they could get two or three bloop hits in a row off him, and it wouldn't bother him. He'd still throw that low fastball, just come right in there with it, where a Stafford might get concerned and try something else.

Sheldon was 15–1 in Class D ball the year before, and that won–lost record is why we kept him. He was a little older, and we needed another pitcher, and I said, "Anybody who won that many games, let's find out if he can win up here." I've always been a strong believer in that—if a man wins in this league and he wins in that league, there's some reason why he wins. He may win 6–5 or 9–8 once in a while, but he wins. You take another pitcher who seems to have all the stuff in the world, but for some reason he don't win. He's losing 2–1 and 3–2 all the time and the other fellow's winning 6–5, and there's got to be a reason. Some guys can get hitters out when they have to, and some can't. That's why earned run averages can be deceiving. One pitcher has a 2.95 earned-run average and another one is 3.50, but the guy with the 3.50 wins because he gets the hitter out when he has to get him out. Sheldon was like that.

A lot of people were second-guessing me that spring, and the mail was coming in pretty bad—get Casey back, and all that kind of stuff. But we put Yogi in left field and then we made the pitching move, and that's when things started getting better. We began winning the games we had been losing.

Whether it was the change in the pitching rotation, or Berra in left field, or Mantle's return to health, or Maris's suddenly blazing bat, in June the Yankee season turned around and for the rest of the year the club played at a sustained high level. The pitching, from being plain bad, became extraordinary. In the first 40 games of the season, through May 31, the staff had only one shutout (Ford's, back in April) and otherwise had never held a rival team to fewer than two runs. But now Sheldon and Stafford each turned in three straight complete-game victories, and the staff produced seven one-run games in two weeks. By the end of the season it had 14 shutouts and 22 one-run games.

And the Yankees rolled.

The enormous home-run power of the team began to display itself. Cerv hit his huge grand slam into the bleachers in the first game of the May 28 doubleheader with Chicago, Maris hit a homer in the second game, Mantle hit one the next day in Ford's loss to Boston, and on the day after that, in Fenway Park on May 30, everything erupted. Mantle hit a three-run homer in the first inning. Maris hit one in the third. Terry started and was routed, but relief pitching stopped Boston the rest of the way as the Yankees scored nine more runs. Berra hit a homer, Skowron hit one, Skowron hit a second one, Maris hit his second of the game and Mantle hit *his* second as the

Yankees buried the Red Sox 12–3. Seven home runs—two apiece by three different batters. The seven in one game just missed the record of eight set by an older Yankee team back in 1939, and it was only the second time in American League history that three players on one team hit two homers in the same game. Six of the seven homers were hit not over Fenway's friendly left-field wall but over the distant fences in center and right. Coates, who pitched the last three innings, had a reputation as a headhunter—a pitcher who throws close to, if not deliberately at, opposing hitters—and he plunked Boston's Jackie Jensen with a fastball. The Boston pitcher, Mike Fornieles, retaliated by hitting Coates.

It was a wild game, and it left the Yankees elated. The next afternoon there was more. Mantle hit his fourteenth homer of the season, Maris hit his twelfth and the Yankees won again. Sheldon pitched well but in the seventh, leading 7–2, he gave up a single and a walk and Houk called for Arroyo. An infield hit let in one run and a wild pitch let in another, and the score was now 7–4. In the eighth Arroyo gave up another run. Make it 7–5. And in the ninth another—7–6. After they scored in the ninth, the Red Sox had the bases loaded with one out, the tying run on third, the winning run on second. Houk in desperation yanked Arroyo and brought in the lefthanded McDevitt to pitch to the dangerous but lefthanded-hitting Vic Wertz. Wertz had driven in the winning run against Ford two days earlier. McDevitt threw one pitch and Wertz hit a sharp ground ball to Richardson. Bobby snapped it up, fired it to Kubek at second for one, Kubek relayed it to Skowron to double up Wertz, and the game was over. The Yankees had won again.

The home runs kept coming. Skowron hit two the next day in Boston, and the day after that in Chicago Berra hit two. Maris also hit one in that game in Chicago, and he hit another the next day and another the day after that, which moved him ahead of Mantle in the home-run race. Back in Yankee Stadium, in a doubleheader sweep of the Twins, Mantle and Blanchard and Kubek hit homers, and in the next four games Maris and Boyer and Berra and Skowron hit homers before the club, in losing to Kansas City, failed to hit a home run for the first time since May 21, the day before Roger put the drops in his eyes. Houk's heroes had hit 32 homers in 17 games, a major league record, and they won 13 of those games to move decisively back into the heat of the pennant race.

The end of the team's home-run streak did not stop Maris and Mantle. Roger hit homers on June 2, 3 and 4, June 6 and 7, June 9, June 11, June 13 and 14, June 17, 18, 19 and 20, June 22. Mickey, trying to keep pace, hit seven homers himself during those three weeks, but even so he fell behind the blazing-hot Roger, 27 to 22.

No one made much note of the home run Maris hit back on May 17, his fourth of the year—Mantle had ten at the time, Gentile eleven, and Colavito, Harmon Killebrew and Bob Allison each had twice as many homers as Maris then—but it marked the beginning of the most amazing stretch of home-run hitting by any player in the history of the game. Mention is frequently made that Maris hit fifteen homers in June, the most he hit in any one month that season, but that admirable statistic (not in itself a record) is artificially tied to the calendar month and does not reflect the extraordinary extent of Maris's hitting. His great surge that began on May 17 ended on June 22, eight days before the end of the month (he hit no homers at all in the last week of June). But in the 37 days (a month plus a week) between May 17 and June 22, Maris hit 24 home runs—24 in 38 games (including the game he appeared in for only half an inning). He hit nearly 40 percent of his 61 homers in 1961 during that astonishing five-week period. No one else—not Babe Ruth or Henry Aaron, not Willie Mays or Reggie Jackson or Ted Williams or Mickey Mantle, not Jimmie Foxx or Hank Greenberg or Ralph Kiner, no one—has ever hit nearly that many homers in that length of time. Ruth came closest. Everyone knows that the Babe hit 17 home runs in September of 1927, a blistering run down the stretch that made it extremely difficult for anyone chasing his record to catch him. But Ruth's great finishing surge began earlier, on August 16, when he had 36 home runs and was still behind Lou Gehrig. Babe hit 24, the last 24 of his 60-homer year, from August 16 through September 30, 24 in 46 days, embracing 41 games, an exceptional feat in itself, but Maris simply blew that apart.

For years, writers commenting on challenges to Ruth's record warned how demanding September would be for anyone trying to surpass the Babe. Maris met that challenge, but he had his great September in the spring, in May and June. His 24 home runs in five weeks was a great baseball feat, and it deserves to be ranked with DiMaggio's 56-game hitting streak as an example of sustained, unrelenting achievement.

When Maris started his great run he was seven homers behind Mantle. When he finished it, he was five ahead. Mickey himself hit 12 in the same period, a demanding rate per game that works out to 51 homers a season, and yet Maris hit twice as many as Mantle did. If Roger had maintained that impossible pace for the entire year he would have hit more than 100 home runs.

But, of course, he slowed down. After hitting his twenty-seventh of the season on June 22 he hit no homers at all for the next seven games while Mantle, in good physical shape again, bravely fought his way back into home-run contention. He hit six homers in a week as June turned into July, four of them in three games.

Then Maris, after his dry spell, responded, and the two moved together almost step for step. In a three-game series against the Senators in Yankee Stadium on the first weekend of July, Maris and Mantle between them hit six home runs. Their combined power was simply breathtaking. Thirteen times between Memorial Day and Labor Day they hit homers in the same game. In early June one or the other of the two hit homers in eight of nine games; later in the month one or the other hit homers in six straight games, and they did that again in July. From May 28 through June 22 there were only four days when fans saw neither of them hit a home run. And the other Yankees were belting them out too. After that streak of 17 straight games with one or more homers, the team hit roundtrippers in 13 of the next 15 games. In other words, in 30 of the 33 games the Yankees played in that period they had at least one home run. Later, in July, the team hit homers in 20 of 21 games. Such sustained power was and is un-paralleled in the annals of baseball.

RALPH HOUK:

The home-run power on that club was unbelievable. I can't believe there was ever a more powerful club in the history of baseball. I mean, we were never out of a ball game. We could be behind three or four runs going into the seventh or eighth inning, and we still thought we could win. I used to get a kick—well, not a kick, really—but I used to shake my head at a lot of the mail I got from fans asking why don't you run more, why don't you steal? [The 1961 Yankees stole only 28 bases, much the lowest total in the league.]

Why would I steal? With a team like that, with the home-run hitters in that lineup, I'd have been crazy to steal. Am I going to give up the chance of a big inning just so I can move a man to second base? It's like playing in Fenway Park, with that short left-field fence. You can't run in that ball park, even if you have a team that's able to steal a lot of bases. You can't take the chance. You never know when some hunky-dunky hitter is going to pop one over the wall and clear the bases, and you can score from first base on a home run as easy as you can score from second. You'd be out of your mind to run there. You're maybe giving up a three-run inning in order to play for one run. It doesn't make sense.

And that's the way it was with that Yankee club. We could blow them out. I *always* felt we were in the ball game. But you'd be amazed by the mail I was getting, complaining that we weren't running enough, complaining that I wasn't stealing enough.

As the pitching solidified and the home-run pace intensified, the club won steadily—16 times in 20 games, beginning with the big Memorial Day victory over the Red Sox. Terry, after his weak beginning (only two victories in his first eight starts—although he was charged with no defeats), suddenly settled down and like Stafford and Sheldon pitched three consecutive complete games.

But the schedule was getting heavy. After having 16 days off during April and May, the Yankees now played games on 32 consecutive days, and in six weeks had only two days off. Houk was keenly aware that the schedule was jamming up and he knew that his pitching, even with a revived Terry and the welcome work of Stafford and Sheldon, needed help to stand up to it. He had ten pitchers but only six of them—Ford, Terry, Stafford, Sheldon, Coates and Arroyo— were contributing significantly. He needed some new bodies.

Ditmar made his first appearance as a reliever early in June and did nothing to help his cause. After covering first base on a ground ball hit to Skowron, he turned and argued with the umpire after the batter was called safe, forgetting about a baserunner on second, who rounded third and scooted home while Ditmar was yelling at the ump.

Two days later he had another disaster. Terry started and pitched well, taking a 5–2 lead into the bottom of the eighth before giving up a two-run homer. He was relieved by Clevenger, whom Houk was still counting on to ease the relief-pitching burden on Arroyo, particularly now that Stafford and Sheldon were no longer working out of the bullpen. However, Tex gave up two quick hits and with runners on second and third Houk reluctantly turned to the hardworking Arroyo again. Louie intentionally walked the dangerous slugger Roy Sievers to load the bases with one out. He had to pitch then to Saturnino Orestes Arrieta Armas Minoso, the magnificent Cuban outfielder better known as Minnie, who was nearing the end of his career but was still a dangerous and productive hitter—as he demonstrated by hitting a fly ball to drive in the tying run. The game went into extra innings, and Arroyo pitched impeccably through the ninth, tenth, eleventh and twelfth before Houk lifted him for a pinch-hitter in the top of the thirteenth. In the bottom of that inning Houk called again on Ditmar, who trudged in from the bullpen to face the powerful Sievers. Art threw one pitch and Sievers hit it for a home run to win the game for the White Sox. John Drebinger called it "the most painful defeat the Yankees had all season." It could have broken the morale of a lesser team.

But the Yankees, now playing excellent ball and aware that they were, bounced back from that defeat to win 6 straight and 11 of their next 12. In one game they scored three runs on a bases-loaded double by Howard, another on a homer by Maris, and four more runs on five singles in one inning. The Yankee offense was not only strong, it was versatile.

But the pitching, while strong, was still thin. Then Ditmar worked five hitless innings of relief, a performance that sparked a trade that, in Houk's view, made the Yankees' season.

RALPH HOUK:

Charlie Finley of Kansas City initiated the trade. He called me in my hotel in Cleveland just before the trading deadline. Finley was always calling, always looking for trades—he called everybody every day, trying to stir something up. I'll tell you a funny thing: When he phoned me in Cleveland he disguised his voice and tried to pretend he was

Roy Hamey, I suppose just to see if I'd say something, tip my hand. I knew it wasn't Hamey but it took me a while to figure out that it was Finley. Charlie used to get a kick out of disguising his voice and phoning people. But that was his first year and I didn't know about that and I didn't know who it was until he finally told me.

Then he said, "Can we do anything? Can we make a deal?"

I said, "I don't know."

He said, "What are you looking for?"

I said, "Well, we're kind of looking for a lefthanded pitcher."

Well, Finley had Bud Daley in Kansas City, and he just popped up and said, "What about this Daley?"

Now maybe Daley wasn't pitching good for him then, I don't even remember, but he had pitched good for Kansas City in 1959 and 1960, and I'd known him in the minor leagues when I was managing Denver and he was pitching for Indianapolis. I thought Daley was a real good lefthanded pitcher then, and I knew he was a battler. He had that little short right arm that he held kind of funny [Daley's right arm was slightly malformed]. I remember that because we used to try to bunt on him. That made people mad, bunting on the poor guy. Well, hell, all's fair in love and war, I don't care if they got funny legs or arms or not. And it didn't do us much good anyway because Daley was a pretty good athlete. He hit .295 for Kansas City one year, which is damn good for a pitcher. I knew Daley was the kind of pitcher we needed, and I figured he could be a big addition to the staff.

So I said, "What are *you* looking for?"

He said, "If we give up pitching we gotta get pitching. What about Ditmar?"

He brought Ditmar's name in, I didn't. Now I'm really getting interested. I figured with Stafford and Terry and Sheldon giving us a lift we could trade Ditmar, we could make that kind of move.

But I said, "I'm not too sure about that." You don't get into it right off when you make a trade. You always act like you're not much interested. But, boy, I was ready right quick.

Still, I said, "I don't know, Charlie. Why don't you let me think about it. Could you call me back a little later?"

I hung up and phoned Hamey right away. I couldn't reach him at first, but we needed a lefthander and Daley was a good one, and I'd already put Ditmar in the bullpen, and I knew Roy would go along with it because he and I sort of agreed on everything. So when Finley called me back I said, "Yeah, I think I'll do that."

He said, "Aaaah, you know you can't make a deal by yourself. I'll have to talk to Hamey."

I said, "I'm not saying I can, but I think we have a trade."

To make a long story short I finally got in touch with Roy, and Roy called Finley and they closed the deal. We had to give him Deron Johnson, too. Deron was a big guy, probably six two, and he became a real good player later on in the National League. But he developed slow and he was a disappointment then, and he didn't do much for Kansas City either. Neither did Ditmar. [Ditmar was in 32 games for Kansas City that season without winning a game and after six more disappointing efforts the next year retired from baseball.]

I liked Art. He was a good man on the club, and it was tough on me when I had to let him go, but we needed the lefthander so bad, and I had to give Stafford and Sheldon a crack at this thing.

Anyway, the trade was made, and it was basically Ditmar for Daley. We were giving up a pitcher we didn't think could pitch anymore, and we were getting the lefthander we needed. It turned out to be a hell of a trade for us. We could go either way with Daley; he could pitch long relief or he could start. And he'd take the ball any time. Bud did a great job for us. I don't think we would have won the pennant without him.

Daley was a very likeable guy, a hard worker, the kind of player you could count on every day. He didn't have a flashy personality but he wasn't one of those quiet guys, either. He was outgoing, he could take a joke and kid around. We had a bunch of guys on that team who liked to win but who liked to have fun too, and he fit right in. He had a nice face, kind of a round face, blond hair, blue eyes. He'd do anything you wanted him to do, start, relieve, middle-line, he never complained. He was happy to be with the Yankees.

Daley could do a lot of things with the ball. He was maybe a poor man's Whitey Ford. He did a lot of the things Whitey did, but he just didn't have the great stuff that made Whitey a Hall of Famer. Buddy was easygoing but he was a very confident person, and a good guy. He lives out in the middle of Wyoming now, has a little business there.

Houk brought up a chubby minor league righthander named Hal Reniff to replenish his bullpen, dropping his fourth catcher, Jesse Gonder. Gonder, a chunky lefthanded hitter, had started off the season with two straight important pinch-hits but had been a disappointment after that. "Jesse would get down on himself," Houk said. "You had to talk to him. At one time we thought he was going to be an outstanding hitter, but he just stayed at one level." (Gonder spent some time in the minors after he left the Yankees but eventually surfaced again with the Mets. He hit .302 in 1963, one of the few early Mets to bat respectably. He also played with the Reds, the Braves and the Pirates.)

Houk started Coates in a doubleheader and got a good performance from him. Ford was winning steadily and Terry, after giving up two hits and a run in the first inning of a game, pitched hitless ball the rest of the way. Needing an extra starter in the press of the schedule (just before Daley joined the club), Houk started McDevitt in the second game of a doubleheader and it cost him. McDevitt was hit hard, the Yankees lost and that was the end for Danny. "I thought McDevitt would do better than he did for us," Houk said. "He was a nice little guy, kind of redheaded, with a sidearmed sinker, but he didn't work out." After Daley arrived McDevitt was traded to Minnesota for infielder Billy Gardner; Houk needed a backup third baseman now that Johnson was gone, and Gardner could also fill in at short and second. The Yankees also signed the veteran first baseman Earl Torgeson, who had been released by the White Sox.

RALPH HOUK:

Roy Hamey liked Torgeson and he was a lefthanded hitter, which was good in our ball park. But we got Earl more for protection than anything else, just in case anything happened to Skowron. We wanted a deeper bench all the time, because we'd lost so much of it to the expansion. We figured Torgeson was a fellow who could maybe come in some day and hit one out for us and win a ball game. We thought he was a good addition to the club because he was a professional, and you don't pick up professionals too easy at that time of year. We were trying not to leave anything unturned, because that pennant in 1961 didn't come as easy as the record makes it look.

Everybody liked Torgeson, but he didn't play much of a part with the club and we had to drop him from the roster before September 1, when you set the players you want in the World Series. But he stayed with us the rest of the year as a coach, just in case we needed him. He was old—that was his last year—but he could still swing that bat a little.

We went for Gardner to protect ourselves in the infield after we traded Deron Johnson. Minnesota was looking for pitching, and it didn't look as though McDevitt was going to help us much, and we had Daley now, so it was a good trade for us. I'd always admired Billy Gardner. I'd seen him in the minor leagues, and he was an intelligent guy, a manager later on with Minnesota and Kansas City. The reason I wanted him as bad as I did was that I knew he could do a pretty good job anywhere you wanted him. He wasn't a bad hitter, and he could play third, he could play second, he could fill in at shortstop. He could play all the infield positions, and he could handle the bat pretty well. He could do things. He played quite a lot for us that season, 40 games or so, and that kind of man is important on a ball club. Billy was fun to have around. He had a very good dry sense of humor, and he could come up with some pretty funny sayings.

I got a kick out of him. When he became manager of the Twins we'd always have something to say to each other at home plate before games. Some managers are uptight before a game, but Billy never was. He's a great guy, a clever man and a good manager. Sometimes he's awfully outspoken around his players, though. I don't know if that helps too much at times.

We added one other pitcher that summer, Al Downing. Al was having a great year at Binghamton, and we brought him right to the majors from A ball. He was a little lefthander and he joined us in Washington at a time when we needed pitchers—we had a lot of games all in a bunch.

Al was very quiet, although now he's a broadcaster in Los Angeles. The thing I remember most about him that year was that he'd fall asleep on the bus riding out to the ball park and go to sleep on it again coming back afterward. He was a real good kid, nice looking, well dressed, never drank or messed around, just an outstanding kid. He wasn't very tall but he was well built, and not a typical lefthander. Most lefthanders are talkative and all that, but not Al. He was very quiet.

He was going good at Binghamton and we were a little short of pitching, so we were thinking of possibly making him a fifth starter. We had it set up so that when he joined us he'd be ready to start right away—and we'd get him in there before he realized what was going on, that he was pitching in the majors. He started in Washington and I think he struck out four of the first six hitters he faced, and I thought, "Boy, where have we been hiding him?" Then he got wild and couldn't get the ball over and I had to get him out of there in the second or third inning.

We used him a little after that but he was still wild. He was probably too young—he was only 20—but after that year he kept getting better and better. He won a lot of games later on for us, and after he left the Yankees he won 20 one year for the Dodgers.

21

Kennedy's summit conference with Khrushchev in Vienna in June did little to ease the tension that summer between the Soviet Union and the West. Khrushchev charged that West Berlin had been turned into a permanent United States military base and that it was being used for espionage and sabotage against East Germany and the rest of the Soviet bloc. Refugees from East Germany were using the city as an escape point. There was easy access to the Western-controlled parts of the city from the Soviet-controlled sector and from neighboring East Germany, and the flow of disenchanted easterners to the West kept increasing.

Khrushchev's words grew angrier, and Kennedy and de Gaulle repeated their determination to defend West Berlin from Communist encroachment. Kennedy said the West had to take a strong stand against the Soviet threat even "at the risk of nuclear war." He called for an increase in the United States army and ordered that the draft pool—the number of men available to be called into military service— be doubled. Baseball, filled with eligible young men, was keenly aware of the military draft (Stafford, who was in the reserve, worried about being called back into uniform; Kubek was drafted after the season ended). The president urged the building of bomb shelters in American cities and towns. Things were getting edgy.

Moscow denounced Kennedy's speech, saying the Berlin issue was being exploited in order to accelerate the arms race. Khrushchev said he did not anticipate war over Berlin and suggested more talks with the West, but his anger over the increasing flow of refugees from East Germany through Berlin was still evident, and the confrontation between East and West persisted.

America's uneasiness was heightened by two more ventures into space, one by the United States, the other by the Soviets. American astronaut Virgil Grissom successfully replicated Shepard's earlier "sub-orbital" flight but then lost his Mercury space capsule when it sank after it parachuted safely to the surface of the ocean. The sinking was unexplained at first, but apparently Grissom accidentally triggered explosive bolts that blew open a side hatch, and he had to scramble to safety from his cramped quarters as the valuable capsule filled with water. It sank with all its equipment to the ocean floor, too far below the surface to be recovered by the rescue gear available in that day. Scientists solemnly warned that the loss of the capsule and the information it contained was a setback for the space program.

Barely two weeks later, as the tension generated by the Berlin crisis continued to spread, the Russians, as though to vaunt their head start in the space race, sent another cosmonaut into orbit. Americans, still smarting over Grissom's failure, were stunned to learn that a Soviet army major named Gherman Titov had circled the earth 16 times and had stayed aloft for more than 24 hours. Khrushchev subsequently announced that the Soviets might build a monster intercontinental missile—and added blandly that it would be used to back a Soviet peace plan.

In baseball the trade deadline, after which no more trades could be made, was midnight on June 15. Even after the deals were completed that sent Ditmar, Johnson and McDevitt away, the borderline players on the Yankees fretted. They didn't want to leave New York. Before the game on June 15 the slumping Hector Lopez, a pleasant man with a fine, quiet sense of humor, was seen huddling behind the water cooler during batting practice.

"Hey, Hector," someone said, "what in the world are you doing back there?"

"Hiding out till midnight," Lopez answered.

Midnight passed and Hector was still with the club and would be for five more seasons.

The Yankees were still in third place but edging closer to the lead. Ford pitched another complete game, Mantle and Maris (who was hitting fifth behind Mickey at this point) were ablaze with home runs. In mid-June the club moved past Detroit into second place, only a game behind the red-hot Indians (who had won 21 of 25 games to move into first place), and went into Cleveland for a three-game series with the new league leaders.

Houk, still hard-pressed for starters—his club had now played 20 games in 16 days, including four doubleheaders—used Coates against Cleveland, and this time it didn't work. The Indians scored six runs in the first two innings and coasted to a 7–2 victory, pushing the Yankees down into third place again. It was the first time since the opening day of the season that Houk's team had been totally out of a ball game. Fifteen of their 21 defeats to this point had been by one or two runs, the close games Houk said they'd been losing instead of winning.

Ford beat the Indians the next night but the Yanks were still in third place—though only one game back—when Terry took the mound against Cleveland in the final game of the series. It was a critical moment, and Terry met the challenge. He was still pitching strongly with the score tied 2–2 after nine innings and Houk stayed with him in extra innings.

Neither team scored in the tenth. In the top of the eleventh Cerv hit for Jack Reed (who had gone into left field as a defensive replacement for Berra) and led off with a single. With Cerv on first base and no one out, Frank Funk, the Indians' good relief pitcher, struck out both Skowron and Howard. However, on the third strike to Howard, the big, bulky Cerv broke for second and stole it successfully. He hadn't stolen a base since 1959, and this was only the twelfth (and last) stolen base of his dozen seasons in the majors. Cleveland catcher John Romano was so surprised that he threw the ball into center field, and Cerv moved on to third base on the error. Blanchard then pinch-

Retired manager Casey Stengel was back home in California, but he seemed to be looking over Houk's shoulder. (New York Yankees)

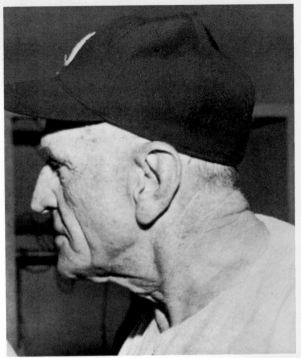

Manager Ralph Houk. (New York Yankees)

Ryne Duren.
(New York Yankees)

Jim Coates.
(New York Yankees)

Youthful Ralph Terry
won 16 games, lost
only 3. (Bob Olen)

Rollie Sheldon.
(New York Yankees)

Bill Stafford.
(New York Yankees)

Bud Daley.
(Anderson Photo)

Bob Cerv.
(New York Yankees)

Elston Howard.
(New York Yankees)

Bill Skowron.
(Bob Olen)

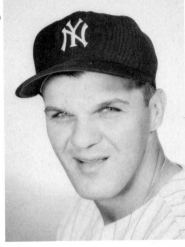

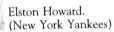

Hector Lopez.
(New York Yankees)

Shortstop Tony Kubek
(left) and second base-
man Bobby Richardson.
(New York Yankees)

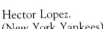

Yogi Berra, in his sixteenth season, still swung a potent bat. (New York Yankees)

John Blanchard, a dangerous home-run hitter. (New York Yankees)

Third baseman Clete Boyer. (New York Yankees)

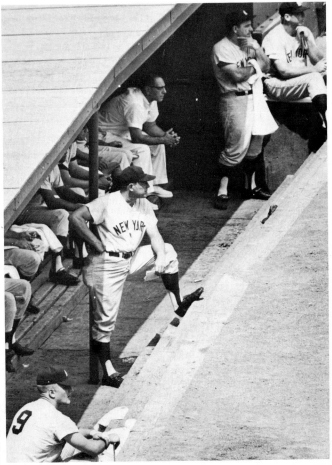

Roger Maris and Mickey Mantle (here with Mrs. Babe Ruth) not only had to battle one another for the home-run crown, but had to cope with the long-dead Babe, too. (New York Daily News)

Manager Houk (foot on step) intently watches the field, as do three of his great stars: Mickey Mantle (top), Yogi Berra (next to Mantle), and Roger Maris (bottom). (New York Yankees)

Surrounded by reporters during his home-run duel with Maris, Mantle remained calm and handled the pressure gracefully. (New York Yankees)

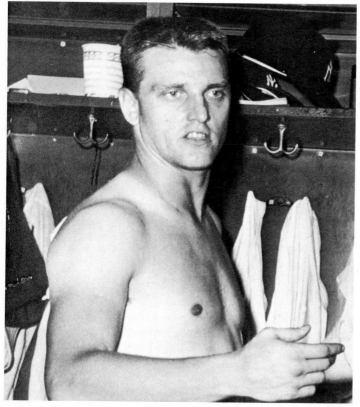

But Maris found it more and more difficult to keep his emotions under control when he was besieged by hordes of reporters asking him the same questions day after day. (Associated Press)

At a "day" for Ford in September, Whitey was only slightly amused at one of his gifts, a giant-size roll of Life Savers, out of which stepped reliever Luis Arroyo. (New York Daily News)

Home runs exploded from Maris's bat. His swing was classic: level, graceful, and powerful. (New York Yankees)

The 1961 Yankees: (from left, first row) Whitey Ford, Bill Skowron, Hal Reniff, coach Jim Hegan, coach Frank Crosetti, manager Ralph Houk, coach Johnny Sain, coach Wally Moses, Earl Torgeson, Clete Boyer, Yogi Berra, Mickey Mantle. (Second row) trainer Gus Mauch, Billy Gardner, Bob Hale, Joe DeMaestri, Tony Kubek, Tex Clevenger, Ralph Terry, Hector Lopez, Bob Cerv, Elston Howard, Roger Maris, Bob Turley, trainer Joe Soares. (Third row) Bobby Richardson, Al Downing, Luis Arroyo, John Blanchard, Bill Stafford, Rollie Sheldon, Jim Coates, batting practice pitcher Spud Murray, Bud Daley. (In front) batboys Frank Prudenti and Fred Bengis. (New York Daily News)

Winning the World Series was the ultimate triumph for a joyful Houk in 1961. (New York Daily News)

Exultant Ford and grinning Mantle share a moment of triumph. Ford won two games in the 1961 World Series after winning 25 during the regular season. (New York Yankees)

hit for Bobby Richardson and singled to score Cerv. Terry held the Indians down in the bottom of the eleventh, and the Yankees won 3–2 to move past both Detroit and Cleveland into first place.

They didn't stay there, at least not for long, but they had won 16 of 20 games and moved confidently on to Detroit, where the next night a huge crowd packed Tiger Stadium and where things turned a little sour for the New Yorkers. The Tigers beat the Yanks frustratingly. Jake Wood led off the Detroit half of the first inning with a single. Bill Bruton followed with another single. Maris booted the ball and then threw wildly past the infield as Wood scored and Bruton raced around to third. Kaline hit a grounder to Boyer, who bobbled it, and another run scored. Boyer made another error in the second inning. In the third, Bruton, who went four for four in the game, singled again and Kaline doubled him home to put the Tigers ahead 3–0. The Yankees got back into the game when Skowron hit a two-run homer in the fifth, but in the bottom of that inning Wood and Bruton again hit back-to-back singles. Maris fielded Bruton's hit cleanly this time and threw toward third in an effort to get Wood, but Kubek at shortstop cut off the throw and fired to Skowron at first base in an effort to trap Bruton, who had made a wide turn toward second. His throw hit Bruton for yet another error, the Yankees' fifth of the game, and Wood raced home to make it 4–2 Detroit, the final score.

The five errors ignited the fires of Houk's temper. He didn't yell at his players, but in the seventh when Skowron was called out at second base on a very close play Houk exploded. He fumed and he stormed and he threw his cap. He kicked dirt. One newspaper account said, "At no time this season has the usually calm major put on anything approaching this explosive demonstration." He was finally tossed out of the game, his first ejection of the season.

The defeat dropped the Yankees back to third place again, one game behind the Indians and Tigers, who were now in a flat tie for the lead, and they fell another game back the next afternoon before another big Detroit crowd when Daley, making his debut with the club, was pounded by the Tigers, giving up four runs in the first inning and three more in the second. It was a bad day all around. Kubek, chasing a pop fly into left field, crashed into Cerv and had to leave the game with badly bruised ribs.

Ford salvaged the final game of the series, shutting out the Tigers 9–0 as the Yankees scored a rare win over their nemesis, Lary. DeMaestri, filling in for Kubek, had three hits in his first three at bats and drove in a run. Blanchard hit two home runs, Skowron another and Maris one.

The Yankees went on to Kansas City, Minnesota and Los Angeles on this 16-game road trip, their longest of the season. Daley did very well in his next start, but Terry, who had done something to his right shoulder in his stirring 11-inning victory over the Indians, was unable to pitch and Houk sent him back to New York to be examined by Dr. Sidney Gaynor, the club physician. Boyer, whose left shoulder was bothering him, was also sent back and the newly acquired Gardner filled in for him at third base.

Houk used Turley in Terry's place against Minnesota, but that didn't work out too well. In Los Angeles, in the last game of the road trip, he tried Turley again against the Angels, who sent Duren to the mound as starting pitcher against his old teammates.

Turley pitched surprisingly well and had a shutout going as the Angels came to bat in the bottom of the sixth. Duren, too, pitched strongly, yielding only one run through six innings. So it was 1–0 in the Yankees' favor as the Angels batted in the bottom of the sixth. Ted Kluszewski led off with a double, went to third base on an infield out and stayed there while another batter grounded out. With two out, Turley walked the next batter, letting a good lefthanded hitter, Ken Hunt, come to bat. Duren was on deck, so Houk had Turley walk Hunt intentionally to load the bases and pitch to Duren.

Duren was a very poor hitter. His lifetime batting average in this, his fifth full season in the majors, was .061. He had not had a base hit since 1958 and, indeed, had only two hits in his major league career. He had one single in 14 at bats in 1957, one in 13 at bats in 1958, and no hits at all in 20 bats in in 1959 and 1960.

Turley pitched, and to the shocked surprise of the Yankees, who knew Duren couldn't hit, Ryne swung and bounced the ball past the mound and over second base. The ball dribbled through onto the outfield grass for a base hit and two runs crossed the plate to put the Angels ahead 2–1. The hit was the only one Duren had all season in 1961, when he went one for 25 for an .040 batting average. The two runs batted in were 40 percent of all the RBIs (five) that Duren had in his entire major league career.

Yet, by God, there he was on first base, his thick-lensed glasses gleaming, his cherubic face beaming. And there were still two men on base, with diminutive Albie Pearson, the leadoff man, following Duren to the plate. Pearson was small (five feet five, 140 pounds) but he was strong, and he was an excellent athlete. Two nights before he had hit a home run off Ford. Now he jumped on one of Turley's pitches and hit a three-run homer to put LA ahead 5–1.

It was the worst inning Houk had to endure all year. He took Turley out after Pearson's homer, and Clevenger and Reniff held the Angels scoreless the rest of the way, but the Yankees lost 5–3 as Duren gained the single most satisfying victory of his career.

RALPH HOUK:

He did beat us in that one game, and got that base hit. I'll never forget that goddamn thing. That was one of the games Turley started, and Bob pitched pretty well that night for five or six innings. But he got a couple of men on with two out and I walked Hunt to bring Duren up. To be honest, I couldn't believe it when the Angels let him hit. Ryne was pitching good, but the score was 1–0 in our favor and I thought sure they'd pinch-hit for him.

The only thing I worried about then was that Turley had a tendency toward wildness and might walk him with the bases full. I was praying, "Don't walk him, don't walk him." I never dreamed Ryne would get a hit. He was a *terrible* hitter. He choked way up on the bat and it was like he was using a hammer to hit a nail. He swung at the ball like that, and the damn thing went through the infield and two runs scored and they go ahead. Then that little Pearson hits a homer and we're behind 5–1. It was unbelievable. I felt like dying.

I remember that Mantle hit a homer in the ninth, but it wasn't enough, and we lost. Afterward Gene Autry came into our clubhouse. Naturally, we filled the park that night. We always did in Los Angeles—hell, we did in most places. People wanted to see Mantle and Maris and—well, the Yankees. That night in Los Angeles they were hanging from the rafters. So Gene Autry comes in, and he's happy. Our clubhouse is so quiet you could have heard a pin drop, and I've always been kind of a bad-tempered loser anyway, but here comes Autry in the cowboy boots and the hat and he slaps me on the back and says, "What a show! What a show! Just great!" Okay, he was in show business and they had a packed house and his team won and Mantle hit one for the fans, and he was happy. Now, Gene Autry has always been nice to me and I like him, but here he was in our clubhouse after we lose one like that and he's slapping me on the back and saying, "Great show! Great show!"

I said something bad about his great show. I don't remember exactly what I said, but it was bad and he left right away.

Every time Gene sees me now, he tells that story. He's never forgotten it. He's really a great guy, but that was his first year in baseball and he didn't realize what it was like in a losing clubhouse.

Duren's victory gave the Angels two victories in the three games played in that series. In fact, the Yanks played three three-game series against the Angels in California that season and lost two out of three games each time. For that matter, the 1961 Yankees didn't do particularly well on the road. Their record in Yankee Stadium was an overwhelming 65–16, still the major league record for most victories at home in a season, but on the road they were only 44–37.

After the loss to Duren the Yankees flew home to New York with a bad taste in their mouths but at least they had a day off when they returned, their first in more than a month. They had played 36 games in 32 days, but they had won 24 of them and had moved into contention.

Back in Yankee Stadium they swept three games from Washington at the beginning of July as Mantle and Maris gorged on Senator pitching. Mantle hit an inside-the-park homer on Friday and two other homers on Saturday to tie Maris, who a week earlier had led him by five. Mantle's second homer on Saturday was a gigantic clout over the 457-foot sign into the left-field bleachers, the second time in his career he had hit one there. Maris responded later in that game with his twenty-eighth to go ahead again, and then hit two more on Sunday.

Washington pitched very carefully to Mantle that Sunday after his powerful hitting in the previous two games and walked him the first four times he batted, but other Yankees took up the slack. Howard followed Mickey's first walk with a homer into the upper deck in left. Maris's first homer was a towering fly down the right-field line, and his second (his thirtieth of the year) ricocheted off the front of the upper deck in right. In the seventh, after Mantle walked for the fourth time, Howard singled, Cerv doubled and Gonder (back with the team briefly) singled. In the eighth, with Kubek on base, the Senators finally got brave and pitched to Mantle, who promptly hit a home run into the upper stands in right. Then Howard singled and Skowron hit a homer over the bullpen into the same distant bleachers Mantle had reached the day before. The final score was 13–4 as the dazed Senators stumbled out of town.

The fielding wasn't bad either. Detroit had a very good ball club that year, a one-season phenomenon, perhaps (the Tigers were sixth the year before and would be fourth the year after), but in 1961 they were a truly outstanding baseball team, with three splendid starting pitchers in Frank Lary, Jim Bunning and Don Mossi, two fine relief pitchers in Terry Fox and Hank Aguirre, the league batting champion in first-baseman Norm Cash (who also had 41 homers and 132 runs batted in, a Triple Crown season in most years), a Hall of Famer in right field in Al Kaline (who batted .324), an awesome home-run hitter in left field in Rocky Colavito (who hit 45 and batted in 140 runs). The Tigers that season actually outhit the Yankees (.266 to the Yankees' .263) and scored more runs (841 to the Yankees' 827). The New Yorkers were clearly superior only in the crushing strength of their home-run attack (60 more than the hard-hitting Tigers) and in their superb but often overlooked defensive play. The fielding artistry of the Yankees tended to be lost in the glow of the hitting, but as a team they had the fewest errors in the league, the most assists, the most double plays, the best fielding average.

Only at first base and in left field was the Yankee fielding less than spectacular. Skowron was a good, competent first baseman, and Berra and the other occupants of left field—Lopez and Cerv—were in the same category: not weak, but not outstanding. But the other six position players—Richardson, Kubek and Boyer in the infield, Mantle and Maris in the outfield, Howard catching—were the best in the league or very close to it.

Houk was particularly pleased with his young infielders—Kubek and Boyer were 24, Richardson 25. Under Stengel, they had been moved in and out of the lineup, playing when and where Casey needed them, but before the 1961 season began Houk told Richardson and Kubek that they were fixtures. They would play second base and shortstop and nowhere else, and he kept his word. For the first time since they played for Houk in Denver they put in a full season side by side, and they meshed beautifully.

Houk was a little slower to give Boyer a clear shot at third base, but even before Deron Johnson disappointed and was traded away, Clete established himself as a bona fide regular. And then Houk had the infield he wanted.

RALPH HOUK:

After Clete played there awhile there were arguments over who was the best third baseman—Brooks Robinson of the Orioles or Boyer. To me, Boyer was as good a fielding third baseman as I've ever seen. He could go to his left or to his right, he could play deep, he could play in close. He'd stay in front of hard-hit balls. He had great hands. He had that outstanding arm. I think he had a better arm than Brooks, although he didn't get rid of the ball as well. And, of course, he wasn't as good a hitter as Brooks, although I think Clete felt he could hit with anybody. And he did have power—when he hit the ball. But he wasn't that good a hitter. He had a little weakness with the curve ball, which a lot of players have. But his fielding, that just spoke for itself.

Clete was one player I might have helped a little. I think I gave him confidence. Casey would pinch-hit for him all the time, and that can get a player down. Casey started Clete in the first game of the World Series against Pittsburgh and then the first time he came to bat he pinch-hit for him, and I don't think he played him again until the fifth game. That didn't make Clete too happy.

Once he got his feet on the ground Boyer was one of the best. With him at third and Kubek at short, it was hard to get a ball through them on the ground. A good third baseman and a good shortstop make each other look better because they cut down that hole between them. Tony really didn't need any help because he had that quick arm from the hole, but when you have a great third baseman like that next to a great shortstop it sure helps. Later on, I had Nettles at third, and he was the same way. Nettles could play the hitters better than any third baseman I ever had. He'd play off the base and get a ball you couldn't believe, and the next time the same guy came up he'd hit one down the line and Nettles would be there. I don't know how he did it.

He was great and Robinson was great, but Boyer defensively rates right up there with them. You can get arguments, of course. When you see a player every day and he's that good, you're inclined to think he's better than the other guys.

I'd pinch-hit for Clete in certain situations—like if they had a sidearm righthander going against us—because Blanchard hit that kind of pitching real well. There's not too many ballplayers like to be pinch-hit for, and you can't blame them. Clete never liked it, and I'd have to try to soothe things over a little bit. He was a tough, hard-nosed kid. Sometimes I'd look the other way after I sent somebody up to bat for him.

He was a handsome kid, too, and he liked girls. They liked him, too, and maybe he ran around a little too much. After he left us he played for Atlanta and hit real well, and then he went to Japan and played there. I think after that Clete hopped from job to job a little, but he's settled down now.

Tony Kubek was a *real good* ballplayer, though I have to laugh when I remember the first ball game he ever played for me. He was only 18 when he came up to Denver from Quincy in I guess it was the Three-I League. He joined us toward the end of the season when we were fighting to get into the American Association playoffs. We were playing at St. Paul and we were one run ahead in the bottom of the ninth with the bases loaded and two outs, and the ball is hit to Tony at shortstop. It did take a kind of a bad hop, but all he had to do with it was throw it to the second baseman for a force-out and the game would have been over, and we'd have won by one run. But instead he made the long throw to first base and the runner was safe and the run scored. The game was tied, and I think we went 11 innings and got beat. He felt pretty bad, but I went over to him afterward and said don't worry about it. He was only a kid.

But he learned. He knew how to play ball. He played for me at Denver the next season and then in 1957 he went up to the Yankees and stayed there. Casey played him everywhere: third base, shortstop, all over the outfield. Tony was good—he was a good outfielder, he could play center field—and he was a good hitter. But he didn't like playing the outfield, and I think he was happy when I told him he was the shortstop. There were some good ones in the league then—Aparicio, Hansen, Versalles—but none were better than Tony.

Over the years since then Tony has changed more than any other ballplayer I've known. When he was young he was shy and quiet, you couldn't get him to talk. He didn't say a word. Now he's a broadcaster, you know, and you can't get him to stop talking. He's a gabber. But he didn't say much back in Denver.

He and Richardson played together in Denver, and they went up to the Yankees together, and they more or less took over up there. Tony was tall and rangy and Bobby was short and chunky, but they were a complement to each other. It was a great thing. They were about the same age, they roomed together, they were both clean-cut kids, they were quiet and well behaved, they never were a problem to the club. They talked baseball all the time, how to do this and how to do that. They helped each other.

In the beginning Casey never thought Richardson could make the double play. And if you can't make the double play, the first thing they say in baseball is that you're scared of the runner. Well, Bobby wasn't scared of anybody. We were talking about him one day when I was a coach under Casey, and we were wondering why he was having trouble getting the ball to first in time on the double play. Tony still wasn't talking much at that time, but he said, "I think Bobby is coming too much toward the bag." We went out and worked on it and Bobby made a little adjustment the way Tony suggested and from that time on he was the greatest thing on the double play you ever saw. Little things can happen, and that little change was unbelievable. Just a step farther out, and it was unbelievable what a difference it made.

Kubek could get on base real good and he was a good contact hitter, just like Richardson. They could move the ball, they could move people around the bases. Kubek hit through the middle—well, he hit all over. He was basically a spray hitter, he hit the ball to all fields. He hit a lot of doubles and he got a lot of them down the left field line, the opposite field for him, or in between the outfielders. He was a line-drive hitter and he had good speed—if he hit a ball in the alleys he could stretch it into a double, particularly if the outfielder had to field the ball on the opposite side from the way he threw. If he had to turn and set, it was hard to throw Tony out at second. He got a lot of doubles that way.

Bobby could really operate with the bat, bunt, hit behind the runner. I had Bobby leading off and Tony batting second a lot, and then later I turned it around and had Tony lead off and Bobby bat second. Tony hit lefthanded but he didn't pull that much, and Bobby could hit to right field better.

Tony was a real good player, but he got drafted into the army after the 1961 season and he hurt his back in the army playing touch football, I think, and it never really got better. I used Tom Tresh at shortstop in 1962 when Tony was in the army, but when he came back I put Tresh in the outfield and Tony at shortstop again. After two or three seasons he had to quit baseball because of his back. The doctors said if he got hit again he could suffer nerve damage, he could even be paralyzed if he got hurt like that again. He was only 29.

And Richardson was a real good ballplayer, too. He planned to quit baseball the same year that Tony did, but we talked to him—we didn't want to lose our shortstop and our second baseman at the same time— and he said, "Well, if Tony quits I'll come back and play one more year." He did, and then he retired from baseball.

Bobby was very, very religious. Now I'm not knocking religion or anything, but sometimes the religious guys were—well, Lindy Mc-Daniel, for instance. He got religion, and kind of overdid it in the clubhouse a little. Bobby was different. The other players liked him so much and respected him so much that it never was a problem. I never heard anyone criticize him or make fun of him. He wouldn't say all that much about religion, but you knew how he felt. I know that sometimes when I had meetings I'd get carried away and say things I really shouldn't have said—I mean, they'd just come out—and I'd glance around and there'd be Bobby, just looking at me.

He's a good decent man. I remember once going out to argue on a play at second base where Bobby tagged a guy and the umpire called him safe. From the bench it really looked like the umpire blew the call, and I went out and started having a big argument with him. I hadn't got to the point of throwing my cap on the ground or anything, but I was yelling, and there's Bobby standing next to me and I hear him say, very quietly, "Ralph, I missed him."

I'll never forget one time when Bobby did get mad. Ordinarily,

Richardson *never* got mad. I don't think he's said a cussword in his life. But he wasn't crazy about Eli Grba, who we lost in the expansion draft to Los Angeles. Grba was pitching against us for the Angels, and he hit Bobby with a pitch. You could see Bobby was sore, and when he got to first base he turned toward the mound and he said to Grba, "I'll punch you in your big red nose." That's the maddest I ever saw Bobby Richardson get. The guys on the bench broke up.

That was a great infield.

Cleveland collapsed after Terry's extra-inning win and played badly the rest of the season. In first place on June 11 with a record of 37 and 19, the Indians won only 41 and lost 64 the rest of the way. They played .661 ball for the first two months of the season, and .390 ball for the rest of it, a depressing turnaround.

With the Indians out of it, the Tigers and Yankees locked together in a fight for first place that lasted all summer. The lead changed hands twelve times. During one 16-day period in July when the lead changed seven times, neither team was ever more than half a game ahead or half a game behind.

The Yankees, who had been a game out of first place on June 12, were still one slim game behind when Detroit came into Yankee Stadium for a doubleheader on the Fourth of July. Ford pitched the first game and gave up a bases-empty homer to fall behind 1–0, but in the bottom of the fifth inning the Yankees flooded across home plate. Cerv doubled, Richardson singled, Maris singled, Mantle was walked, Howard tripled to right, Skowron singled—and the Yankees led 5–1. Ford yielded another run in the ninth, but he pitched a complete game and the Yanks moved into first place by four percentage points.

With Terry still bothered by his ailing shoulder—he hadn't pitched now for almost three weeks—Houk gave Turley the start in the second game. It was his last start that season, and he survived only into the third inning. Houk replaced him with Coates and later Arroyo and Sheldon and Stafford. Lary was pitching his usual strong game for the Tigers and led 2–0 into the eighth. Then Maris hit a homer with Kubek on base to tie the score. Coates and Arroyo had pitched well, but in the ninth Sheldon gave up two walks and a single to load the bases. With powerful Colavito at bat, Sheldon went into a full windup, and the Tigers pulled a stunning triple steal, Chico Fernandez sliding across home plate under Sheldon's throw to put the Tigers ahead again, 3–2.

With one out in the last of the ninth Skowron beat out an infield hit. Blanchard hit a little foul pop-up along the third-base line but catcher Dick Brown and third-baseman Steve Boros ran into each other going after it and the ball fell to the ground. Given another chance Blanchard singled, sending Skowron to second. Then Gardner, playing third base for Boyer, flied out for what should have been the final out of the ball game. But Skowron moved over to third after Gardner's fly and when Lopez, batting for Sheldon, scratched an infield hit, Skowron scored the tying run.

Stafford came in to pitch the tenth, the Yankees' fifth pitcher against Lary. With two out and Boros on first base, Brown hit a ground rule double that sent Boros to third. Eschewing a pinch-hitter, Scheffing let Lary bat for himself. Stafford had two strikes on the Tiger pitcher when Lary, surprisingly, squared away and laid down a perfect bunt along the third-base line. Stafford scrambled after the ball but Boros slid home safely, and the Tigers were ahead again, 4–3.

It still wasn't over. Kubek opened the last of the tenth with a single, and after Richardson popped up Maris came to bat. Scheffing, who had not pinch-hit for Lary, now decided to take him out of the game; he brought in the lefthanded Aguirre, who got Maris to pop up for the second out. With Mantle at bat, a passed ball (Brown was having a hard time behind the plate) sent Kubek to second with the tying run.

That left first base open, and the Tigers walked Mantle intentionally. Berra followed with a long drive to deep center that was caught for the second out, Kubek moving to third on the play. Now Scheffing removed Aguirre and brought in Terry Fox, his righthanded reliever, to pitch to Skowron, and Moose hit another fly ball that was caught for the final out. It was a great ball game, but it put the Tigers back in the league lead.

Detroit left after that one-day holiday visit, and Cleveland and Boston came into the Stadium. The Yankees defeated the Indians twice on successive shutouts by Sheldon and Stafford, and then beat the Red Sox three straight to regain first place. But in the final game of the four-game series with Boston, the last game before the first All-Star break (there were two All-Star games that year, as there had been in 1959 and 1960 and as there would be in 1962 before sanity triumphed and the number was returned to one), the Sox jumped all over Terry, who was making his first start in 24 days. The Yankees lost and fell a half game back into second place as the season stopped for three days while the All-Stars headed for San Francisco.

The All-Star voting then was done by players, coaches and managers, and in this balloting by their peers Mantle, Maris and Kubek were named to the American League's starting team. Ford, now 16–2 on the season, was the American League's starting pitcher (for the second straight year and the third time in his career). In short, four of the American League's nine starters were Yankees.

Stengel, as the manager of the previous year's American League champions, ordinarily would have been the All-Star manager, but with Casey gone from baseball (and no one inclined to invite him out of retirement to manage the All-Stars) the league gave the honor to Paul Richards, whose Orioles had finished second in 1960, rather than to Houk, the manager of the incumbent champions. Houk didn't mind. The three days off were a welcome respite. Richards picked nine pitchers for the squad, including two from Detroit and Ryne Duren (!) from the Angels, but only Ford from the Yankees. Among the extra players Richards selected were Howard and Berra. He also invited Houk to be one of his coaches, but Ralph suggested he take

Frank Crosetti, who was in his thirtieth season with the Yankees, in his place.

That All-Star Game, on Tuesday, July 11, was the memorable one played in Candlestick Park, where the game began in warm, sunny weather and ended in the chill, swirling wind that made Candlestick an infamous name in baseball. Ford pitched against the National League's Warren Spahn, went three innings and gave up a run. The powerful winds whipping around Candlestick slowly changed what had been an orderly game into a wild one. Seven errors were made— by teams of All-Stars—and the National League's little pitcher, Stu Miller, was buffeted so hard that he lost his balance on the mound and was charged with a balk (in baseball myth, Miller was "blown off the mound"). The American League scored two runs to tie the game in the ninth before losing it in the tenth. All in all, it was a weird game that contributed substantially to the indelible reputation Candlestick has had ever since.

One happy story that came out of the Candlestick game revolved around a bet Ford made on how well he would do against Willie Mays. Ford and Mantle had reached San Francisco on Monday, the day before the game, and had played golf at a club where Horace Stoneham, the owner of the San Francisco Giants, was a member. They were told by Pete Stoneham, Horace's convivial son, that if they needed anything at the club or at the pro shop to just sign his father's name to the tab. Ford and Mantle went a little overboard and along with golf incidentals they ended up buying golf shoes and shirts and sweaters and ran up a bill of $200, all on Stoneham's tab. That night Ford saw Stoneham at a pre–All-Star Game party and with some embarrassment explained about the tab and said he and Mantle would pay him back.

Amused, the amiable Stoneham said, "Wait, I'll make a deal with you. Double or nothing. If you get Willie out the first time you pitch to him tomorrow, forget about the tab, we're all even. But if you don't get him out, you two owe me $400. Okay?"

Ford said, "Let me talk to Mickey." He found Mantle and explained the bet. Mickey didn't want any part of it—$400 seemed like an awful lot of money, even for a man making $70,000—but Ford (one of whose nicknames was Slick) talked him into going along with it.

In the first inning the next day Mays came to bat with two out and a man on second. In center field Mantle watched tensely. Ford worked carefully and got two strikes on Mays. Then, he says, he loaded up the ball and threw Willie a spitter that broke wickedly down over the plate for called strike three. It was only the third out of the first inning, but in center field Mantle shouted with exultation, smacked his fist into his glove, jumped in the air and came running in toward the dugout pumping his arms and grinning as though Ford had just gotten the last out in the World Series.

It was, as Ford likes to say, a real money pitch. But, then, he was the Yankees' money pitcher, and never more so than in 1961. Houk's decision, made soon after he was named manager, to have Whitey start every fourth day paid off handsomely. "Every fourth day" usually means approximately every fourth day, but in Ford's case it was exact. The many postponements early in the season threw the plan off rhythm for a few weeks, but by the middle of May Ford's schedule was running like clockwork. From May 21 through all of June and all of July and to the very end of August, Ford started *every* fourth day, with only two exceptions: he missed a start in July because of his appearance in the All-Star game in San Francisco, and in mid-August he started one day late when his regular turn fell on an off day in the schedule.

Otherwise, he was on the mound every fourth calendar day for nearly three and a half months, and the results were impressive. He made eight straight starts in June and won all of them, the first time a major league pitcher had won eight games in one month since Schoolboy Rowe did it for Detroit in 1934. But Ford didn't stop at the end of June. He won five more in July and extended his winning streak to 14 straight before losing.

He would finish the season with a record of 25 wins and 4 defeats. In his previous decade in the majors, he had started 30 games or more only once, and in the three seasons before 1961 he had started 29 times each year. Now he started 39 times, an increase of 35 percent.

Under Stengel he'd been called on to do a bit of relief pitching on an average of four times a year. In 1961 he did not relieve at all. During his last three years with Casey, Whitey won 42 games and lost 26, a winning percentage of .617. In his first three years with Houk (1961–1963) he won 66 and lost 19, a .776 percentage. His average won–lost record from 1958 to 1960 was 14–9. From 1961 to 1963 it was 22–6.

In a word, he flourished under Houk. While he made many more starts, Houk kept a close eye on him in late innings and would call for Arroyo to come in from the bullpen at any sign of Ford tiring. Ford understood this and went along with it willingly. Sometimes he would glance over at the dugout when he felt he was losing his stuff. By the time of the San Francisco All-Star game, when Ford's record was 16–2, Arroyo had relieved him nearly a dozen times already and would relieve him another dozen before the season was over. Ford even quipped, "I'll have a great season if Arroyo's arm holds out," a gag that backfired to some extent, with careless observers undervaluing the work Ford did and overvaluing Louie's contribution to his performance. Arroyo finished the season with a remarkable 15–5 record of his own, but five of those victories and one of the defeats came in games Ford started in which Arroyo relieved with the score tied or the Yankees leading. Louie was a splendid relief pitcher, but he was not impeccable.

Ford's most significant contribution to the Yankees' success in 1961 was as a "stopper," the pitcher who wins the next game after his team has lost. Ford was 12–0 in games he started after the Yankees lost, and the team was 17–1. As a starting pitcher he stopped losing streaks of two games or more eight different times. Only once all season did a Yankee losing streak continue in a game Ford started; that was early in May when Arroyo lost in relief after Ford left the game in the eighth inning, leading 5–4.

And Ford won the big games, the games the Yankees had to win. In May, with Ford starting, the Yankees beat Detroit after losing two in a row to the Tigers. A week later, when the club had lost four straight and dropped to fourth place, the nadir of their season, Ford beat Baltimore. In mid-June, after the Yankees had again lost two straight to Detroit, Ford shut out the Tigers, and he beat them again in the first game of the big July Fourth doubleheader to put New York in first place (momentarily, at least). In mid-July, after the Yankees had lost three out of five and the pitching staff had given up 42 runs in five games, Ford stopped the White Sox 5–1. In September he started the first game in another key series with Detroit and the team won. He put the final nail in the Tigers' coffin in mid-September when he beat them 11–1. Ford started 6 games against Detroit in 1961 and the Yankees won all 6; the Tigers won 8 of the other 12 games the teams played.

Ford, blond-haired, blue-eyed, red-faced, was short for a pitcher, about five feet ten, and his practice of wearing his uniform pants tucked in at the knees like old-fashioned knickers made him look like a little boy, small and vulnerable. But he was powerfully built through the back, the shoulders and the arms, and his guile on the mound was backed by strength. He could throw hard when he had to. His powerful wrists and hands enabled him to take an exceptionally strong grip on a baseball, and when he was able to get a little dirt on the ball and thus raise the gripping surface along the seams just a bit, he could throw a startling pitch that broke almost straight down. This was probably the "spitball" Ford was so often accused of throwing. He did throw the spitter occasionally—against Mays in the All-Star game, for example, if Ford's own story isn't an embellishment—but the "dirt ball" was used more frequently. And it wasn't just a matter of putting dirt on the ball. Ford's strength and technique were as important as the mystic added ingredient. He was a master of his craft.

Because he completed only 11 of his 39 starts that season and was relieved so frequently by the admirable Arroyo, Ford received an undeserved reputation for being a pitcher without stamina. But he pitched into the seventh inning in 29 of his first 30 starts. In today's lexicon, a "quality start" is one in which a starting pitcher completes six innings and gives up three or fewer earned runs. By that standard, Ford had 16 quality starts in his first 17 games in 1961 and 30 in all for the season, plus 3 other performances that if not technically "quality" were certainly admirable. He pitched scoreless ball and had two outs in the fifth inning in one game when he had to leave with a hip injury; after the Yanks clinched the pennant he pitched five innings in a tuneup for the World Series and left leading 4–3; and after giving up five runs early in another game he settled down and pitched scoreless ball through the tenth inning.

Ford led the American League in innings pitched with 283, and in his 39 starts averaged seven and a third innings (or one out in the eighth) per game. His personal record was 25–4 but the Yankees were 34–5 in games he started, an .872 winning percentage. With the other starting pitchers, the Yankees were .610 on the season; the second-place Tigers were .623. Not to dismiss Mantle and Maris or what they meant to the team, but an argument can be made that Whitey Ford was the most valuable player on the 1961 Yankees, and by extension the most valuable in the league. He gave the club stability, a sense of confidence built on the knowledge that "Whitey's pitching tomorrow" and that Whitey would probably win. The confidence such a great pitcher generates cannot be measured, but in the case of the 1961 Yankees it was an extraordinary help in keeping the team from collapsing altogether in the depressing early weeks of the season, as well as in raising it to its sustained, pennant-winning accomplishment later on.

RALPH HOUK:

I can't remember Ford ever being anything but an outstanding pitcher, even in the seasons when he didn't win all that many games. He didn't pitch as many innings then. One of the reasons we felt we could go with Ford every fourth day was the fact that we had Arroyo out there in the bullpen. With Louie pitching so well, I could take Whitey out of there after six or seven innings. We could protect a lead with Arroyo and not wear Whitey out. That's one of the big reasons we decided to pitch him every fourth day. I had a lot of confidence in Arroyo and so I wasn't afraid to take Whitey out if I felt he was getting tired. Or if he felt he was.

Usually, when I went out to the mound I'd already made up my mind to take the pitcher out. Whitey was the only one I'd ask, "How do you feel?" He'd tell me if he didn't have it anymore, and if I had Arroyo ready I'd bring him in. Sometimes I could see Whitey taking looks out at the bullpen, and that was a sign he felt he was losing something. Whether he knew I saw him doing that I don't know, but I knew he was looking. If I had Arroyo ready Whitey might say, "I guess you better get him." If I didn't have Arroyo ready—well, I usually didn't take Ford out if Arroyo wasn't ready. I'd say, "You can get this next man, can't you?" And he'd say, "Yeah," kind of half agreeing with me.

But if Whitey said, "I'll get this guy out," even if I had Louie ready I'd leave Ford in, and nine times out of ten he'd get the guy out. I remember one game he was going along fine and then in the eighth they got to him for two or three runs. I went out, but he said, "I'm all right," and I left him in. He got the next five men and the game was over.

I can remember only one time when he stayed in when he shouldn't have when I had Arroyo ready. It had to be the top of the ninth at home against the White Sox, and I'm pretty sure Minnie Minoso was the hitter. A tough hitter. I think the bases were loaded with two out, and I went out to the mound. Arroyo was ready and I'm expecting to make the move, but the second I got there Whitey said, "Skip, I got him out real easy last time." Last time. He didn't say anything about this time. I said, "Well, okay. Get him out now." I no sooner got back to the dugout when Minoso hit a humpback liner to center field for two runs, and they wind up beating us. Damn, I was mad. I had Arroyo *ready*, I fully intended to bring him in. That's why I always took pitchers out before I got to the mound, because I didn't want to be talked out of anything. If they know they're leaving, they can't put up an argument. After the game Whitey said, "Skip, I'm sorry. I'll never say that again." But, oh, I was pissed.

In spring training that year, 1961, Whitey looked so good. He really had a great spring. He was throwing the ball perfect. He came to spring training in real good shape, which was one of the reasons his arm looked good. He was throwing the ball outstanding, and he never had a bit of trouble with his arm all season. He had a little difficulty with his legs, or his hip, I guess it was, but not his arm.

I saw him at a basketball game in New York during the winter after I was made manager, and I asked him if he thought he could start every fourth day, and he said sure, he'd like to try it. I think the only time I deliberately didn't pitch him every fourth day once the season really got going was at the end of August, just before a big series with Detroit. I pitched somebody out of turn and held Whitey out an extra day so he could start against the Tigers, because that was a series in which I knew we had to hold our own against Detroit or we'd be in trouble. Whitey pitched the opener on a Friday night and we won, and that was a big win.

Ford was some pitcher. He'd change according to the situation, and when the situation got tough, he got tougher. If they got the lead runner on in a tight game, the first hitter in an inning, and the next hitter, say he's a righthanded batter, tried to hit to right field—that is, hit behind the runner to move him around to third—Whitey wouldn't let him do it. He'd keep that ball in, in, in, in, and it would be impossible for the batter to push the ball to right. Ford wouldn't let him. All of a sudden you got the guy popping up, and you got your one out, and now the inning's a lot easier to get out of. Whitey knew about things like that.

He was a student. He kept a book on the hitters, and he knew what he was going to do when he went out on the field. We kept pitching charts then, where people hit balls and what they hit them off and all that kind of stuff. It was kind of new to keep charts then, and not all the pitchers paid much attention, especially the younger ones. You'd get on them about it and they might look at the charts a little for a day or so, but they didn't stay with them, they didn't study them. As great a pitcher as he was and as experienced, Whitey was one of the few on the staff who'd come in and say, "Where's that chart? What's it say again?" He'd go over them, study them. He kept track of what the hitters were doing, what pitches got them out. He'd look at those charts and he'd say, "You know, I think I'm going to do this to get this guy out, because this is what he did the time before." When he went out to the mound, he was ready.

He was a professional. People talk about him and Mantle and Billy Martin doing this and doing that. Whitey was a pretty happy guy, and he liked to go out and have a few drinks and have fun, but if you listen to him and Mickey and Billy you'd think that all they ever did was stay out late and raise hell. Well, you can bet that whenever Whitey did anything like that it was *after* he pitched, not before. The night before, he was in bed. He'd get a good night's sleep. He was ready when he pitched. A lot of people figured he was just a happy-go-lucky guy who happened to be a great pitcher, but he *worked* at his profession. He made a job of it, and he earned everything he got.

You try to tell young pitchers that, and they pay attention for a little while, but that's usually the end of it. Whitey worked at his job every day. He made notes. He knew what the hitters were doing, and what they were hitting, and where they hit it, and what the count was when they hit it, what he got them out with the last time he faced them. He could set hitters up so good he used to amaze me. He'd go along and he wouldn't be striking anybody out, but now they've got a man on third base and nobody out—and Ford strikes out the batter, he doesn't let him hit the fly ball. He always had a pitch ready. He'd have the batter set up for the pitch, but he wouldn't use it until he needed it. He was great that way. He was great on making a batter hit into a double play. Or if a man had been hitting the ball up the alley between outfielders, Whitey would end up where the guy was hitting the ball to center. He'd just move the location of the pitch a little and the guy swings the same way and he hits it, but now it's an out.

It's like what we did with Mark Belanger, the great-fielding shortstop Baltimore had. Belanger couldn't hit, but we couldn't get him out. He'd bloop the ball into right field all the time. He didn't hit the ball good, just bloop it, but he kept getting those hits. Our guys would make good pitches, and Belanger would thumb 'em into right field. One day we're going over the Baltimore hitters and we come to Belanger, and somebody—I don't know who it was, it might have been Whitey—said why don't we throw the ball right down the middle and let him hit it, like in batting practice. You watch Belanger take batting practice, and he'd hit fly balls all day to center. Sure enough, we got him out from there on like nothing. Just threw the ball right down the middle, a nice straight fastball, and he'd hit fly balls to center instead of those bloop hits to right.

That's the way it was with Whitey. He didn't overpower a lot of hitters, but it was amazing what he could do with them. He always knew what was going on.

He was the best pitcher I ever managed, and there's no question about that. Real smart, real real smart.

Ford remembered that season fondly. "I saw Ralph during a basketball game in Madison Square Garden," he said. "I guess Kansas was playing, and that's why he and Bette were there. It was just after he was named manager, and he asked me if I could start every fourth day. I was tickled when he suggested it. I always wished Casey would have let me, but I'd never done it before. Well, once or twice I did, and in fact once I pitched with two days' rest. We were short of pitching and I told Ralph I could pitch, and he went in and told Casey."

Ford had physical problems the previous season but he said, "Even though I never started regularly before on every fourth day, I wasn't worried about it. I was in good shape, and I wasn't the type of pitcher that depended on being strong or having speed, throwing fastballs all the time. I didn't throw that many pitches anyway. I always thought I could have pitched every fourth day.

"But looking back at that season now, I can't help wondering how I won eight games in June. I can hardly believe that. And I was 19–2 in July and I remember Warren Spahn saying, 'How the hell can you have 19 wins by the All-Star game?'

"I was in good shape all year, although I did have that hip thing. I guess landing on my right foot, for some reason, made my right hip bother me on and off. If I took it easy for a couple of days it would clear right up. When I was pitching and I felt it, I'd tell Ralph and he'd get me out of there. And once in a while I could feel a blister coming on my finger, and I'd get out of a game an inning or so before it might pop up. You could feel it getting hot, the finger, and if you got a blister there you might have to miss a few games, so I'd tell Ralph. He'd put Arroyo in, and that's all I've heard about ever since.

"Louie really did seem to go in all the games I pitched, and he had a great year, but late in the season the papers were always saying Ford and Arroyo, Ford and Arroyo. I'm thinking, 'Christ, here I am 23 and 3 or something, and all I hear about is Arroyo.' Everybody was saying I couldn't complete a game. A few years before that I led the league in complete games but I never heard that brought up.

"But I really enjoyed those years when Ralph managed and he let me pitch every fourth day. And then when Yogi came in as manager in '64, I was the pitching coach, and I'd pitch whenever I wanted to. I think the first ten games we played that year, with the rainouts, I had five decisions. The other guys would kid me about that.

"I had fun. The nights after I pitched I never could get to sleep anyway. I'd be awake until five in the morning. So those were the nights I'd go out. I had a lot of fun."

24

After the All-Star game, Mantle and Maris continued the home-run rat-a-tat-tat they had begun just before it. Each hit a homer in Chicago in the first game after the break as Stafford beat the White Sox. Mantle hit another one the next day as Sheldon lost to the Sox, and the day after that Maris hit one to help the Yankees win despite another shaky performance by Terry, who lasted only three innings. Although Houk tried at first to use Turley to plug the pitching hole created by Terry's lingering trouble with his shoulder, it was Daley who did the job. Never overpowering, sometimes pitching in hard luck (he lost 7 of his first 11 decisions for New York), Daley nonetheless threw the ball well and helped greatly to steady the pitching staff while Houk waited for Terry to return to form.

On the Sunday after the All-Star game, in rain in Baltimore, Daley pitched beautifully and won 2–1. Mantle hit his thirty-second homer for the Yankees' first run, and in the ninth, with the score tied, he doubled home the game winner. The Orioles managed to put the tying and winning runs on base in the last of the ninth with only one out, but Daley got Ron Hansen to hit the ball on the ground, and Kubek turned it into a sparkling 6-4-3 double play to end the game.

It was still drizzling on Monday when the Yanks and the Orioles began a twi-night doubleheader. Ford pitched a six-hit shutout in the first game as Mantle hit his thirty-third homer, his fourth in five games.

Before the second game began there was a moment of silence when it was announced over the public-address system that Ty Cobb had died that day in California at the age of 74 (his estate was later reported to be worth $11 million, which would have caused a hushed silence, too). The rain that had fallen intermittently during the first game started up again. Mantle and Maris, along with Boyer, hit homers in the early innings, but when the rain fell even more heavily the game had to be stopped. After waiting more than an hour the umpires called it off. Because five innings had not been played, it was not an official game and the home runs were washed away (else Maris would have had 62 for the season).

That was a bad day all around for Maris and Mantle in the home-run derby, as it was beginning to be called. More and more frequently, the stories on their homers included mention of Ruth's pace in 1927 (the Babe was back in the news again). Maris, with 35 homers, was now 19 games ahead of Ruth, and Mantle, with 33, was 8 games ahead, but that same day Commissioner Frick made his feelings about the pursuit of Ruth's record official. He issued a formal ruling that said no batter pursuing the Babe would be credited with equaling or breaking the record unless he accomplished it within 154 games, the length of the season when Ruth hit his 60.

"Ford Frick threw a protective screen around Babe Ruth's record of 60 home runs yesterday," one newspaper said with cynical accuracy. Frick said a player who hit 60 *after* the 154th game would be given recognition but added—much to his later chagrin—that such a record would go into the record book with "a distinguishing mark" to show that it had been made in a 162-game season. He didn't mention other records that might be broken because of the eight extra games in the schedule, nor did he mention an asterisk, a word that was to haunt him the rest of his life. All he said was "a distinguishing mark," but the baseball writers took it from there. They assumed that the distinguishing mark would be an asterisk, and because Frick's ruling aroused such strong feelings on both sides of the matter, "with an asterisk" became a catch phrase that eventually entered the language as a term for a qualified success. Frick and "asterisk" became closely identified, so much so that when he wrote his autobiography a dozen years later he called it *Games, Asterisks and People*, even though he devoted barely a page in the book to the whole Maris–Ruth contretemps.

In 1961, though, his ruling was big news, and it served to make the home-run race not a contest between Maris and Mantle but one between Maris and Mantle and Ruth—or, to be more accurate, eventually between Maris and an artificial barrier at the 154th game of the season. From the day of Frick's ruling to the end of the season the publicity attendant on the home-run derby grew and grew, and Maris became, like Mantle, an intensely public figure.

The Yankees left rainy Baltimore for Washington, where Mantle hit 2 homers the next day to tie Maris at 35, and another the day after that to move into the lead. Mickey had hit 8 home runs in nine games, including the one that was rained out in Baltimore. He had hit 6 homers since Roger's last one, and in the previous 26 days had hit 14 to Roger's 8.

The team moved on to Boston for a three-game set with the Red Sox, and in the first inning of the first game in Fenway, Maris hit a homer to tie Mantle. Mickey, batting right behind him, immediately hit one himself (nine now in ten games) to retake the lead. Berra hit a two-run homer in the fourth, but the Yankee pitching that day was as bad as Boston's and New York was behind 8–6 going into the ninth inning. Boston reliever Arnold Earley, who had pitched hitless ball since entering the game in the sixth inning, retired the first batter in the ninth but then nervously walked both Maris and Mantle. Berra singled to right to score Maris, and when the ball was bobbled Mantle advanced to third and Berra to second. Even though that was the only hit Earley had allowed, he was lifted in favor of Mike Fornieles, Boston's best relief pitcher, who walked Skowron intentionally to fill the bases and then got Howard to pop up. Down to his last out, Houk sent Blanchard in to bat for Boyer, and John hit a grand-slam home run to give the Yankees a spectacular 11–8 victory (Arroyo held the Sox scoreless in the bottom of the ninth).

The Yankees beat the Sox again the next day in another wild game. Neither Maris nor Mantle hit homers, which disappointed the large

Boston crowd (their "twin assault on Babe Ruth's record" was "packing in the customers," according to a news story), but the Yankees had a 7–1 lead in the third inning. The Red Sox fought back to go ahead 9–8, scoring the tying run when Arroyo fielded a bunt and threw wildly past third and the go-ahead run when Richardson dropped a double-play ball at second base. When the slick Yankee defense made errors, it was man-bites-dog news. Boston was still ahead by a run when the Yankees batted in the ninth. Boyer was scheduled to lead off the inning, but again Houk sent Blanchard up to hit for him, and again Blanchard hit a pinch-hit homer. With the game now tied, Houk let Arroyo bat for himself, and Luis, a good hitter (he batted .280 that season), made up for his error by slicing a double off Fenway's left-field wall. Richardson then made up for *his* error by punching a single to center on which Arroyo, running as hard as his little legs could carry him, scurried home to put the Yankees ahead by a run. Kubek followed with a booming double—Tony had 38 doubles that season, second in the league—that scored Richardson, Arroyo held Boston scoreless in the last of the ninth, and the Yankees had another amazing victory.

Back in New York there was a small entr'acte, an exhibition game with the San Francisco Giants that was notable mostly for the fact that it drew a crowd of 47,368 despite 92-degree heat in New York. The crowd was composed principally of old New York Giant fans who had come to see Willie Mays, who was playing his first game in New York since the Giants left for California three and a half years earlier. When Willie left the game after driving in two runs to give the Giants a 2–1 lead, an enormous, appreciative cheer rose from the crowd. When Mantle, who accounted for the Yankees' only run with a homer, left the game an inning later there was only perfunctory applause from the National League fans who had crowded into the Stadium. It was as though the Giants were the home team, the Yankees the visitors, and it foretold the subsequent popularity of the still embryonic Mets. (An echo of this occurred 24 years later, in 1985, when Tom Seaver, the ex–Met star who had moved on to the Chicago White Sox, won his 300th game against the Yankees in New York. The crowd in Yankee Stadium was heavy with Seaver rooters, to the extent that at one point the fans began cheering, illogically, "Let's Go Mets! Let's Go Mets!")

In midsummer the cold war heated up. President Kennedy called for an additional 217,000 men for the armed forces and asked Congress for a $3.4-billion fund to meet the worldwide threat of the Soviets. As the flight of refugees to West Berlin continued, the East Germans, under Soviet direction, built a wall across Berlin, abruptly splitting the city in two with a physical barrier that blocked the escape routes the refugees had been using. East Germans trying to get to the West grew frantic as the wall rose. Streets were blockaded; subway and elevated lines were cut off. Commuting from homes in the East to jobs in the West was halted. East German soldiers reinforced the police guard at the Brandenburg Gate, once the symbolic and now the actual passage between the two sectors.

The entire border between East and West Germany was sealed. The Western allies angrily protested, and West Berlin mayor Willy Brandt urged President Kennedy to use "political action," not just words. The cold war was heating up. The United States ordered almost 27,000 sailors who had been due for release from the navy to remain in uniform. Additional American troops were sent into West Berlin, and tanks and soldiers from the Western countries took positions along the border. The Soviets accused the United States of provocation. Vice-President Johnson flew to Berlin from Washington to make a firsthand analysis of the situation. News broadcasts were filled with reports from Berlin, and there were scare headlines every day.

When the East Germans declared that they might shut down Western access to any part of Berlin (the city was completely surrounded by East Germany) the United States said such a step would be considered an aggressive act and issued a "solemn warning." The East Germans eased their stand, and slowly the tension abated. The wall stayed up, but the Western allies continued to move freely in and out of West Berlin. A growing rift between the two Communist giants, the Soviet Union and China, became more evident, and that seemed to soften the chances of the Russians going to war with the West. The split became wider when China publicly disagreed with a Soviet-held view that the "war" between Communism and capitalism did not have to be won by arms.

25

The day after the exhibition game with Mays and the Giants, the Yankees played a twi-night doubleheader against the White Sox at the Stadium. It was a spectacular night for Roger Maris, who trailed Mantle 37 homers to 36 going into the doubleheader. In the fourth inning of the first game Roger hit a home run to tie Mickey at 37. Mantle followed him to the plate and hit his thirty-eighth to regain the lead. In the eighth inning Maris hit another homer to tie Mantle again, and in the fourth inning of the nightcap he hit another to go ahead 39–38. In the sixth inning he hit yet another, his fourth of the night and his fortieth of the season, to move two ahead of Mickey. The Yankees won the first game 5–1 behind Ford, the second 12–0 behind Stafford.

Turley went on the disabled list to have his arm examined, although he went on it almost accidentally. Even though he wasn't able to pitch well there was nothing functionally wrong with his arm. However, the Yankees had picked up a stocky little lefthanded pinch-hitter named Bob Hale from Cleveland, and they had to make room for him on the roster. Since Turley wasn't being used anyway, he was asked to go on the disabled list for a while, although Houk saw to it that he was back on the roster in time to be eligible for the World Series (he didn't pitch in the Series, but at least he was part of the show.)

Hale, in his late twenties, was nominally a first baseman, but he had been in twice as many major league games as a pinch-hitter as he had playing first base. With the Yankees that year he had only two hits but one was a home run, his last as a major leaguer, which made him forever an integral part of the major league record for home runs the Yankees set that season. Hale retired the next season and went back to college. He earned a Ph.D. in education and in time became principal of a public school in Chicago, where he was able to command the respect of potentially obstreperous students who were somewhat awed to discover that plump, baldheaded Mr. Hale had played for the 1961 Yankees.

RALPH HOUK:

How we got Bob Hale is kind of a funny story. What happened was, I always liked Hale as a pinch-hitter, and when Cleveland put him on waivers we claimed him automatically just to let the Indians know we were interested in him. That is, in case they wanted to move him later on, like in September, when the rosters get bigger, or in the offseason. We didn't have room for him then, but we didn't think they'd let him go for the waiver price. That's the way waivers worked. You put a lot of players on the waiver list that you weren't planning to get rid of, just to get the lay of the land to see who might be interested in what players. Then you withdrew the waivers and made a deal later on.

It didn't work that way this time. The Indians didn't withdraw the waivers and, by God, we had Hale. And we had to take him, because they were irrevocable waivers. Now we had a problem, because while we liked him we didn't need him at that particular time. But we had him, and we had to keep him on the roster, and we had to make room for him. We were really up the stump. Hamey and I were sitting there saying, what are we going to do now? And then it worked out that Turley could go on the disabled list temporarily. Before September we dropped Earl Torgeson, made him a coach until the end of the season, and put Bob back on the active roster.

But it just shows you how little things can catch you because we *were* interested in Hale, and he was on waivers. When we said let's claim him, we never dreamed we'd get him and then, oh, Christ, we had him.

Hale was a stocky-built kid, kind of a full face, chunky. He was quiet, pleasant. I never realized he was such a bright man, that he'd become a Ph.D. I just liked the way he swung a bat. And he was a pull hitter. I said, "Here's a guy we could use." I was thinking "Here's a fella might win a couple of ball games for us some day . . ."

The season moved on. When the Yanks beat the White Sox the day after Maris's four-homer doubleheader, Blanchard hit home runs in his first two at bats. It was the first time John had played since his successive pinch-hit homers in Boston, and that meant he had now hit four home runs in four at bats, equaling a major league record set by Jimmie Foxx in 1933 that has often been tied but never surpassed. When Blanchard came to bat again with a chance to break the record, he hit a long fly to right field that missed being a fifth home run by a foot or so. Mantle also hit a homer in that game, his thirty-ninth to Roger's 40. He was now 22 games ahead of Ruth's pace, Maris 23 ahead.

RALPH HOUK:

Blanchard had an amazing year. He was quite a guy. Johnny was a big, good-looking fellow, pretty quiet unless he got a little giggle juice in him. He was like a nice big shepherd dog, one of those easygoing people who don't exert themselves too much except on occasions. You had to sort of tell John what you wanted done at first—he didn't volunteer a whole lot. But he sort of grew up, and he became a big part of that club in 1961, especially when he started to hit those home runs.

Blanchard could really hit. He didn't run real good and he wasn't a great catcher but he had a good arm, a power arm, and he did everything fairly well. We played him in the outfield once in a while, and he could judge a fly ball good and catch it and he could throw from out there. Sometimes, you know, catchers develop that one throw to second base and you put them in the outfield and their ball doesn't carry, but his did.

John wasn't one of those rah-rah guys—he sort of felt his way into things. He wasn't as hard-nosed as some ballplayers are, but he loved to win and he loved the Yankees. He liked his role. He didn't care about playing every day. He just liked being there and being part of the team. A heck of a guy, very likeable. Later on he got to drinking a little too much and he had some difficulties, but he got that straightened out. His wife almost left him, but they're back together now in Minnesota and that's great. He's got a nice family. Johnny's a good guy.

The Yankees completed a four-game sweep of the White Sox behind Terry, who at last was back in form, pitching strongly for the first time since the middle of June. With Terry back, with Daley pitching well, with Ford and Stafford and Sheldon winning consistently, with Coates helping Arroyo in the bullpen, with Reniff and Clevenger, and the promising Downing around if he needed them, Houk's pitching was at last both strong and deep.

The Tigers, in a minislump, lost three straight during the last weekend in July, just before the two-day break for the second All-Star game. Here was a chance for the Yankees to break away, to open a substantial lead. Instead, they lost three out of four to Baltimore as the powerful Yankee bats were stifled and stopped. Only when Ford beat the Orioles 5–4 for his nineteenth win (and thirteenth in a row) did the club do anything at the plate. That was on Saturday, when Berra hit a home run. They were shut out the previous night, and they were able to score only once all afternoon in a Sunday doubleheader that the Orioles swept.

When Sheldon got off to a bad start in the second game of the Sunday doubleheader, Houk brought Arroyo on in the second inning. He didn't like to use Arroyo that early, but he wanted badly to win this last game before the All-Star break. Arroyo, behind 1–0, pitched shutout ball from the second through the eighth, leaving in the bottom of that inning for a pinch hitter when the Yankees finally—after 16 scoreless innings—pushed a runner across home plate to tie the score,

1–1. But to Houk's annoyance, Baltimore quickly regained the lead in the top of the ninth, 2–1.

It was a very hot day, and Houk was seething inside and out. In the last half of the ninth, losing by a run, the Yankees rallied against starting pitcher Milt Pappas and filled the bases with nobody out. One clean hit and the Yankees would score two runs and win the game, and Houk could go off on his All-Star break in a happy frame of mind. Pappas got behind on the count to Boyer, and manager Richards abruptly took him out of the game, replacing him with Dick Hall, a six-foot-six-inch, herky-jerky relief pitcher. Hall got a second strike on Boyer and then threw a pitch that Clete and the rest of the Yankees felt was low and outside. Home plate umpire Ed Hurley called it strike three. Boyer slammed his bat on the ground. Houk yelled angrily from the dugout in protest. He could not go out onto the field to protest because of the rule that calls for automatic ejection of a manager if he comes out of the dugout to dispute a ball or strike call. Shouting at the umpire, Houk sent Lopez up to pinch-hit. The Yankees still had a great chance to win or at least tie the game. The bases were loaded, and there was only one out. The tying run was on third, only 90 feet away from home plate, and the winning run was on second.

But Lopez hit Hall's first pitch into a fast double play and the game was over, just like that. The Yankees had lost. It was unbelievable. One moment they had the bases loaded with nobody out, and two pitches later the game was over and they'd lost. Houk erupted. All the pent-up frustration of the losing weekend and the long hot afternoon burst through. He ran from the dugout at umpire Hurley, who was coming toward the Yankee dugout to leave the field. Shouting furiously, Houk had to be pulled away from the umpire by his coaches. Hurley, describing the incident later, said, "He definitely bumped me. I'll have to report it to the league."

Houk went off fishing on Monday during the second All-Star game in Boston, which ended in a rained-out 1–1 tie after nine innings. Mantle played, but Maris, who had missed two of the Baltimore games with a slight muscle pull, appeared only to pinch-hit. During the game it was announced in the pressbox that American League president Joe

Cronin had fined Houk $250, which was a big fine, and had suspended him for five days, which was a drastic punishment. Houk missed seven games during his suspension. Crosetti managed the team in Houk's place, and Sain made the pitching changes. Houk would make out the starting lineup each day but had to be off the field and out of uniform by game time. More than a quarter of a century later Houk was still steaming over the incident.

RALPH HOUK:

Damn right. It was a *terrible* pitch. You see, we had the bases loaded and nobody out and Boyer's the hitter, and he's got the count to three and two. Hurley called him out on a ball this far outside. If Boyer walks the game is tied, and Hector's ground ball wins it. But Hurley calls it a strike! It was this far outside! It was not only outside, it was low! It was a terrible pitch.

Boyer went crazy, and so did I. You can't really see from the bench, you know, but that pitch was a ball. I yelled a lot but I didn't come out of the dugout because I didn't want to get thrown out of the game—you can't come out to argue balls and strikes. And, hell, we still had the bases full and only one out—we still had a shot. So you say to yourself, okay, let's get on with it. Let's win this thing. And then, boom, the game was over.

It was awful. It was awful, awful. It was a hot day, and we lost two, and what a way to lose. It was one of the worst days—well, I've had a lot of bad days, and you remember the bad days more than you remember the good ones. And when you lose a game like that you're always thinking there was something you could have done to win it.

So now the game's over, and that's when I charged Hurley. He was coming toward the dugout and I didn't give him a chance to say anything. Hurley could have been a real good umpire, but he had a chip on his shoulder for a lot of players. He didn't like Mantle, for instance. He'd follow Mickey all the way toward the outfield after an argument, jawing at him. Unbelievable. If a player looked at him crossways, Hurley would follow him. He wasn't an umpire you could talk to.

So I charged him. The word was that I shoved him, which I really didn't. I don't think I even touched him, but he couldn't get into the dugout and everybody was all around him. It was a mess.

The next day was a day off because of the All-Star game and Bette and I decided to get out of there. I said, "Let's just get away from everybody." We took the kids and drove up to Norwalk, Connecticut, and we rented a little boat and a three-horsepower motor and went out on Long Island Sound to do some fishing. We went past the lighthouse and we were out there catching these little fish, porgies, and what with the kids and tending to the lines we weren't paying attention to where we were. A kind of wind came up and the tide was wrong, and when we looked up we had drifted the wrong way. We were way the hell out on the sound. We started up the engine, but those three horses weren't strong enough to get us back in against the wind and the tide. We weren't making any headway at all. We tried not to show the kids we were worried, but I was scared and Bette was too. The other boats had all gone in. It was Monday, and there weren't too many out there to begin with. Finally, I don't know what happened—the wind died down and the tide changed, or something—but after a long time we got back in.

Now we're in the car and we're on our way home to New Jersey, and that's when I hear the news about being suspended. It came over the car radio, and I didn't even know about it. Bette said, "Oh, good, now we can go back and do some more fishing." But that was a bad time.

I still get upset thinking about it. I can *see* that pitch. I ran into Boyer at an oldtimers game in Orlando, and the first thing we talked about was that pitch. He said, "Ralph, I swear to God it was that far outside."

I guess I was a bad loser. I remember there was a place in Washington where a lot of the players would get off the bus to eat when we were on the way back to the Shoreham from the ball park after a night game. I can't remember if it was a Chinese restaurant or an Italian restaurant or what. I never went there myself. I didn't go to places where the players went; I don't think a manager should. The players get enough of you during the game. Let them have time to themselves afterward.

Ordinarily, the team bus takes the players from the ball park right to the hotel, but in Washington they'd got into this habit. There was a traffic light or a stop sign right there by the restaurant, and the bus would stop and they'd hop off. But this night we'd blown a ball game to the Senators, and I was sore. I don't remember now how we lost it, but I remember we looked terrible and I was mad. Somebody was late getting to the bus after the game, and that teed me off because I was very strict about punctuality. I raised hell when he got on the bus, and I guess I blasted the whole ball club.

Now we're moving along and the bus finally gets to that stop sign and several players get up, and Yogi says, in this low voice, "I don't think we better get off tonight."

And not a soul did. I felt kind of bad about it.

But on a ball club you have 25 grown men making a lot of money, and they have to pay attention to you. You run the team, and they have to know that, and I think they do. Even today, ballplayers haven't changed as much as people think they have. They're still little boys. They love to win and they love to joke, and that's why they haven't changed as much as you read they have. Sure, they make all this money, but once they walk into that clubhouse and put the uniform on, they're little boys again. They want to look good in front of people. They want to do well. They're competitive, or they wouldn't be good athletes. People say, "What's it like to manage players making so much more money than you are?" but I've never had to give that a thought. You can call down a guy making $800,000, and you're not making half that by a long shot, and you chew him out and ask him what's going on with him out there in the outfield or wherever he plays, and he feels terrible. You might think he'd say, "Who the hell are you to talk to me like that?" but I never had that experience. It never came up. You're the boss, and they accept that.

Of course, I was fortunate in that every place I've managed I've had leaders on the club, players that the other players look up to—Kaline and Freehan in Detroit, Yastrzemski and Rice in Boston. With the Yankees it was Mantle and Berra, super people. They controlled that end of it. If somebody got out of hand they'd take care of it. They'd say, hey, let's stop that stuff. And that helps. That helps a lot.

26

Houk's absence didn't appear to hurt the club, which won six of the seven games he missed, including the last five in a row, although Ford was twice frustrated in his attempt to gain the twentieth victory he'd been waiting on for ten years. In his first attempt, with the score tied in the eighth, Ford himself punched a single to left to drive in two runs to put the Yankees ahead, but in the ninth inning he gave the runs back before he could get anyone out, and the score was tied again. Arroyo had to come on and prevent any more scoring. In the last of the ninth, with Ford out of the game, Maris singled, Mantle doubled him to third and Howard walked to load the bases. After Berra popped up, Cerv hit a grounder to third base. The throw went to the plate but Maris slid in hard and the catcher dropped the ball. The Yankees won—but the victory went to Arroyo.

In his next start, against Minnesota, Ford went 10 innings, but the game went 15. Whitey gave up a homer in the top of the tenth to fall behind, but Blanchard hit a homer in the bottom of the tenth to tie it. Ford left for a pinch-hitter, and Arroyo pitched the next three innings, Reniff the last two. In the bottom of the fifteenth, the Yankees filled the bases with one out. Berra hit a ground ball to Harmon Killebrew at third base. Killebrew did not try for an out at the plate but instead elected to go for an around-the-horn double play. He threw to second baseman Billy Martin, who in his wanderings around baseball after leaving the Yankees had joined the Twins earlier in the season. Martin made the out at second and relayed the ball to first, but Berra, running awfully fast for a 35-year-old catcher, beat Billy's throw as the winning run scored. It was Reniff's first major league victory, and Ford was still on hold at 19.

RALPH HOUK:

Hal Reniff was a little fat guy with a kind of erratic delivery. It was effective, but after the real good hitters saw him a few times they could hit him without too much trouble. We tried to make a starter out of him, but he had more luck relieving. He had his streaks where you thought things were going real good and then all of a sudden he'd be in trouble on the mound. We used him a lot in losing games, to save somebody else.

Hal was a sort of happy-go-lucky guy. He was fun-loving. Not the kind of a guy that went out and drank and had trouble with the curfew, not that kind of stuff. He just liked to have fun. I don't think he ever took things seriously enough, and maybe he overestimated his ability a little bit.

He was a good guy. People liked him. He fit in well. But Hal wasn't a pitcher you'd go to when you *had* to win a game. No way. But he was a good man on the club.

Meanwhile, Coates, who had started a few times before Daley joined the team in June, was again pressed into service as a starter in August when the Yankees played five doubleheaders in three weeks. He did very well for three or four games before tailing off again and going back to his long chores (Coates, 5–3 as a starter, was 6–2 in relief).

Ditmar pitched against the Yankees for Kansas City, gave up a homer to Mantle and hit Maris on the right leg with a fastball. After staying in the game long enough to score a run, Roger left to have icepacks put on the bruise. Houk returned and the Yankees continued to play good ball, extending their winning streak to nine straight. The Tigers won six out of eight at the same time and still fell four games

behind. Ford finally won his twentieth, a 2–1 victory over Los Angeles, and the Yankees completed a great home stand, winning 15 of
19 games despite those three bad losses to Baltimore.

They spent most of the rest of August on the road, watching Maris
and Mantle hit home runs. Neither was able to shake off the other,
and their battle for the lead in the chase after Ruth's record fascinated
the players, as well as the press and the public. At the second All-
Star game at the end of July Maris led, 40 homers to 39. On August 2
Mantle hit his fortieth to tie Roger. Two days later Maris hit his forty-
first to go ahead again. Two days after that Mantle hit two to leapfrog
into the lead, and the next day he hit another. He was batting .319
and was the popular favorite to break the record. Maris was hitting
.284, which was respectable (only four Yankees, Mantle, Howard,
Blanchard and Kubek, were batting higher) but not impressive enough—
it wasn't .300.

Hitting .300 was a standard of excellence in 1961 that was a relic
from the 1920s and 1930s, when all really good hitters were expected
to bat .300 or very close to it. In considering Mantle's popularity that
season it should be noted that he finished the year at .317, almost
exactly what he was hitting early in August, whereas Maris's average
fell 15 points to .269. A .269 batting average sounded *awful* in those
days when the .300 mystique was so strong. Yet Maris's .269 was 13
points above the league average in 1961. If he had played 25 years
earlier, in 1936, and had batted 13 points above the league average,
Maris would have hit .302.

After that splurge in early August neither hit a home run for four
days, with Mantle still out in front by two, but then the Yankees went
into Washington for four games on a hot August weekend. Maris
ended the brief home-run drought by hitting his forty-second in the
fifth inning of a Friday night game. Mantle riposted by hitting his
forty-fourth in the eighth inning of the same game. Maris hit another
on Saturday, his forty-third, and in the first game of a Sunday doubleheader hit yet another to tie Mantle at 44. That Maris homer was
lined into the bullpen in deep right-center field, about as far as a ball
could be hit in old Griffith Stadium without going completely out of

the ball park. A few innings later Mantle hit one to the same spot. It was his forty-fifth and put him back in the home-run lead.

That was the zenith for Mantle as far as position in the home-run battle was concerned. Maris hit another homer in the second game, another on Tuesday night and two the next afternoon—seven homers in six games—to take a three-homer lead.

By now the sports pages were filled with Maris and Mantle stories, many of them detailed analyses complete with charts showing how many games were left in the season, how far ahead of Ruth the two were, how many homers they had to hit to tie Babe's record or break it, and so on.

There were efforts to explain the boom in home-run hitting. Ted Williams, in his first year of retirement from the game, said that it was because expansion had diluted pitching. "They're batting against guys they never would have seen in previous years," he said. Al Lopez said the ball was livelier. Hal (Skinny) Brown, the Baltimore pitcher, was more specific. He said the ball was wrapped tighter and felt smaller and that the seams were flatter. The Spalding Company, which made the ball, insisted that the "coefficient of restitution" (that is, the rebounding quality) of the baseballs was the same as a year earlier.

Yet the stories kept coming. An article in August claimed it was not just the balls, but the bats, too. At an oldtimers game in Yankee Stadium, Wally Pipp and Emil (Irish) Meusel, who had played with and against Ruth, said the Babe had hit his homers with a big 50-ounce bat, not the 33-ounce lightweight bats the modern players used. Some leaped on that theme and argued that the success of the present-day players was due in large part to the superior equipment—from bats and balls to better playing and living conditions.

Mantle, who had fallen five homers behind Maris at this point, reacted negatively to the criticism. He said, "I think if Roger breaks Ruth's record he should get full credit. All this talk about the ball being livelier and the bats being livelier gives me a pain in the ass. What sport hasn't changed? They got steel-shafted golf clubs now that can hit a ball a hundred yards farther than the old wooden shafts they used to use. Does that mean the golfers today aren't as good as oldtime golfers?

"They keep saying the baseball is livelier. If it is, how come I can't hit the ball as far as I did five years ago?" In the 1950s Mantle had hit several tremendously long home runs, notably one in Washington that an enterprising Yankee publicity man named Arthur Patterson measured. Patterson said it went 565 feet, and Mantle's titanic blasts quickly became known as tape-measure home runs.

"I hit balls back then that were supposed to be the longest ever hit in different parks," Mantle said. "I'm hitting the ball just as hard this year, but I'm not getting the distance I did then, and I'm not hitting for as good an average. Why? Because the pitchers are slicker and smarter now than they were then. Those oldtimers talk about Ruth swinging a 50-ounce bat. Hell, throw me nothing but fastballs and curves like they did then and I could swing that 50-ounce bat too. But today you got sliders, screwballs, forkballs, knuckleballs, change-ups, all sorts of pitches. I know they're not all new pitches, but more pitchers know how to throw them, and they have better control over them, and most of them mix them in with a good fastball. You got to use a light bat so you can control your swing and change it at the last instant if you have to.

"I'm tired of all this talk about the oldtimers. I don't think we'll ever see a .400 hitter again, but that's no knock on the hitters today. The pitching is just so much better. The game is improving all the time. I know the pitching has—at least, it has in the ten years I've been up here."

RALPH HOUK:

A lot of people think you use a light bat to hit a fastball pitcher, but most batters I've known use the light bat against breaking-ball pitchers. They use a heavier bat to hit a fastball pitcher because then they're usually swinging in one plane. Mantle knew that. Mickey knew a lot of things. There was nobody like him when it came to playing ball.

I never saw him more determined than he was in 1961. It seemed like he'd always get the big hits. I thought it was going to be his greatest year and he did have a great year, but it could have been so much more if he hadn't got hurt. You don't know what he might have done.

Roger got the MVP that season but I thought he and Mickey were really co-MVPs. I don't see how you could separate them. Mickey was the leader and I think he meant more to the team, but Roger won an awful lot of games for us. You could hardly cast your vote for one and not the other. Ford and Arroyo didn't hurt either.

But Mantle was the biggest help to me. He really grew up that year. I think the fact that he knew I was depending on him to keep things going made him take on more responsibility. Casey being gone kind of took a load off his shoulders and made it easier for him, and the other players thought so much of him. Like the way he'd come back after an injury. He'd be hurt and not able to play, and then he'd come back and—wham!—first time up he'd hit one. He was amazing. Just amazing. All the players liked him, and they all respected him. When you have a player that good who plays as hard as Mantle did, it just sort of makes the other guys play harder too.

Mickey had great natural ability. I remember the first time I saw him, in spring training in Phoenix in 1951, the year the Yankees and the Giants traded training camps for one season. We had that precamp in Arizona, the instructional school, and that's where I first saw him. Oh, he could run. He could flat-out motor. He was skinny-looking then compared to what he was later, but he could hit from both sides, and he had a great arm. There wasn't anything he couldn't do. If only he hadn't got hurt so much. . . .

But he played so hard that he was always getting hurt. His body moved so quick. I don't mean just speed. I mean quickness, reacting to things, the way great athletes do, like the way a hitter reacts, or the way a great baserunner sees a chance and just *goes*. He was amazing, he was so quick. In some people, like a Mantle, the mind sees something and the body reacts instantly. You can't teach that. You can help someone to use his feet right, or his hands, certain things like that, and you can help make them quicker, but you can't make them quick. That's just there.

I've talked to doctors about this, and I don't know if I ever got the right answer, but there's something in some people that makes them quick and other people slow, something from the brain to the energy or the muscles or whatever it is that makes you do things faster. Something in Mantle made him move so fast that sometimes his legs or his body couldn't take it. He'd swing so hard or he'd run so hard that he'd hurt something. His muscles wouldn't hold up. The muscle up here was so strong that it would pull the muscle down there. Something had to give.

It's like Mark Fidrych, who I had when I managed Detroit later on. Fidrych was the greatest thing that came along in baseball at that time. After he hurt his arm I got mail saying I overpitched him. I never overpitched him one inning in his whole life. I protected that kid. When you have something like that come along you guard it with your life. He could throw the ball in an area this small, one pitch after the other. The ball would just naturally sink, and he would put it right in there, over and over again.

I think what happened to Fidrych was what used to happen to Mickey, except when it happens to a pitcher it can be worse because he depends on one thing, his arm. Fidrych was so competitive that something in him would say, I gotta get this hitter out, and he'd exert himself so much that something had to give. There was nothing you could do about it, but when he lost that pitch that was the end of it—he lived by that sinker. What a shame. He was unbelievable. His attitude was perfect. He never complained. He loved everything.

I tried to protect Mantle, too. I didn't like him stealing bases because I was worried about his legs, I was afraid he'd get hurt. I had my own signs with him for stealing. He'd get on first base and if I went like this, that meant he could go [Mantle stole 12 bases in 1961, almost half the team's total], and if I went like that, no. I usually wouldn't let him go, and he'd get mad at me. But I felt strongly that any base he stole had to be only to put the tying or winning run over there.

They walked him a lot, and that was because I had him hitting fourth, behind Roger. I got a lot of letters about that, too. People wanted Mickey to be the one to hit the 61 home runs, not Roger, and they used to write me telling me to bat him third and Roger fourth. It was probably true, Maris was probably getting more pitches to hit with Mickey out on deck waiting to hit behind him. I moved Roger up and down in the batting order for a while before he settled in to batting third, but I had Mickey hitting fourth all the way. I wasn't concerned about records. All I wanted was the pennant, and I thought that was our best lineup, with Mickey hitting fourth.

When there was a base open, they'd walk him. That would burn him up. A lot of times they'd walk him damn near on purpose even with nobody on second, and then he'd want to steal, he was so mad. He'd look in at me on every pitch, and I'd signal, no, nope, no. Oh, he'd be sore.

He was great for me. I'm not sure he believed me in the winter when I talked to him about being the team leader. He might have thought I was kidding, snowing him a little. But you have to have someone who is the leader, the one the others look to, and you have to let him know you consider him the leader. I told Mickey that, and I told the press. The writers couldn't quite figure that out—I guess Mickey was still a kid to them—so they went to Mickey and talked to him about it. I don't know what he said to them but, damn, he became the leader and he was ideal.

A leader has to be a good ballplayer to start with, because how can you lead a club if you're not one of the stars? Mickey was a great ballplayer, but it was his attitude toward winning, going all out, trying all the time, that made him such a good leader. He was probably the most unselfish ballplayer I ever saw. If you won a game and he had a bad day, looked terrible, struck out three times—you'd never know it. He was just happy we won. He'd make jokes about himself, laugh about it, say things like "You guys really did it today." But if he had a great day, homers and everything, and we lost, he'd sit there feeling as down about the game as everybody else. You'd never have known he had a good day.

He was a tough ballplayer who loved to win. You get guys like that on your team and it makes it easy for a manager.

27

During the summer another plane was hijacked to Cuba, this one an Eastern Airlines flight from Miami to Tampa. Castro said the 37 passengers on the plane could return to Miami but that the United States and Cuba would have to negotiate about the return of the plane. While Cuba was holding it, two other gunmen hijacked a plane over Texas and held it for nine hours at the El Paso airport before giving it up. Five days later a Pan Am jetliner was hijacked and diverted to Havana. Castro released the Pan Am plane quickly without comment, but he held the Eastern Airlines plane for several more days before it was finally returned.

If the cold war eased, it nonetheless went on. Late in the summer the Soviets said they would resume atomic bomb tests, and President Kennedy responded by saying that while such testing was a peril to the world it meant that American hands were now free as far as nuclear testing was concerned. Khrushchev again blamed the West for creating tension. He said that despite renewed testing there would be no nuclear war over Berlin, claiming that the Soviet aim in resuming the bomb tests was to shock the Western countries into a parley on Germany and disarmament. After Russia exploded a third test bomb, the United States and Great Britain called for a ban on atomic testing in the atmosphere—although Kennedy said America would resume testing underground. At about the same time, he made a speech at the United

Nations warning of the peril of atomic war, and Khrushchev said he was willing to meet again with the president. Despite all the noise, the crisis slowly subsided. But it had been a hairy summer. No wonder they started dancing the twist at the Peppermint Lounge.

The Green Bay Packers gave a new five-year contract to Vince Lombardi, who was about to begin his third season as the Packers' head coach. The Pack had been 1–10–1 in 1958, but in 1959, Lombardi's first year, they improved to 7–5 and in 1960 they had won the National Football League's Western Conference with an 8–4 record, before losing to Philadelphia in the NFL championship game (this was still years before the Super Bowl). Now, in 1961, they would win the NFL title and begin Lombardi's reign of glory.

At the other end of the scale, the Philadelphia Phillies, in their second season under 35-year-old manager Gene Mauch, lost 23 games in a row.

Charlie Finley in Kansas City fired manager Joe Gordon and replaced him with Hank Bauer, Houk's old friend. Finley said his general manager, Frank Lane, had fired Gordon. Lane called Finley a liar. Finley fired Lane. Later he unfired him, but at a public peace session asked Lane if he had really called him a liar. Lane said yes, because, he said, Finley had not told the truth "when you said I fired Gordon." Finley was also chastised by Commissioner Frick for holding a mock "Appreciation Day" at the Kansas City ball park for a sports columnist who had been critical of the Athletics' owner.

Finley traveled to California and announced that he was thinking of moving his ball team there. He returned to Kansas City and said that wasn't so, that he was definitely going to keep the Athletics there. Seven years later he moved the club to Oakland. In 1961 Finley said Kansas City fans weren't supporting the team. His critics argued that local fans were just tired of rooting for losing teams. After the Athletics moved there from Philadelphia in 1955 the team had been last or second to last every year, and in 1961 it had a splendid chance of becoming the first team in American League history to finish tenth. As it turned out, the A's avoided that sorry fate by winning on the last day of the season to gain a ninth-place tie with the expansion Senators.

Three other events cast their influence into the future. The Grove Press issued Henry Miller's *Tropic of Cancer,* 27 years after that sexually explicit novel had first been published in France, opening the way for specific "frankness" in books, magazines, movies, television and stage plays. President Kennedy signed a bill allowing NFL teams to bypass interstate commerce restrictions and pool their income from television, a significant step in improving the financial strength of all professional football and in expanding television coverage of the sport. And in California Richard Nixon, who less than a year earlier had lost to Kennedy in the presidential election and had presumably retired from politics, began his comeback by announcing that he would run for governor of California in 1962.

Interest in the home-run race was so great that headlines began to say things like M&M FAIL TO CONNECT, as though not hitting a home run was news. In Cleveland in August the Yankees beat the sagging Indians twice before a crowd of 56,000, by 20,000 the largest paid attendance in Cleveland all season, and despite the double defeat the crowd cheered loudly when Mantle hit a home run and almost as loudly when Maris hit one.

Two days later in Los Angeles, on August 22, Maris hit his fiftieth homer of the season, the earliest by far that anyone had ever reached 50. The previous record date was September 4—by Ruth in 1927 and Foxx in 1932. In Los Angeles, Stengel was asked which of the two he thought would break Ruth's record. In a dig at Frick, Casey growled, "How the hell would I know when I don't even know where the finish is? I know the young fella with the fine swing has a fine chance since he already got 50, but don't overlook the other fella. He hits a ball a mile from either side of the plate and when he gets hot there ain't nobody stopping him."

Where the media focus had previously been largely on Mantle, now it began shifting toward Maris, who was ill-prepared to handle it.

Mantle, after hitting two homers in Minnesota at the end of August to move within three of Maris, took some of the pressure off himself with self-deprecatory humor. The press noted that in 1927 when Ruth and Gehrig had staged *their* great home-run duel, the two ended the season with a total of 107 homers, Ruth hitting 60 and Gehrig 47. After hitting his forty-seventh and forty-eighth in Minnesota against the Twins, Mantle joked, "I caught my man. Now Roger has to catch his." The big question, of course, was: Would he?

Total 100-percent attention on Maris and Mantle was delayed just a little while longer by the heated pennant race. The Yankees had been trying all summer to shake loose from Detroit, but the Tigers had gotten rid of their doldrums and they moved close in again. They were too good a ball team to give way easily, although the Yankees, like some massive, irresistible force, had slowly but steadily squeezed the Tigers out of the lead. The New Yorkers had pushed into first place for a day in mid-June, again for a couple of hours during the July Fourth doubleheader, again for three days just before the first All-Star break, again for three days after it. Their pressure was relentless. The Tigers recaptured first place three times after the first All-Star game, but when the Yankees swept the White Sox on July 25 to move into first place again, Houk's troops were there to stay. They held a half-game lead for a couple of days, then a full game, then two games. They edged up to two and a half, to three and, during their nine-game winning streak in August, to four.

And still Detroit would not give in. For two and a half months, while Mantle and Maris led the greatest home-run assault in history, while Ford was winning 16 of 17 games, while Arroyo was heading toward a league-leading 29 saves, the Tigers stayed with the Yankees, seldom more than a step behind. In August, when the Yankees accelerated their already torrid pace and played better than .700 ball for the month, the Tigers matched them exactly, winning 22 games and losing 9, just as the Yankees did. They actually played better than New York in the latter part of the month, cutting the Yankee lead from four games to three to two, and when they came into Yankee

Stadium on September 1—the first time the teams had met since the July Fourth doubleheader—they were only a game and a half behind. They had beaten the Yankees 6 times in 11 games so far during the season. If they could take 2 out of 3 now in September, they'd be only half a game behind, with a month left in the season. If they could sweep in New York, the Tigers would be in the lead.

28

It was clearly the showdown of the season. On Friday, September 1, a humid, sultry night with temperatures in the mid-eighties, a crowd of 65,566 was in Yankee Stadium for the first of the three games between the Tigers and the Yankees. Houk held Ford out of the pitching rotation for one extra day—the first time since early May that Ford's pattern of pitching every fourth day had been deliberately interrupted—so that he could go against the Tigers in the opener. Don Mossi, the fine lefthander, pitched for Detroit. Before the game Mantle and Maris, who were rooming together with Bob Cerv in an apartment in Queens, arrived at the Stadium in a white convertible. They sprinted past the crowd gathered to see them ("Mickey, sign this Mickey," the fans cried, and "Roger, Roger, hey, Roger") outside the players' entrance to the Stadium. In the locker room as they undressed and put on their uniforms they were surrounded by sportswriters. Photographers besieged them on the field before the game. Everything they did attracted attention. There were roars from the crowd when one or the other reached the seats in batting practice.

In the Yankee half of the first inning, after Kubek, batting second, singled, a tremendous roar greeted Maris as he came to bat. The roaring continued through each pitch but stopped abruptly when Roger struck out on a three-and-two pitch. Mantle stepped in and there were, astonishingly, a few boos from the crowd mixed in with the greater sound of cheers. Then Mickey struck out, too.

Mossi continued pitching scoreless ball and so did Ford, but in the fourth inning Whitey strained his hip and after getting two Tigers out in the fifth inning called time. Houk went out to talk to him, and a moment later Ford walked slowly off the field, unable to pitch any more that night.

Daley replaced him, and the scoreless duel continued, through the sixth, through the seventh, through the eighth. In the top of the eighth, the score still 0–0, Bruton singled with one out and Kaline followed with a base hit down the left-field line. Bruton stopped at third but Kaline, seeing Berra running toward the foul line after the ball, turned first and raced for second. It seemed a certain double, but Berra backhanded the ball, stopped, turned and fired a perfect throw into second base and Kaline was out. It was an amazing play, particularly for a catcher playing the outfield, and it stunned the Tigers. Daley got Cash to pop up, and the inning was over, the threat denied.

The Yankees pinch-hit for Daley in their half of the eighth but failed to score, and Arroyo retired the Tigers one-two-three in the top of the ninth. Maris and Mantle were the first two hitters in the bottom of the ninth, which lifted Yankee hopes, but Mossi, still pitching strongly, retired them both, getting Mantle on a called third strike that angered him. Mickey had gone oh for four for the night (three strikeouts and a popup) and after yelling at the umpire he flung his batting helmet from the dugout onto the field.

With two out and the bases empty, Howard singled off Mossi and so did Berra. Skowron, batting seventh, bounced a base hit past third base and Howard, running from second, scored to give the Yankees a stunning 1–0 victory. If the Tigers had won, they'd have been only half a game behind; now they were two and a half back.

A crowd of more than 50,000 turned out for the second game on Saturday afternoon, when Terry started against Frank Lary. In the fourth inning with the Yankees behind 2–1, Maris doubled and moved to third base when the ball was mishandled. Mantle, who was three behind Roger in the home-run race, gave up the chance to hit one and instead laid down a drag bunt, beating it out as Maris scored to tie the game. In the sixth inning, with the bases empty and two out, Maris went to a three-and-two count against Lary and then hit a pitch into the right-field seats to put the Yankees ahead 3–2. In the eighth Maris hit another home run as the Yankees battered the Tigers for four runs to take a 7–2 lead, the final score.

Maris's first homer was his fifty-second, which equaled the number Mantle had hit in 1956, his Triple Crown year, when he became the first Yankee other than Ruth to hit 50 homers in a season. Roger's second homer made him second only to the Babe for most homers by a Yankee in a single season. Mickey was now five behind him again. Worse, in the sixth inning as Mantle batted after Maris's first home run, he swung so hard at a pitch that he pulled a muscle in his left forearm. He stayed in the game, even though he couldn't swing the bat properly. "He had no business playing, but I let him stay in," Houk said. "He could still field, and he asked me to leave him in the game. He told me he'd bunt whenever he had to hit."

The Yankee lead was now up to three and a half games, and the Tigers desperately needed to win the final game of the series on Sunday. Mantle's forearm was so sore when he arrived at the ball park that Houk did not plan to use him. But Mickey took physiotherapy treatment in the clubhouse and found that he was able to swing the bat. After putting a couple into the seats in batting practice he said he could play.

"I was pretty pumped up," Mantle said. "I didn't want to get out of the lineup if I could play at all."

Houk let him play, which pleased a third successive big crowd, this one more than 55,000 (the total attendance of 171,503 set a new Yankee record for a three-game series during the regular season). The Tigers scored quickly off Stafford in the first inning and led 1–0. With two out in the Yankee half of the first, Maris singled off Jim Bunning and Mantle, bad arm and all, hit a home run down the right-field line to put the Yankees ahead. Berra followed with another homer, the Yanks added another run in the fifth and were leading 4–2 after seven, with two innings to play.

They seemed headed for a sweep, which would shove the Tigers four and a half games behind with only 19 games left in the season, but it was a very hot, humid afternoon, and after Stafford completed seven innings Houk lifted him for a pinch-hitter. He called on Arroyo—for the third straight day—to handle the last two innings. When Arroyo took the mound in the eighth he threw just six pitches. The first was hit for a single by Bruton. Kaline hit the second for another single, moving Bruton to third. Colavito hit Arroyo's third pitch sharply, but on the ground to Kubek, who went for the double play as Bruton scored. The score was now 4–3, but Arroyo's next three pitches were strikes to Cash, and the odd, brisk inning was over. The Yanks still led by a run. In the ninth Arroyo walked Dick McAuliffe and struck out Chico Fernandez. Dick Brown topped a ball in front of the pitcher's mound, and Arroyo grabbed it and threw to first base. His throw glanced off Skowron's glove and the runners moved to second and third. Suddenly the old pennant race seemed much tighter again. A Tiger base hit would score two runs and put Detroit ahead with only the last half of the ninth to play. And if they could hold the Yankees then, the Tigers would return from the depths of an imminent four-and-a-half-game deficit and be only two and a half behind, with morale restored and hopes high of still catching New York.

Houk had Arroyo walk pinch-hitter Bubba Morton intentionally to fill the bases, but Jake Wood upset that strategy by singling. The Tigers had scored the two runs and they led 5–4. The Yankees were losing, and the pennant race *was* very much alive.

Mantle led off for New York in the last of the ninth and electrified the crowd by hitting his second homer of the game, his fiftieth of the season, to tie the score. It was the first time two players on the same team had hit 50 homers in the same year. It was the second time in his career that Mantle had hit 50; only three other hitters—Ruth,

Foxx and Kiner—had ever done that. And it came the day after he suffered the muscle pull in his arm so painful that he couldn't swing the bat—so painful, in fact, that he was unable to play the next day in a Labor Day doubleheader against Washington.

Berra followed Mantle's homer with a single, and Arroyo sacrificed him to second. Skowron was walked intentionally and Boyer flied out to right. Two out now, score tied, two men on and Elston Howard up. Howard was batting ninth. He had struck out hitting for Stafford in the seventh inning and had stayed in the game to catch.

Now, the last man in the batting order, he hit a towering three-run home run that won the game 8–5 and, as it turned out, ended the pennant race. The Tigers, now four and a half games back, were finished.

After the game a reporter commiserating with Bob Scheffing, the Tiger manager, said something about Yankee luck.

"There's nothing lucky about that club," Scheffing said. "They're just good. They're one of the best-balanced teams I've ever seen. They've got everything. No matter who they take out, they've got someone else on the bench to keep them going. Imagine having a hitter like Skowron batting seventh. Imagine a hitter like Howard coming up ninth."

RALPH HOUK:

A lot of people think we won that 1961 pennant easy, but it wasn't until we beat them those three straight in the Stadium that we started to pull away. I was so concerned before that series that I pitched somebody out of turn just to have Whitey ready for the first game. My staff was rested, and some of them couldn't believe I'd do that, mess with the rotation like that, but I told them, "I'm pointing to one thing, and that's the Detroit series." I knew we had to hold the Tigers off. They were the team we had to beat. I maneuvered around to get Ford and Terry and Stafford in there, the guys who could beat them, or at least the ones I thought could beat them. We had to beat Detroit. We pointed for that series all summer.

I wanted to be sure to win one game from them and I hoped we'd win two, but I can't say I expected we'd sweep all three. It sure wasn't an easy sweep. I was really bothered when Ford had to leave in the first game. Whitey's hip used to go out on him every once in a while, and that worried me then because he'd been pitching real good. But Daley did very well when he came in. Daley did a lot of good things for us that season, and pitching that good in that game was one of them. And then Arroyo wrapping it up.

When Yogi made that throw he saved the game for us. If Kaline was safe at second, we'd have walked the next man and they'd have had the bases full and only one out. Instead, it's one man on and two out. I'll never forget that throw, and I don't think Yogi will either. Or Kaline. He still talks about it too. Some things just stand out in your mind, and that's one of them. It was a great throw, just unbelievable.

And Mickey dragging that bunt in the second game to score Roger. That was typical of Mantle. He wanted to hit home runs, but he'd do things like that to win ball games. Then he pulled that muscle and wouldn't come out of the game. He said, "Don't take me out. I can still get on base." He was the hardest guy I ever managed as far as getting him out of the lineup was concerned. He couldn't stand being on the bench. He really couldn't.

The third game, that was one great ball game, and it showed what I've always said about that 1961 club of ours: we were never out of a ball game. We had so many good players. I remember once against Kansas City when Hank Bauer was managing the A's. Every time Hank made a move, I could top him with a better move, like bringing in a Blanchard or a Howard, because I had so many players. We beat them, and Hank looked at me and threw up his hands as if to say, "What are you gonna do?" We had players that could hit the long ball, and if we could get something going, sooner or later somebody would pop one and we'd be right back in the ball game, or ahead of them, or in the clubhouse with the win.

That was some game, that last one with the Tigers. Detroit fought like hell and all three games could have gone either way, but we won 'em all and that was the end of the Tigers.

We continued to win after that, and they continued to lose. We opened it up real fast then. We just blew it out. Everybody thinks we won the pennant easy, but that's when it all happened—within a week, boom! That was the biggest series of the year.

Mantle's forearm spent two hours in physiotherapy the next day before he reluctantly conceded that he was simply unable to swing the bat. He sat out both games, except to go into the field in the ninth inning of the first game as a defensive substitute. The Yankees didn't miss him or Maris, who went oh for eight in the doubleheader. They beat the Senators twice while the dazed Tigers were losing their fourth in a row. Suddenly, astonishingly, the Yankees were *way* out in front in the pennant race. In little more than 24 hours—from the middle of the ninth inning on Sunday, when the still-feisty Tigers were three outs away from being only two and a half games behind—Detroit had fallen to six games back.

The Yankees won again the next day, and the floundering Tigers lost a doubleheader to fall 7½ games behind. They continued to lose—9 in a row before they could stop their slide—while the Yankees, riding high, carried the string of victories that began with their 1–0 win over Mossi to 13 straight before stopping. A week after leaving Yankee Stadium the Tigers were 11½ games behind. Never has a tense, season-long pennant race fallen apart so rapidly and so completely.

PART FOUR

Roger Maris and the Home-Run Ordeal

29

With the pennant race now definitely settled, the baseball writers had little more to dwell upon than Maris and Mantle and their chase after the home-run record. Ford, having the greatest year of his career, was all but ignored. "It was the damndest thing," Ford said, "I'd been with the Yankees for ten years and for ten years I'd been hoping to win 20 games. Now I win 25, and all anybody asked me about was home runs."

Other players were disregarded, too. Consider the Labor Day double-header when the Yankees swept two games from the Senators while the Tigers were losing, the *coup de grace* day that broke the pennant race apart for good. The Yankees won two important, exciting games. Sheldon pitched seven good innings in the opener and left with the score tied 3–3. In the eighth Blanchard hit yet another of his dramatic home runs to give the Yankees the victory. Young Reniff, who had pitched well in relief since Houk brought him up from the minors in June, got credit for the win, his second against no defeats. In the second game Daley, whose pitching had meant so much to the Yankees, pitched a complete game for his tenth victory of the season. Boyer homered in that game, Howard and Skowron hit back-to-back doubles, Cerv tripled and Boyer drove in the winning run with a sacrifice fly. The legitimate heroes of the day—Sheldon, Blanchard, Reniff, Boyer, Howard, Skowron, Cerv—all were ignored. That was the day Mantle's forearm was so sore that he could not play, and Maris went oh for eight in the doubleheader, and *those* were the big stories of the day: MANTLE HURT, MARIS HITLESS.

The demise of the pennant race coincided with their latest burst of homers. During the week after Detroit died, Mantle hit a homer on Tuesday, Maris on Wednesday, Maris on Thursday, Mantle on Friday, Maris on Saturday, Mantle on Sunday. Their rhythmic one-two punch was unrelenting and irresistible. There had been a lot of attention paid to the two before, but now it became almost unbearably intense—and sometimes ridiculous. A stripper in Texas began calling herself "Mickey Maris."

"One of the hardest things for Roger," Mantle said, "was the recognition he started getting. Everywhere we'd go, people would want his autograph. I'd been through all that for ten years, so it wasn't that new to me, but it got to where we couldn't go out to eat, couldn't go downstairs in the hotel. Roger didn't like that. He wasn't crazy about that at all. He'd always been kind of private, away from things, and now he couldn't be."

Maris had moved well ahead of Mantle, but when Mickey's two home runs in the final Detroit game gave him 50 to Roger's 53 he seemed to be back in the race. At the least it kept the M&M firm in business as a twin attack force on Ruth. But Mantle was fighting a losing battle. Even though he hit those two homers against the Tigers after pulling the muscle in his forearm, when the injury forced him to miss the doubleheader the next day he lost a golden chance to gain ground as Maris went hitless. Home-run champions almost always hit in streaks—they're hot for a while and then cool off—and Mantle's arm injury came when he was hot.

When he got back in the lineup again on the day after the doubleheader, after taking physiotherapy again, he came to bat for the first time in the second inning and hit the first pitch six rows deep into the upper stands in right field, a tremendous home run that tied the game 1–1 and moved him to within two homers of Maris (53 to 51). It was an astonishing moment but it was Mantle's highwater mark in his duel with Maris. He never came that close to Roger again.

But it served to complete the swing of emotional support in his direction. To the fans and the press, Maris was a superb, mechanical home-run-hitting machine—unemotional on and off the field, efficient, cold, reserved. One writer quaintly referred to Maris as a "sobersides." Mantle, on the other hand, had become gallant, the wounded hero striving against adversity. His emotions on the field, once dismissed as childish, now seemed the legitimate reactions of a brave, frustrated man. He was no longer the *bête noire* of Yankee fans. Now Maris was the upstart, and Mickey at last was the rightful successor to Ruth and DiMaggio. Mantle had become the popular favorite.

Roger hit a home run the next day, breaking an oh for 16 slump, and he hit another the day after that, his fifty-fourth and fifty-fifth of the season. He was the second-greatest home-run hitter in Yankee annals, but nothing he did seemed to capture the heart of that great animal, the crowd. Sure, he'd been warmly applauded when he came to bat the first time in the first game against Detroit on September 1, but that was really a welcoming cheer—the Yankees had been on the road when Roger hit his fiftieth and legitimized, so to speak, his pursuit of Ruth. And Mantle at that time was still being booed reflexively by a few diehards. Maris hit two homers against the Tigers, but then he slumped, which most fans find unforgivable, before starting to hit again, while in the meantime Mantle had become the courageous, injured darling of the masses.

The crowd's attitude toward Maris shifted, and he was having trouble holding even their mild affection for him. He later blamed this vaguely on the Yankees—management, presumably—who, he said, "wanted Mantle to break the record, not me. They did everything possible to assure that. They wanted to reduce my chances." That petulance had very little basis in fact. The Yankees, staff and players alike, may have wanted Mantle to break the record but, if anything, Maris got the preferential treatment. As Mantle said, "I think if I batted third all year I might have broke the record." Ford said, "If the players were rooting for Mickey, they never showed it. I can't remember one instance of a guy saying, 'I hope Mickey beats Roger.' If anybody ever said anything like that I never heard it. I mean, I was pulling for Mickey. I knew him better, I hung out with him all the time. It wasn't that I didn't like Roger. I liked him very much. But Mickey was my buddy, and I was pulling for him. But not out loud."

Maris lacked whatever quality it is that generates public affection. Not even a remarkable thing he did at bat one day that week seemed to impress anyone. Only three homers ahead of Mickey at the time, he came up in the first inning with Kubek, who had tripled, on third base. There was one out. The infield was playing respectfully deep for Roger. Maris skillfully bunted and beat it out for a hit as Kubek scored.

The sportswriters were amazed.

"Why bunt?" they asked afterward.

"Why not?" Maris replied coldly, in his best, contemptuous, you-don't-know-much-about-baseball tone. "They were playing deep, and I knew I could get Tony in. We still have a pennant to win." The run, the game, the pennant—these were still paramount in Maris's eyes, which was an admirable, if unappreciated, attitude for a ball-player in his position to have.

In his very next time at bat, as though to emphasize how versatile a ballplayer he was, Maris hit his fifty-fifth homer. He was four ahead of Mickey again. Mantle hit one the next day, but Maris hit another one the day after that, his fifty-sixth, the same number Hall-of-Famer Hack Wilson had hit in 1930, which has remained the National League record for more than half a century. That homer gave M&M 108 for the season, surpassing the 107 Ruth and Gehrig hit in 1927.

Maris was now in a pretty good position to break Ruth's record. His bat was hot again, and he needed only four to tie the Babe, five to beat him. He had 20 games left in the season, 12 before Frick's arbitrary 154-game barrier. To tie the record in 154 games Maris needed to hit an average of one homer every three games, and so far during the season he had been hitting them more frequently than that, about one every two and a half games. He had already overcome the bogeyman of Ruth's fabulous 17 homers in September. He didn't have to accelerate to beat Babe; he could even ease off a little.

For the 162-game season, Maris needed a homer only every four games—a much slower pace—to pass Ruth. The numbers get a little heavy here but Maris to this point had been hitting homers at a rate that would give him 61 for a 154-game season, 64 for a 162-game season. He could slow down to a 51-homer pace and still reach 60 in 154 games, equaling the Babe, and he could slow down even further, to a 41-homer pace, and surpass Ruth's mark in 162 games.

But more and more attention was fixed on whether he could do it in 154 games, and at that point he seemed a good bet to do it. He still had a doubleheader in the Stadium against the inept Indians before the Yankees left on their last road trip of the year, and the road seemed no obstacle. Maris hit homers away from home as frequently as he hit them in the Stadium, and the first two stops on this trip were in Chicago and Detroit. Tiger Stadium in Detroit was always a good home-run park, and Maris had hit 13 homers off Chicago's pitching. It was accepted almost as a matter of faith in 1961 that the addition of the two expansion teams was the big reason why Maris was hitting so many home runs (which helps explain in part Frick's fervor in protecting Ruth; he didn't want the Babe's mark supplanted by a "cheap" record). Yet almost 25 percent of Roger's home runs to this point (13 of his 56) had come against the White Sox, one of the better teams in the league, and he had hit only four against the expansion Angels, whose home games were in little Wrigley Field. Go figure.

But even though Mantle hit his fifty-third in the first game of the Cleveland doubleheader, Maris failed to connect. Perhaps Roger was distracted, because it was a wild, tumultuous afternoon. The Yankees extended their winning streak to twelve games and their lead over Detroit to 11½. An exuberant crowd of 57,826 raised the Yankees' season attendance to 1,657,031, its highest in ten years, with five home games still to play. (They finished the season with 1,747,725, the best in the league.) In his first season as manager Houk was drawing more fans with his team than the colorful Casey had in any of his last nine years with the Yankees.

It was a crazy doubleheader, as it had been a crazy weekend. The day before, Saturday, had been Whitey Ford Day, arranged by the Yankee front office, which appreciated what Ford had done even if everyone else was overlooking it. The pitcher was showered with gifts, some of them furniture and appliances for his home. When Ford saw them all he quipped to his wife Joan, "Now we'll have to buy a bigger house to put this stuff in." One of the gifts Ford received was a huge, man-sized roll of Life Savers, which was trundled onto the field and presented to him. Before the puzzled Ford could do or say anything, the Life Saver package was opened and Arroyo, Ford's relief-pitching lifesaver during the season, stepped out. The crowd roared with laughter and Ford accepted the joke with good nature, although privately he was a little annoyed by it. He was proud of his pitching that season, and he didn't like it being devalued.

Ford did not pitch on his Day but he did start the next day in the first game of the Sunday doubleheader. He was given a big lead and then uncharacteristically blew most of it, giving five runs before Houk replaced him with Coates in the third inning. Ford's hip was still bothering him on and off, which troubled Houk because he was counting heavily on Ford in the World Series. He planned to start him in the first game (not hold him out the way Casey had in 1960) and come back with him in the fourth game, and, if necessary, again in the seventh. An injured Ford was a serious matter but after the doings of that zany afternoon, amid the usual storm of questions about Maris and Mantle, no one thought to ask about Ford.

During the first game of the doubleheader two young men from Long Island jumped onto the field from the low outfield stands and charged toward the Cleveland center fielder, the highly strung Jimmy Piersall, a longtime Boston Red Sox star before moving on to Cleveland, who had never been a favorite with Yankee fans. The volatile Piersall squared off against his attackers, punched one and when the other turned to flee deftly kicked him in the behind. Both the trespassers were collared by the police, to the approval of the crowd, and after play resumed Piersall drew a tremendous cheer when he made an amazing catch near the fence—he grabbed Blanchard's bid for a home run while colliding with right-fielder Willie Kirkland. And in that game Coates, who was credited with the win, threw knockdown pitches at Cleveland's Vic Power while Power was standing on first base.

RALPH HOUK:

Jim Coates hated all hitters. He was a big old boy from Virginia, lives there yet, kind of a hillbilly, very tall and lanky. He looked like you'd picture a Kentucky mountaineer would look, and he more or less talked like that.

Jim had a real good fastball—it didn't sink, it kind of rose a little— but he had to have his control to be effective. Usually it wasn't too bad, but sometimes he'd get the fastball in areas where the hitters could get to it, and that would hurt him because he was a strikeout pitcher. He had to strike out a lot of hitters to win. He'd give you five or six strong innings, and maybe after that a little bit of the fastball left.

He was really mean out there on the mound. He had a temper, and he'd throw at batters and he got to be a pitcher people disliked. The guys on the team liked him but I don't think they enjoyed playing behind him too much, because there was always a problem developing. Jim would throw at somebody, and they'd throw at our people, and someone would end up getting tossed out of the game. I know some of our players were pretty happy a couple of years later when we traded Coates to Washington for Steve Hamilton. Sometimes he'd throw at hitters when we were ahead in a game and he'd wake the other club up. I didn't like to get on Jim, but there were times like that when I had to.

Sometimes it could get to be pretty funny, like when he threw at Vic Power that time. I think he hit Power or walked him, but now Power's on first base and Coates kept throwing at him. Power is standing there on the *base* but Coates kept throwing over there, throwing the ball right at him.

He was rough out there. I remember him and Jim Piersall in Cleveland—that was probably the funniest thing I ever saw on a ballfield. Coates was on the mound warming up before the start of the first inning. Piersall was leading off for Cleveland and he came out of the dugout swinging four or five bats, and he stood about ten feet from home plate watching Coates throw his warmup pitches, the way hitters do. I guess Coates and Piersall had some kind of verbal battle. Maybe Coates said something, maybe Piersall did, I don't know. But about the second warmup pitch, Coates threw a ball just as hard as he could right at Piersall. Coates knocked him down, and the guy wasn't even at bat. The bats went flying in every direction and Piersall landed on his ass, and then the two of them went at it, and Coates hadn't even thrown a ball in the game yet.

But Jim was a pretty important pitcher for us. I used him in a lot of different ways: spot starter, middle relief, even to finish some ball games, and he'd always take the ball. He was a worker. He was like one of those oldtime ballplayers you read about, a guy who went home when the season was over and worked in a sawmill, things like that. He had a nice family, too.

He was very confident. He was a hard-nosed guy all right, but I liked him. And he sure helped us a lot in 1961.

After all the fuss in the first game, another furor developed in the nightcap. Boyer hit a drive down the left-field line that appeared to clear the railing for a home run before bouncing back onto the field. Plate umpire Joe Linsalata waved his arm in a circle, indicating a home run, and Boyer slowed to a home-run trot as he rounded second. But Piersall came sprinting across the outfield toward third-base umpire Charlie Berry, the senior member of the umpiring team, who had run out along the left-field line to make the call. Piersall had seen the ball hit the top of the fence, not clear it, before ricocheting away. So, in fact, had Berry, who had made a gesture indicating the ball was in play. The home-plate umpire had misinterpreted Berry's gesture.

Meanwhile, the Indians' left fielder picked up the ball and threw it to third base where the jogging Boyer was tagged out. Boyer was indignant. After all, he had slowed down only after the plate umpire signaled it was a home run. The Yankees gathered around angrily, Houk leading the argument. The discussion raged. Berry explained to Houk that the ball had indeed hit the fence and had remained in play and that Boyer was, yes, out at third. He said to Houk that the misunderstanding had been his fault because he hadn't signaled clearly, and that Linsalata had misread his call. It was too bad Boyer was out;

it was a shame; but unfortunately that didn't change the circumstances. The umpires were not responsible for baserunners, who were on their own. In short, the decision stood and Boyer was out.

After quite a bit of shouting and arguing Houk and the Yankees reluctantly accepted the decision, but the fans, basking in that sense of outraged moral self-righteousness a crowd sometimes acquires, would not. For 17 minutes they booed and jeered and mockingly waved handkerchiefs at the umpires before finally settling down and letting play resume.

Newspaper and television reports ran pictures of Piersall booting the interloper and of Houk and Boyer and the others in the furious argument over the false home run, but the headlines were about Mantle's homer and Maris's lack of one. Roger had wasted 2 of the precious 12 games he had left before the 154-game deadline.

Still, as the Yankees left New York to begin the road trip there was optimism that he—and possibly even Mantle—would catch Ruth in the ten games remaining. True, it would be a real long shot for Mickey, and it wouldn't be easy for Roger, but they had hit home runs in bunches so often that there was an air of expectancy as the team headed west for Chicago.

30

But the three games in Chicago turned out to be a disaster, taking Mantle completely out of the running and just about cooking Maris's chances of passing Ruth in the prescribed time. And it was in Chicago that the alienation between Maris and the press flared into outright war. Wave after wave of reporters and photographers, most of them unfamiliar to Maris, asking the same old questions, asking what he thought were stupid or rude questions, asking him to pose for the same photographs that had been taken of him a hundred times before, were rapidly becoming the bane of his life.

One writer asked him, "Do you fool around on the road?"

"I'm a married man," Maris said.

"I'm a married man myself," the reporter said, "but I fool around on the road."

"That's your business," Maris said.

The tenor of such questions, which he usually tried to answer honestly, was wearing him down. He felt the reporters were distorting what he said and what he did and what the ball club was doing.

RALPH HOUK:

Roger Maris was just as nice a guy as you'll ever want to meet, but that season really got to him. I think it really started in Minnesota

late in August just before we came back home to the Stadium to play
the Tigers. It had been bad enough before that, with everybody coming
around asking the same questions all the time. What about Frick?
What about expansion? What about the lively ball? *Everybody* asked
if the ball was livelier. Oh, yeah. Every year, if somebody happens to
do a little better than they usually do, right away they start asking
questions about the lively ball. Or the bats. Maris had a great answer.
He said the players were livelier.

But then in Minnesota it began to get worse. He'd hit his fiftieth
homer, so all of a sudden it was serious. Maybe he *was* going to bust
Ruth's record. We flew in from Kansas City, and in Minneapolis they
were all over him—him and Mickey both—as soon as the bus got to
the hotel from the airport. That was the first year the Twins were in
Minnesota, you know, and they were all excited about baseball. There
were mobs of people all around, and not just kids. Roger's brother said
there were old ladies who all they wanted to do was touch them.
They'd put their hands out and touch Roger or Mickey on the back
and then snatch their hands away. Mickey and Roger, they couldn't
even take the elevator down to the hotel lobby, it was so jammed with
people waiting to see them. They'd have to go down a flight of stairs
and sneak out the back way.

Then after we swept Detroit in the Stadium it got bad everyplace.
The newspapers figured the pennant race was as good as over, and
they didn't have anything else to write about except Mantle and Maris.
You never saw so many writers and photographers in your life. There
were writers there from everywhere, from Podunk, and they were always
around Roger and Mick asking questions. They were all going to get
the big story.

I remember after that doubleheader with the Indians, when Whitey
got knocked around and I had to take him out in the second or third
inning. His hip was bothering him again, and I'm sitting there thinking
here's my big Series pitcher and he's hurting, and I don't know how
bad it is, and what if he can't pitch in the Series? I was wondering
what I was going to tell the writers, because I knew they were going
to be all over me about it after the game. It was the damnedest thing.
Nobody asked me a thing about Ford. They were all around Maris and
Mantle.

That's about when Roger started having trouble with the press. He
was a good guy. He always talked to the writers. He'd never had any
trouble with them. But he didn't realize that talking to them was one

thing, and having every last thing he said printed in the paper was another, especially when every story was in the headlines. He couldn't say anything that wasn't picked up and printed.

I'm pretty sure it was after that doubleheader with the Indians that it started. Roger went oh for eight or something, I know he had a bad day, and the crowd was getting on him. When you play right field in the Stadium you're real close to the fans in those lower stands—or you were then before they rebuilt the place in the 1970s. You felt like they were sitting on your shoulders. You could hear everything they said, and they could really blister you. I used to sit out in the bullpen, and I know.

So Roger had a bad day and the fans were getting on him bad, and he didn't like it. After the game some writer asked him what the crowd in right field was like, and without even thinking about it Roger says, "Terrible. They're the worst fans in the league."

He just said it, you know. So the guy asks him some more questions and Roger says he's booed every time he makes an out, and he said something about the fans weren't like that in Kansas City, where he used to play. He was just popping off. He was mad—he had a bad day and the fans booed him and he didn't like it.

But when the story comes out, here's Roger Maris blasting the Yankee fans like he'd called a press conference and made a speech about it. It was a big story, and that shook him up. Hell, he'd just been blowing off steam.

That kind of thing kept happening. He'd say things honestly, without thinking about them, and they'd be exaggerated. Somebody asked him if he really wanted to break Babe Ruth's record and Roger said, "Hell, yes," and that was big news. Why wouldn't he want to break the record? Rogers Hornsby, I think it was, said, "Wouldn't it be a shame for a hitter like Maris to break the Babe's record?" and Roger said screw Hornsby. He just said it, half kidding, but the writers were jumping on things like that, and now that's in the headlines: Maris Rips Hornsby.

The first game in Chicago was played in a steady rain and had to be called in the sixth inning. The Yankees won it 4–3 for their thirteenth straight, but not even that impressive streak was the news. The headlines said MARIS, MANTLE HELD TO SINGLES. In the game Maris had a mild disagreement with plate umpire Hank Soar. The reporters asked him about it, and his answer was blown into another major story. "Soar is usually a good umpire," Maris said, "but he was off tonight." He explained that he hadn't been getting many strikes to swing at (that is, pitches over the plate) but that Soar had been calling strikes anyway. "I've been swinging at bad pitches," Maris said, "and I made up my mind tonight that I'd swing only at strikes. Like I said, I didn't get too many, yet they were being called strikes."

It was just a routine ballplayer's gripe, but it, too, was headline news. Stories ran all over the country saying Maris was complaining that he wasn't getting a fair shake from the umpires. Roger had always been a moaner, as many ballplayers are, but now every moan was magnified.

He also complained that he'd been called out on strikes on a pitch he had planned to bunt, meaning that if it had been in the strike zone he would not have taken the pitch. In other words, it was a ball and the umpire was wrong in calling it strike three. A disbelieving reporter questioned the whole story by saying, "*You* were going to bunt? Why would *you* bunt?"

Bristling, Maris said much the same thing he had said several days earlier when he had laid down the successful squeeze bunt in Yankee Stadium. "Why not?" he demanded. "There was a man on third. They weren't expecting a bunt. It would have scored an important run." Maris remembered, if the reporter did not, that it had been a close game and that the Yankees wanted to win it.

Others asked over and over again how he felt about the rain that had shortened and ended the game. When he expressed indifference, his questioners wouldn't accept it. They moved in, asking again if he hadn't been annoyed about losing valuable times at bat because of the rain.

"We won," Maris said. "Look, right now winning the pennant is as important to me as breaking the record. If we're rained out leading in the sixth inning in every game from now to the end of the season, it'll be all right with me."

That generous attitude was all but ignored, but when he talked about the umpiring he was made to look as though he was whining about unfair treatment. Maris continued to respond to reporters, but he was getting increasingly irritable. He had a country man's wariness of strangers, and more and more of the writers asking pointed questions were people he didn't know. He didn't much trust the reporters he did know, either. Some ballplayers have rabbit ears. They hear every critical remark yelled from the stands. Maris had eagle eyes—he seemed to have read or been made aware of everything derogatory that was written about him, particularly those stories that distorted things he had said or done. He'd made casual remarks, as in criticizing Soar, and they were magnified. He didn't know how to banter with reporters, fend them off without antagonizing them, and now he was becoming increasingly defensive around them. Only his antagonistic remarks seemed to interest them.

When Maris read the stories he reacted badly to them. After reading one column about his exploits he commented, "That guy ought to forget about writing." Stories hinting that he and Mantle, who were good friends, were feuding particularly annoyed him. "Some of these guys like to make things up," he said. "That kind of shit makes me mad."

Mantle, on the other hand, grinned when he was asked what he thought about the press coverage.

"I only look at the box scores," he said.

Really?

"Well," he said, "I read the headlines, but not the stories." Pressed for more detail he said, "I look at the batting leaders, and I read the box scores to see what the pitchers are doing—whether they're giving up lots of walks, things like that."

He was becoming deft at handling reporters, although after a bad day he could be as gruff and curt with them as ever. Also, now that he was hopelessly behind in the home-run race he was getting less attention. "This is great," he said one day, sitting alone at his locker while Maris was surrounded at his. He did not have the pressure that Maris continued to have each day, with writers gathering around Roger in the dugout, clustering near him at the batting cage while he waited his turn to hit, closing in around his locker after every game. Someone suggested to Maris that the only time he had privacy was when he was alone out in right field. "The only time I have privacy," he said, "is when I'm taking a crap."

In Chicago he said to Mantle, "I can't take this any more." Mickey said, "You got to."

31

The rain in Chicago persisted, and though the Yankees and the White Sox tried to play the next day, the game was called off after three innings. The stories predictably noted the big news: Maris singled, Mantle popped up. Writers digging around for rainy-day stories talked to former home-run kings Hank Greenberg and Ralph Kiner for their reaction to the question of whether a new homer record would count if it was not made within 154 games. It's probably unfair to assume this so many years after the fact, but the feeling persists that if either Greenberg or Kiner had come out in agreement with Frick that it had to be done within 154 games (the schedule in effect when both Greenberg and Kiner were hitting their homers) it would have been a big story. But when Greenberg said he hoped both Maris and Mantle would break the record and that it didn't matter if it took 162 games, and Kiner said substantially the same thing, their comments were barely noticed. Rooting against Roger was news, rooting for him wasn't. Joe Cronin, the American League president, was similarly ignored. Cronin had disagreed with Frick's decision back in the summer, and now he said, flatly, "A season is a season. If he does it during the season, it's a new record."

Frick testily replied, "You don't reach the 100-meter record in a 100-yard dash. There will be two records: one for 162 games, one for 154."

Berra raised a wonderful Yogiesque question at this point. "What if one guy breaks the record in 154 games," he asked, "and then the other guy passes him in 162?"

The pressure to get it done in 154 games intensified as the date grew closer and the news coverage kept growing. The Yankees still had two games left with the White Sox, to be played in a twi-night doubleheader. Mantle, coming down with a cold, went oh for seven in the doubleheader, but Maris had three hits in eight at bats, not a bad night's work. But none was a homer. The White Sox won both games, ending the Yankees' monumental, pennant-winning streak, but headlines said only, SOX STOP MARIS, MANTLE.

After the doubleheader Mantle, still stalled at 53 home runs, said philosophically that he was out of the chase.

"I figured if I hit a couple here, I might have been able to do it," he said, "but I don't think I can now, not even in 162 games." He said he had no excuses. "The wind tonight favored a pull hitter like me, but I just didn't hit a ball good all night. I didn't get under the ball in either game."

Everybody had to get Maris's reaction to Mantle's remarks about being out of the home-run derby. Maris seemed surprised and with his usual candor said, "Mickey shouldn't concede. He's too good a competitor to concede." He was asked if *he* would concede if he realized he had almost no chance to break the record. "No," he said. "I may not do a thing in Detroit over the weekend, but I'm going to keep on thinking I can break the record until I've had my last chance."

Back to Mantle went the inquisitors, hoping perhaps to exploit this possible rift, this difference of opinion, but Mickey waved off the question. He was out from under the pressure now. The writers still came to him, but not the way they zeroed in on Maris.

The stories written about Maris's reaction to Mantle's "concession" upset Roger, who felt they made him sound as though he had been criticizing Mickey when he thought he was praising him. "That's it," he said. "From now on I'm not talking to anybody."

The Yankees moved on to Detroit for four games that might have been the series of the year in the pennant race if the Tigers had not collapsed. Now interest revolved entirely around Maris and his chance to beat Ruth in 154 games. He had only seven games left, four in Detroit and three in Baltimore, seven games in which he had to hit four home runs to equal Ruth's record, five to break it. The homerless series in Chicago had all but destroyed the possibility. He was still at 56 and while Detroit was a good home-run park, Memorial Stadium in Baltimore was not. Maris hadn't hit a homer there all year, except for the one that had been washed out in July. Time was growing very short.

In Detroit, playing in his second doubleheader in two days, Maris made out eight straight times before singling in his last time at bat in the second game. Ironically, it was in this doubleheader that the Yankees as a team broke the existing major league record for most home runs in a season. Berra hit the one that tied the old record at 221, and Skowron broke it with number 222 (the club went on to hit another 18 before the season ended to finish with 240, a mark that has stood for more than a quarter of a century and seems now almost as remote as Ruth's 60 did before 1961).

Maris was growing increasingly edgy. He was really disturbed by the fans booing him when he made out. "I'd already gone through all that," Mantle said. "When I came up I was supposed to be the next Babe Ruth, Lou Gehrig and Joe DiMaggio all rolled into one, and for a few years there it didn't look like I was going to do a lot. I knew what it was like to have the fans on you."

Roger was so nervous that his hair was beginning to fall out. After the doubleheader in Detroit, his brother Rudy came into the clubhouse and the two retired to the trainer's room to talk. By custom and tradition the trainer's room is off limits to reporters. With a herd of writers and cameramen waiting for him impatiently, Maris stayed in the trainer's room for a long time, talking with Rudy and with other Yankees who wandered in and out. The writers were furious. They appealed to Houk to make Maris come out, but Ralph, not that patient with reporters himself, reacted angrily.

When Maris finally did come out of the trainer's room and was surrounded by the press he was caustic and sarcastic. He felt the stories out of Chicago quoting him as criticizing Mantle for conceding had been unfair, and now he said, "I don't want to talk about the record. What do you want? You want me to concede? Okay, I concede. All right?" He refused to answer any questions.

If you feel, as William Congreve did, that hell has no fury like a woman scorned, you've never seen a sportswriter scorned. Ford's twenty-fourth victory in the opener, the Yankees' hundredth victory of the season in the nightcap, the team's new home-run record, all were pretty well overlooked in the flap about Maris's retreat to the trainer's room. Even the staid *New York Times* ran a story the next morning headlined MARIS SULKS IN TRAINER'S ROOM AS FUTILE NIGHT CHANGES MOOD. The story was written by Louis Effrat, an esteemed veteran of the *Times* sports staff who had been sent on special assignment to cover Maris, and it was typical of the outraged reports on Maris's cantankerous behavior. The story said, somewhat snidely, that Maris had previously made himself available to questions and that "Often it has been difficult to get him to stop talking. Here it was different. . . . While [Mantle] answered all questions and volunteered information, Maris . . . remained in the trainer's room and sulked."

"Sulk" seems an inflammatory word to use to describe a man's conversation with his brother, but almost all the sportswriters were harshly critical of Maris. They had asked Bob Fishel, the public relations man, to go into the trainer's room and get Roger to come out. Fishel returned and reported that Maris said he wasn't coming out, that he wasn't going to talk to reporters anymore, that he was tired of being "ripped by writers in every city."

Such a reclusive attitude was a "sudden and decided change," one reporter wrote. This was a different Roger Maris, he told his readers, from the man who in Chicago refused to count himself out of the chase. Other stories were harsher. Few made allowances for the possibility that Maris was bitterly disappointed by his inability to hit even one home run in the two successive doubleheaders in Chicago and Detroit, nor that Maris, probably more than anyone else, recognized that with only five games left, three of them in Baltimore, his chances of hitting the four homers he needed just to tie Ruth had gone out the window. No one suggested that Maris might be depressed and just didn't want to answer any more questions on why he hadn't hit any. Maris was wrong, of course. When you're a major league player and a baseball writer asks you questions, you'd better be ready to answer them.

The ballplayers were still on his side and were rooting for him, and not just his teammates. The Tigers' Frank Lary said, "I hope Maris breaks Ruth's record. That would shut up some of these oldtimers." When Lary pitched against Maris a day or so later, he walked him in the first inning on four pitches and the fans in Tiger Stadium booed. When Maris batted again in the third inning, Lary threw a fifth straight ball and the crowd booed again. He came across the plate with a fastball then and Maris hit it against the roof of the stadium for his fifty-seventh home run, his first in seven games. The ball bounced back onto the field, where Al Kaline picked it up and tossed it into the Yankee dugout so that Maris could have it as a souvenir.

Despite his declaration the day before, Maris did not retire to the trainer's room after the game on Saturday but stayed at his locker and answered questions. It was obviously an ordeal. He seemed listless and tired. He didn't smile. He spoke barely above a whisper. He answered the questions carefully and without embroidery—and still managed to get himself in the soup again. A Detroit writer, hoping to build a little feature story around the home run, asked Maris what he thought of Kaline's act of throwing the ball to the Yankee dugout. Maris said it was nice of Kaline to do it. It was suggested to Maris that what Kaline had done was more than that, that it was a particularly decent gesture by a very thoughtful man. Maris, always literal and direct in his thinking, said, "It was nice of Al, but anybody would have done the same thing." Now Maris was putting down Al Kaline.

One reporter, reacting to Maris's subdued behavior, decided to do his own deep-dish analysis of Roger's subdued behavior. "Is Maris excited?" he wrote. "Inwardly, perhaps. On the surface he appears— or, rather, tries to appear—bored." Maris couldn't win either way.

RALPH HOUK:

In Chicago—and that was a bad series for him—he said something about Mantle and it came out as though he was criticizing Mickey. They got along fine. They were friends. The story didn't bother Mickey but Roger says, no more, no more talking to the writers.

So then we go to Detroit for another doubleheader there. Roger had a bad night. At least, I know he didn't hit a homer, and some Detroit fan got on him and Roger told him off. When he came into the clubhouse the reporters were all around him. He wouldn't talk to them. "Go talk to Kubek," he said. "Go talk to someone who had something to do with the game." We still hadn't clinched the pennant, but the writers didn't care about the pennant. To hell with the pennant. They wanted to talk to Maris.

I guess you can't blame them, Roger was the big story, but he just wasn't going to talk to them. He went into the trainer's room with his brother, where the writers couldn't go. They could see him in there—it was kind of like a cage more than a room—but he was sitting on a table with his back to the door and he wouldn't come out and he wouldn't talk to them.

They asked Fishel to get him out, but Roger told Fishel he wouldn't. Now they come to me. Oh, god. I said, "Well, he's not in the mood to talk." That didn't go over so well. This one writer says to me, "Get him out of there."

By this time I was getting kind of sore myself. Here were all the other players sitting around, players who had done well, and nobody was talking to them, nobody even looked at them. I was still worrying about the pennant—we lost four out of five games that week and you can blow a big lead pretty fast in this game. So I got mad.

"Are you telling me what to do?" I said.

"Well, he shouldn't be in there," he said.

"That's his business," I said.

He said, "We can't go in there and his brother can. How come his brother's in there?"

I really got sore then. I may even have shoved him a little. I know I yelled.

I said, "Are you telling me how to run my clubhouse? Are you trying to tell me I shouldn't let a man talk to his brother?" I said, "Are you looking for a story? I'll give you a story. I'll give you the whole story. He didn't hit a home run and he cussed out a fan. That's it."

Roger finally did come out, but when he did he was very sarcastic, and boy, they came down on him hard. Oh, there were a lot of stories that day. I talked to Roger afterward, and so did Mickey, and he understood. He began talking to the writers again, but he didn't like it much. He didn't want to talk to them. He was under such pressure all the time. I know he was getting a lot of mail from people who didn't want him to break Babe Ruth's record, bad letters, you know, and all that kind of stuff, and it finally got to him.

On Sunday in Detroit Maris hit a long drive in the seventh inning that just missed clearing the fence for a home run—he had to settle for a triple—and with it drove in a run that put the Yankees ahead. After the Tigers tied the score to send the game into extra innings, Maris hit a home run in the top of the twelfth to win it. That homer, his fifty-eighth, tied him with Foxx and Greenberg for second place on the all-time list behind the Babe, and it meant that the only man who ever hit more than he had in a 154-game season was Ruth. He was in very select company now, and he was besieged with questions after the game. "What were you thinking?" he was asked, in that profound cliché that sportswriters and broadcasters love to ask. "What were your thoughts?"

"Truthfully," Maris said, "when I hit it I thought, 'There's two runs that'll put us ahead.' " Pressed for more, he said, "When I stepped on home plate I thought, 'I've got 58 homers now.' " Dutifully, he added, "Here in the clubhouse I'm thinking it's a great thrill to know I'm second to Babe Ruth."

He was asked again and again how he felt when he hit the home run, didn't he feel excited, didn't it mean a great deal to him. He refused to rise to the bait and give a stock answer to a stock question. Once again he answered honestly. "You always feel good when you hit one," he said, "but you don't go losing your head about it. Maybe if I make 60 I'll lose my head, but up to now I haven't."

He was asked how much chance he had now to hit 61. Maris didn't mention the 154-game barrier. Referring to the 162-game season, he said, matter-of-factly, "I should be able to do it but I can't be sure. I could go into another slump and maybe not hit any. Don't forget, except for the last five games in Yankee Stadium I'll be playing in Baltimore and Boston. Those are two big ball parks for a lefthanded hitter."

Houk said he thought Maris would break the record—meaning before the end of the season. Berra said, "He's a cinch." Mantle, closer to the problem and more realistic about it, said only, "He's got a hell of a shot."

They were all talking about breaking it in 162 games, as Maris had, but if Roger spoke in terms of the 162-game season, inwardly he was burning to do it in 154. He needed two more home runs and he had three games to get them in, but all three were in forbidding Baltimore against the Orioles and their great pitching.

32

The Yankees had a day off before opening in Baltimore, and the rainy-day stories continued to deal with home runs. Maris was asked if he could remember his first major league homer. He said he remembered hitting it but not the pitcher he hit if off (it was in 1957, off Jack Crimian of the Tigers). Mantle, whose cold was getting worse, said with tongue in cheek that he remembered his first home run but couldn't remember his last one, it was so long ago. He hadn't hit one since the team left New York.

Houk, asked about his first home run, said, "Me? No, not me. I didn't hit any. I didn't get to play that much. But in 1947, my first year up, I hit a pitch off Frank Papish of the White Sox down the left-field foul line and the ball hit the foul pole. If you hit the foul pole today, it's a home run, but back then it depended which way the ball bounced after it hit. If it bounced fair, it was a homer. If it bounced foul, it was a double. This one went foul, so it was called a ground rule double, and that's the closest I ever came to hitting a homer in the majors.

"At the time, I didn't worry about it. I was young and strong and I figured I had a great future ahead of me. I thought I'd hit plenty of home runs. Never did though."

In Baltimore on Tuesday the Yanks and the Orioles played a doubleheader. Ford pitched another fine game in the opener but lost 1–0, his fourth defeat of the season. Lefthander Steve Barber, who won 18 games for the Orioles that year, third in the league behind Ford and Lary, shut out the Yankees and stopped Maris in his tracks. Mantle was too sick to play and sat on the bench throughout the doubleheader, except to pinch-hit against Barber with two out in the ninth inning, when he struck out to end the game.

Maris, oh for three against Barber, went oh for five in the second game against starter Hal Brown and reliever Hoyt Wilhelm. Barber threw fastballs in the first game, but Brown and Wilhelm threw nothing but curves, offspeed pitches and knuckleballs, tough balls to hit for home runs. Maris did pull one screamer down the right-field line into the seats, but it was foul.

Now he had only one game left, and he still needed two home runs just to tie Ruth. After the doubleheader some reporters asked Houk about the ethics of Baltimore's use of junk-ball pitchers like Brown and Wilhelm against Maris, indicating that it would have been more sporting to have given Maris a chance by using a fastball pitcher in the second game too. Houk refused to take issue.

"I can't fault that," he said. "They're still fighting for second place."

There's a story that pops up every now and then that Paul Richards, who had managed the Orioles since 1955, warned Wilhelm before the Yankee series that if he threw Maris even one fastball he'd be fined $1,000. That fits well with the image of the grim, harshly competitive Richards, but it falls apart when it is recalled that Richards resigned as Baltimore manager a month before the season ended, and that the more genial Lum Harris was the Orioles' manager when Maris and the Yankees came to town in mid-September.

In any case, Maris had only one chance left in the 154-game time frame. "Success after the deadline would give the Yankee star an asterisk in the record book," a sportswriter wrote. Maris said, "As far as Mr. Frick is concerned I only have one game left to break the record. As far as I'm concerned I still have nine games left."

Nonetheless, he was desperately hoping to hit two and at least tie the Babe. The tension around him was enormous. Even the urbane, unflappable Ford said, "You know, I'm really nervous." The army of press, radio and television people following Maris was larger than ever.

RALPH HOUK:

When we got to Baltimore Roger was in pretty bad shape. We played the doubleheader the first night there and he didn't hit any homers, and now it's the 154th game and he came to me and said, "Ralph, I don't feel good. I'm not playing."

He looked awful. Maris was a very sincere and good guy, but there are some people who just can't take the atmosphere of the press, all that coverage, all the people, all the cameras, all the bullshit that goes with it, and he was one of them. The pressure just got to him. His hair was falling out, not in clumps, like some of those guys wrote, but it was coming out, and it was turning gray.

He said, "I'm not playing," and he was kind of crying. It was sad. It was just we two in the office alone. He said, "Ralph, why don't you just get me out of there?"

Well, I talked to him and I said, "Hey, Roger, you gotta play." I talked about the people in the stands who'd come to see him, and this and that, and finally I said, "Look, Roger, why don't you go out and hit in batting practice and let me put you in the lineup. You start the game, and after an inning or two I'll take you out if you want. We can say you're sick." We talked a little bit more, and he went out and played, and that was the end of it. Nothing more happened. That was the night he hit his fifty-ninth home run, and that was the night we clinched the pennant. I'll never forget that night.

In the first inning, batting against Milt Pappas, Maris lined out hard to right field, but in his second time at bat, in the third inning, he hit another line drive that carried over the fence at the 380-foot mark for his fifty-ninth home run. That moved him ahead of Foxx and Greenberg and everyone else into territory only he and Ruth had ever explored. A 32-year-old Baltimorean named Bob Reitz caught the ball and held tightly on to it as ushers and guards gathered around him. He was brought under the stands to meet Maris, who came off the field between innings to talk to him. Reitz did not offer to give the ball to Maris. He said he wanted money for it. How much? Twenty-five hundred dollars, he said. Maris just shook his head. They talked for another moment or two, and then Maris said, "Are you really going to keep that ball?" Reitz nodded. "Good luck to you," Maris said and returned to the ball game.

He needed one more home run now to tie Ruth. The Orioles brought Dick Hall in to pitch, and when Maris faced him in the fifth he hit one hard line drive foul to right and then struck out. In the seventh he got his bat on one of Hall's pitches and lifted a powerful drive high up toward the right-field seats—but it curved foul by ten feet.

In the Yankee bullpen Coates yelled, "Come on, Roger, baby, hit it to me." Stepping into the batter's box again, Maris hit a long fly in Coates's general direction, but the ball was caught in right center field, close to the fence.

His final time at bat, his last chance to catch Ruth, came in the ninth inning against Wilhelm, who had relieved Hall. Maris fouled off one of Wilhelm's knuckleballs, then half swung at the next pitch and topped the ball along the first-base line, where Wilhelm fielded it, almost apologetically, and tagged Maris out.

It was over.

The attention paid to Maris's efforts obscured the biggest moment in Ralph Houk's career, the night the Yankees clinched the American League pennant. In the clubhouse Houk and the rest of the Yankees whooped it up a little but except for the perfunctory photographs they were pretty much ignored by the mobs of media people, who surrounded Maris, almost pinning him to the wall of the locker room. Despite the crush Maris was remarkably under control.

"I tried," he said calmly, "I tried hard all night, but I only got one. I wanted to go out swinging, but I never did get a chance to swing good against Wilhelm." Asked about Frick, Maris said, "The commissioner makes the rules. If he says all I'm entitled to is an asterisk, that's all right with me. I'm happy with what I got." He looked around at the other Yankees celebrating the pennant. "From now on," he said, "I'll concentrate on straightening myself out for the World Series. I've been swinging at too many bad pitches."

A story out of Baltimore said, "Ruth's record, which has been in the books since 1927, remains unmatched. Maris is resigned to an asterisk in the record books." That wasn't exactly true. Maris might have said politely that he was happy with what he had, but he didn't have 60 yet and the Yankees had eight games to play. The record was still there for the taking.

Back at the hotel the Yankees held a small party to celebrate their pennant. Some of the boys made a night of it, but Maris didn't and Mantle stayed for only a drink or two before going back to his room and going to bed. He stayed there all the next day, not going out to the ball park because of his cold—or virus, as the players called it.

For the fourth and last game in Baltimore, Houk fielded a makeshift, post-party lineup with rookie Tom Tresh at shortstop, Bob Hale at first base, Jack Reed in center field, and Billy Gardner at third base. Maris played but did not hit another home run. Even then the head-lines read, MARIS FAILS. If you read nothing but headlines that September, you'd have felt that the famous home-run chase was largely a litany of failure. It's not surprising Maris was so often sour.

In New York Frick, asked to comment on Maris's fifty-ninth homer, waffled a little. He said, "There will be no asterisk in the record book—just a double listing. As for that aterisk, or star, I don't know how that popped up because I never said it. I certainly never meant to belittle Maris. I feel he should end up with more than 60."

Frick said once again that his decision to have two sets of records was made only because he felt the 162-game schedule was temporary. "I'm certain we'll go back to the 154-game schedule," he said, meaning that inflated records made during what he presumed would be only a brief interregnum of 162-game seasons should be noted as something out of the ordinary. He said he expected four more clubs to be added to the existing majors in a very short time, which would give each league 12 teams—or, he said, there might be a realignment into three 8-team leagues. Either way, he said, the old 154-game schedule would work nicely, and he expected it to be restored. In a 12-team league, each club would play every other one 14 times (11 rivals times 14 games per rival equals 154). In an 8-team league each team would play each rival 22 times (7 × 22 equals 154). As mentioned before, it was not possible to have that kind of balanced scheduling in a 10-team league with a 154-game schedule. Thus the 162-game slate. Thus, the eight extra games and the fuss about the home-run record.

Frick did not anticipate two things: that it would be seven more years before baseball expanded again, and that at that time each league would be split into two divisions, further upsetting the old idea of neatly balanced schedules. Nor did he take into consideration the satisfaction that the clubs (and, by extension, the players) would derive from the added income they gained from gate receipts, parking fees, concessions, television and radio revenue and the like from those eight extra games each year. Eight extra games was a 5-percent increase over the old season, and to the marketing experts who were taking over control of the game 5 percent was—and is—a substantial figure. In short, once the 162-game schedule was put in place, there was little chance of ever going back to the 154-game level. Never mind balanced scheduling. Never mind records. Just put the money in the pot.

It's kind of sad about Frick. He was a nice man, and he loved baseball, but he was living in a reverse time warp. His mind was fixed in the 1920s and 1930s, and here he was being buffeted around by the turbulent, changing sixties.

From Baltimore the Yankees traveled to Boston for two games, their last stop on the monstrous road trip that had started almost two weeks before in Chicago. Mantle, whose cold wasn't much better, insisted on playing in Boston, and in his first time at bat hit his fifty-fourth homer, a tremendous poke into the bullpen in right. Ford, who left after the fifth inning leading 4–1, won his twenty-fifth game. Maris had a hit and a walk and scored twice but hit no homers. Nor did he hit one the next day in Boston, a Sunday. Mantle didn't hit one either, and the headlines were back to their old chant: MARIS AND MANTLE FAIL TO CONNECT.

The team returned to New York for the final week of the season, with five games left for Maris. He had hit only three home runs in 15 games, and on Tuesday night only 19,000 people were on hand in Yankee Stadium to see him hit number 60. It came in his second time at bat, in the third inning, when he lifted a fly to right that carried against the front of the upper stands for a home run. The crowd made up for its size with its exuberance and cheered wildly until Maris reluctantly came out of the dugout and waved his cap to the fans he had derided a few weeks earlier.

A curtain call like that, so common today, was an extraordinary event in that era, almost unprecedented. Five years earlier, in May 1956, Dale Long of the Pirates accomplished the extraordinary feat of hitting a home run a game for eight straight games. No one before had ever hit homers in more than six straight, and no one would after him until 1987, when Don Mattingly equaled his record. When Long hit one in his eighth straight game, the crowd cheered so loudly and for so long that his Pirate teammates made Long go out of the dugout and wave his thanks so that the game could go on. Long's curtain call was almost as big a story as his home runs, and Maris's bow in 1961 had much the same effect. Red Barber, who had been broadcasting major league baseball for more than 25 years, was almost beside himself with excitement as he described Maris coming reluctantly from the dugout to wave to the crowd. Things like that just didn't happen then. Nor, for that matter, did 60 home runs.

Maris said afterward, "This is easily the greatest thrill of my life." The Yankees won the game, 3–2, but in the top of the ninth inning the New York crowd was rooting for Baltimore to tie the score or even go ahead, so that Maris might have one more chance to come to bat and perhaps hit his sixty-first.

The sixtieth home-run ball bounced back onto the field, but now Sam Gordon, a restaurant owner in Sacramento, California, offered $5,000 to anyone who might catch the ball Maris hit for his sixty-first homer. Gordon said he would put the ball on display in his restaurant and then give it to Maris. Spectators clustered in the lower right-field stands and bleachers the next afternoon, Wednesday, when the Yankees played the Orioles again, but were disappointed when Maris did not play. Neither did Mantle.

"I had a real bad cold," Mantle said, "and I was taking antibiotics but it just wasn't getting any better. I remember we were coming home from Boston on the train and Mel Allen, the broadcaster, said he knew this doctor who took care of a lot of people, who maybe could help me. I went to the doctor and he gave me some kind of shot. I don't know what it was but, damn, it hurt. I don't think he injected me where he should have. I think the needle hit me in the hipbone. I know it hurt like hell. I felt like he paralyzed me. I yelled and I said, 'God, that really hurts.' He took and rubbed it and he said, 'Don't take a cab back to your hotel. Walk it out. Walk back.' And

I did. It was something like 14 blocks from where his office was on Park Avenue to the St. Moritz Hotel, where I was staying. Oh, that thing hurt. I don't know what he did, but it got infected. I woke up in the morning with a 104-degree temperature, and I couldn't move my leg. That was the morning my wife was coming into New York to be with me during the World Series, and I couldn't get out of bed to go meet her."

Mantle tried to play that night when Maris hit his sixtieth, but he had to leave the game after one inning. He had an abscess on his hip and the infection was so bad that he could hardly walk, let alone run. Dr. Gaynor, the team physician, took him to Lenox Hill Hospital in Manhattan, where the abscess was lanced and drained and packed. Mantle stayed in the hospital and was there for the rest of the week, the wound slowly healing but still draining.

Maris showed up at the ball park on Wednesday but, once again, asked Houk for the day off. His wife was in town, there was no game scheduled the next day and he could have a nice little respite, a 48-hour vacation from the tension. Houk said okay and Roger, neatly dressed and looking at peace with himself, left the ball park. It seemed an extraordinary thing to do. There were only four games left in the season, and he still needed one more homer to pass Ruth, yet he chose not to play. Houk told the wondering press that Maris said he was "too bushed" to play, but he added, "Roger's exhaustion isn't physical. It's mental. He hasn't had a moment of peace for the last two months. All things considered, I think he's handled himself beautifully. He's been living in a madhouse."

When Maris returned to the club on Friday night he said, "I feel more relaxed than I have in a long time." He went hitless as the Yankees beat the Red Sox 2–1, although he walked twice on three-and-two pitches and scored the winning run in the ninth inning. That afternoon Houk and Mantle's wife, Merlyn, visited Mickey in the hospital and reported that his fever was gone and that he hoped to be ready to play in the World Series, which would begin the following Wednesday.

On Saturday Maris again got few good pitches to hit and went one for three as the Yankees beat the Red Sox. Once again the crowd in Yankee Stadium was relatively small. The left-field sections were all but empty, while fans, eager to catch the $5,000 home-run ball, jammed into the stands and bleachers in right.

Now it came down to the last day of the season, Sunday, October 1. After getting his fifty-eighth homer in Detroit on September 17 Maris had hit only two home runs in two weeks—memorable home runs, it's true, his fifty-ninth and sixtieth, but still only two of them—and he had been at 60 since Tuesday. Attendance in Yankee Stadium on that momentous Sunday was only 23,154—although it should be noted that a crowd that size on such an occasion was not as small in 1961 as it would be now. Nevertheless, it demonstrated that for all the glamor of home runs and for all the attention given to Maris, a game between contending teams in a close pennant race would have attracted far more people to the ball park than the last shot at the home-run record did.

In this last game under intense pressure, Maris was remarkably relaxed. He told teammates in the Yankee bullpen, "If you catch the ball, don't throw it to me. Hang on to it. It's worth five grand." Before the game Fred Opper, a photographic assistant who knew Maris only to nod to, paused and spoke to him. "I hope everything works out today the way you want it to," he said. Maris nodded his thanks but said nothing. During the game Opper and a friend went out to the lower left-field stands to watch the game. "There was nobody out there," he said. "Maybe half a dozen people scattered around. Everybody was over in right field."

Tracy Stallard, a big, amiable, hard-throwing righthander, was on the mound for Boston. In Maris's first time at bat, Roger sliced a fly ball to left field that brought an "Oooh!" from the crowd, but it was caught without difficulty by left-fielder Carl Yastrzemski. Opper said, "Just for a second, it looked as though the ball was going to carry into the left-field seats. I thought, wouldn't that be funny, with all those people jammed into right field."

In the fourth inning, with Stallard still pitching, the score still 0–0, Maris swung at a fastball on a two-and-nothing count and lifted a high fly to right field that floated into the throng in the lower stands. It was his sixty-first, the record-breaker.

Nineteen-year-old Sal Durante, from the Bensonhurst section of Brooklyn, was at the game with his fiancée, Rose Marie Calabrese, and his friend John Tortorella. They had come by subway all the way from Brooklyn and had reached the Stadium an hour early. Durante jumped on to the seat when Maris hit the ball. As the ball dropped into the crowd another fan tried to trap it with his coat but the lithe, slender Durante raised his bare right hand and caught the ball over his head. He made the catch so easily that some of the people scrambling around him thought the ball had fallen and went down on their knees to look under seats for it. Ushers moved quickly to protect Durante and took him under the stands and through the passageway under the structure to the corridor behind the Yankee dugout.

Maris meantime had made his circuit of the bases, running fairly quickly in his balanced, even stride, his arms held low, his eyes on the ground. He crossed home plate, touched hands with teammates gathering to greet him and quickly disappeared into the dugout. The crowd was cheering uproariously and again Maris was forced to come out of the dugout onto the field to acknowledge the salute. Maris was smiling, almost shyly, as he waved his cap at the crowd. He ducked back into the dugout, but his teammates lifted him into view again. They kept pushing the smiling Maris out of the dugout to take bows and wave his cap. They had a lot of fun, their affection for their sometimes dour teammate obvious.

When things settled down a little Yankee officials took him back through the tunnel from the dugout to meet Durante. They posed for pictures, Maris congratulated Durante on his good luck, wished him well and returned to the field. (Sam Gordon made good his promise. He not only paid Durante $5,000 for the baseball, but he gave Sal and Rose Marie a honeymoon trip to California—his restaurant was in Sacramento. They were married on October 29, 1961, at St. Finnbar's Church in Bensonhurst. Not long before their twenty-fifth wedding anniversary in 1986 they and their three sons, Bob, Tom and Sal, Junior were guests of the Yankees at the Stadium.)

Maris played the rest of the game but struck out and popped up in his last two times at bat. Stafford and Daley combined to shut out the Red Sox and give the Yankees their 109th victory of the year. The final score was 1–0, with Maris's homer the margin of victory. It was the 240th and last home run that the Yankees hit that season.

In the clubhouse after the game, Fred Opper stood at the edge of the throng of reporters and photographers around Maris. At a pause in the questioning Roger glanced to one side and saw him standing there. Remembering Opper's wish before the game that everything would work out the way he wanted it to, Maris smiled and nodded and said, "I guess it did."

Maris appeared in 161 of the 163 games the Yankees played in 1961 (including one tie). He hit 30 of his home runs in Yankee Stadium, 31 on the road. He hit 49 against righthanded pitchers and only 12 against lefthanders, but then the switch-hitting Mantle hit 42 of his 54 against righthanders and only 12 against lefthanders, which seems to indicate that his switch-hitting advantage against lefthanded pitching didn't mean much, if anything, particularly in Yankee Stadium, with its vast left field.

While news stories about the sixty-first home run made some mention of the 154-game dispute, their emphasis was simply that Maris had topped Ruth, as indeed he had. It's impossible to give proper weight and balance to the variables that exist in different baseball seasons—liveliness of the ball, size of the ball parks, quality of the pitchers, impact of relief pitching, night baseball, day baseball, and so on. The essential fact is that with his sixty-first home run Maris broke Ruth's record. He had 590 at bats and 94 walks in 1961 for 684 plate appearances (not including whatever minor number of sacrifices or hit-by-pitcher stats he might have had). In 1927 Ruth had 540 at bats and 138 walks for 678 plate appearances, an almost identical figure. Maris hit one homer for every 11.2 times he came to the plate; the Babe hit one every 11.3 times. No matter how you slice it, Maris was a valid record-breaker, a legitimate successor to the Babe.

Why did he hit so many homers in 1961? Well, why did *everybody* hit so many that year? The American League averaged 153 homers per team in 1961 compared to 136 a year earlier, an increase of more than 12 percent. That can readily be attributed to the addition of the two new expansion teams, which supposedly diluted pitching strength in the league. But in 1961 the National League, which had not yet expanded, also went up in homers, from 130 per team to 150, a 15-percent jump, a greater increase than the American League had. No one has ever been able to explain that.

Maybe it was just 1961. It was a very strange year. Whatever caused it, and in spite of Frick's ruling, in spite of expansion, in spite of the livelier ball, if such existed, in spite of everything, Joe Cronin was right. A season is a season, and in the season of 1961 Roger Maris broke Babe Ruth's record.

It didn't do him much good. He broke the record and was named Most Valuable Player in the American League for a second straight time, but his life in baseball went downhill from then on. In 1962 he hit 33 homers and batted in 100 runs and despite those impressive figures he was considered to have had a disappointing season and was dismissed by short-sighted critics as a flash in the pan, a one-season phenomenon. But his home-run hitting from 1960 to 1962 was hardly that of a flash in the pan. He hit 133 home runs in three years, which is better than Mantle ever did, or Henry Aaron, or Hank Greenberg, or Reggie Jackson, or Ted Williams, or Mel Ott, or Willie McCovey, or Hack Wilson, or Mike Schmidt.

But Maris had things working against him. One was that low batting average, particularly in his 61-homer year. It was awfully hard for baseball traditionalists to recognize that a .269 batting average was not nearly as important as the fact that Maris led the league in runs scored and runs batted in. Few people would put Maris on a level with Al Kaline, the Tigers' fine rightfielder, now deservedly in the Hall of Fame, but in 1961, when Kaline "outhit" Maris by 55 points (.324 to Maris's .269), Roger had 42 more home runs than Kaline had, 60 more runs batted in and 16 more runs scored. In Maris's three big seasons, 1960–1962, when Kaline was in the middle of his career and reaching or approaching his best or second-best career figures in hits, doubles, triples, homers and runs scored, Roger averaged 23 more homers a year than Kaline, 37 more runs batted in and 17 more runs scored. And he was in Kaline's class as a fielder and a baserunner. Yet suggest that Maris was a better ballplayer than Kaline—as he might have proved if his later career had not been chopped down by chronic injury—and baseball people look askance.

The splendor of Maris's 1960 season is often overlooked in appraising the performance he gave in 1961. Among other things, he was well on his way to hitting more than 50 home runs in 1960 before he was hurt in August. Maris's resentment of the incessant publicity he received in 1961 stemmed in part from a contempt he felt for the ignorance some of the writers displayed. Although they had named him Most Valuable Player in 1960, much of the press had not really noticed that he had hit an amazing number of home runs during that pre-expansion season. When he did the same thing in 1961 they looked upon him as a one-year phenomenon, a freak created by expansion, which wasn't true. Maris didn't suffer fools gladly, and a lot of the media people besieging him in 1961 were, he felt, just that.

Maris broke the most sacrosanct record in baseball, yet few really admired him for it. He was probably the most misunderstood and least appreciated of American sports heroes. For a good part of the 1961 season, even though he was the incumbent MVP and from June on was head-to-head with Mantle in the home-run race, he was clearly the villain in the Chasing Babe Ruth drama. Mantle got the early season publicity—how many games ahead of Ruth and so on—and even after Maris caught up and passed him, Mantle seemed the obvious choice to eventually finish on top. But Maris did, and the fans and the press resented it. Mantle never showed any sign of resentment himself, although the injuries and illnesses that beset him during the season, which eventually knocked him out of the home run battle, must have frustrated this highly competitive man. Another player might have moaned that if he hadn't been injured or if other circumstances had been different the results of the home-run race might have been the other way around. (Willie Mays every now and then can't help mentioning that if he and Henry Aaron had changed places, if

Henry had had to cope with the adverse conditions in San Francisco's Candlestick Park while Willie basked in the home-run heaven that is Atlanta's Fulton County Stadium, Willie might well have broken Ruth's career record instead of Henry.)

In 1961 Mantle batted fourth all season and Maris third for a good part of it; it has been argued that if Mickey had batted third and Roger fourth, Mantle might have been the one to hit 61 home runs. He had more home runs per official times at bat in 1961 than Maris did, but he was walked many more times. His presence behind Maris in the batting order tended to make other teams "pitch" to Maris, put the ball over the plate in an effort to get him out rather than walk him to first base and then have to pitch to Mantle with a man on. Not that Maris didn't walk a lot, too—he had 94 for the year to Mantle's 126, and the batters following Mantle in the order (Skowron, Howard, Berra, Blanchard) were no slouches either. But there is no doubt that Mickey was in the tougher spot for a home-run hitter.

Yet in 1961 and all the years since, Mantle never appeared to mind Maris taking the coveted record and the concomitant fame (and wealth) away from him. He got along well with Maris, despite unfounded rumors that the two hated each other, and he got along well with all his teammates and with most rival players too. For all his sullenness with the press, his pouting with Casey Stengel, his fits of temper on the field or in the dugout, Mantle was never a prima donna in his relationship with other players. DiMaggio quietly insisted on being recognized as number one when he was the Yankees' star, and he maintained a kind of regal reserve with the other players that could turn into chilling coldness when he was displeased. Mantle never seemed to worry about his status, yet in the latter part of his career he received the same deep respect from his teammates that DiMaggio had, and with it a warmth and affection that not even DiMaggio had commanded. His teammates admired DiMaggio; they loved Mantle.

The sportswriters in 1961, pleased to find the "new" Mantle accessible and even genial, inevitably (if often subconsciously) compared him to Maris and found Roger lacking. Mickey had learned to be diplomatic with the media; Roger was literal and sometimes painfully direct. He had almost no sense of public relations. He could not give easy, glib answers to anything. While this didn't bother Maris's teammates, who both liked and admired him, it disturbed many reporters and broadcasters. Maris spoke the literal truth, and that jarred and upset people expecting ritual responses to their questions. He hated to go to banquets. His job, he felt, was to play ball. If there was money to be made by appearing at a banquet, he'd go, but he wouldn't put on a show. Once, when he was presented with a sterling-silver dish, he accepted the gift, said, "Thank you for this platter," and sat down.

Maris tended to alienate people. He was too sensitive to criticism to attract affection and admiration, and his personality would not reshape itself to meet the demands of people he came into contact with. He never forgot grudges. A year or so after he broke Ruth's record someone asked him to pose with Hornsby, the oldtime batting hero who had been contemptuous of Maris's skills as a hitter (and who later referred to Maris as a "bush-leaguer"). Roger refused. "I don't want to pose with him," he said. "He's always ripping me." The sheer impudence of that—who does this .269 hitter think he is, refusing to pose with the great Hornsby?—cost him a tremendous amount of good will, and never mind that Hornsby was a pretty sour man himself.

In 1963 Maris suffered a succession of leg injuries and missed more than 70 games. When he did play, his performance suffered. Booed by the fans for not running hard on ground balls to the infield, he reacted angrily. He played much better in 1964, but in 1965, after he hurt his hand sliding, he lost much of his old power. He missed 100 games that season and 40 in 1966 and complained constantly about the hand injury, even though the Yankees said doctors could find no evidence of serious injury. He wasn't happy with Houk after Ralph moved to the front office to become general manager in 1964 and by 1966 said he wanted to quit baseball. The Yankees traded him to the St. Louis Cardinals and Maris stayed in the game after August Busch, the Cardinals' owner, gave him a lucrative contract that included the promise of a Budweiser beer distributorship in Florida. Maris stayed two years with the Cardinals, and though he was able to play only about two thirds of the time he helped St. Louis win two pennants and a World Series, and he was happier than he had been in years.

After the 1968 World Series he retired from the game at the age of 34 and spent the rest of his life as the nominal (and prosperous) head of the beer distributorship. His brother Rudy was the active force in the business, but Maris worked at his end, which, in one of the great paradoxes, required him to be friendly and convivial with customers and prospects. Perhaps not so paradoxical at that, because despite his unhappy public image, Maris could be a warm, friendly, engaging man when he was out of the public eye. He had an exceptionally happy married life and was a close and attentive father to his six children.

RALPH HOUK:

Roger was unpopular because the fans wanted Mantle to break the record, and I guess the press did too, though it really wasn't until Maris came along that Mickey became a hero. They booed Roger something awful, and they kept on booing him. It got so bad that later he didn't want any part of New York anymore. After the 1966 season he told me he wouldn't come back. Just definitely would not come back to New York, not as a player, not as anything else. He wasn't coming back, and that's all there was to it. He was going to quit baseball. When Roger left the Yankees, he was pissed off at the world.

Then we made the deal with St. Louis. What we did, we gave him his free agency, really, and he agreed to go to St. Louis because he was from that general area anyway.

That was the best thing that ever happened to Roger because, jeez, they really took care of him, gave him that Budweiser dealership in Florida as part of the deal. He brought his brother Rudy in, and Rudy took over the paperwork, that sort of thing. Rudy ran the business and Roger was sort of the figurehead. He worked at it, but he was more or less the front man.

Roger changed a lot then, too. He was in the selling business and he had to appear at dinners and play a lot of golf with customers and prospects, things like that. I saw quite a bit of him for a couple of years there, and he was always talking with people. Roger was peculiar that way. If you got him at the right time—a sportswriter, anybody— he'd sit and talk and be as nice as you want. Other times he wouldn't. That's just the way he was.

Basically he was a nice guy. I always liked Roger. And he was a great ballplayer.

Other great athletes—Ruth, Jack Dempsey, Joe Namath, Muham-mad Ali—had their great fallings-out with press and public but even-tually won their way back to popular acclaim. Except for the cheers of crowds welcoming him to the few oldtimers games he attended, Maris never regained the spotlight. Of course, that was the way he liked it, which was something the press and the public failed com-pletely to understand, particularly in 1961.

He and Mantle remained good friends for the rest of his life, and Mickey, who had been unnerved by his father's early death from Hodgkins disease, a form of cancer, grieved when Maris was afflicted with cancer in his forties. After Roger died in December 1985, at the age of 51, Mantle was one of a group of Maris's close friends who made the long trek in the depth of winter to his funeral in remote Fargo, North Dakota. It was characteristic of the Maris family, which had lived in Florida for nearly 20 years, to have the requiem mass and the burial in the distant North, in Roger's hometown, where he grew up. His grave is in a quiet, tree-studded cemetery north of town, on the edge of the prairie. The small, distinctive headstone of dark, polished stone is in the shape of a baseball diamond. On it, beneath the name Maris, is a small figure of a baseball player swinging a bat, along with the numerals "61–'61" and the words "Against All Odds." Separate from the headstone is a small footstone that says, "Roger Eugene Maris, Sept. 10, 1934– Dec. 14, 1985."

The great irony of Maris's life came after his death. In 1961 he was looked upon as a usurper by the defenders of tradition, a pretender to Babe Ruth's crown. But when he died the great asterisk controversy was mentioned only in passing. The average reader looking at the headlines that had so often denigrated Maris saw him only for what he was: the man who broke Babe Ruth's record.

PART FIVE

The World Series

34

The World Series was an anticlimax to some, but not to Houk. While his club was heavily favored to defeat the Cincinnati Reds, Houk didn't think the Series would be the walkover the experts were predicting.

Even though the Pittsburgh Pirates had won the World Series from the Yankees in 1960, it was generally agreed before the 1961 season began that the National League pennant race would be wide open. Five of the eight clubs in the league were given a chance of winning—the Pirates, the St. Louis Cardinals, the Los Angeles Dodgers, the San Francisco Giants and the Milwaukee Braves. Only Chicago, Philadelphia and Cincinnati were considered hopeless outsiders. The Cubs and the Phillies upheld this low opinion of their abilities by finishing last (Phils) and second to last (Cubs), but the Reds, who were sixth in 1960, 20 games below .500, fought their way to the top under Manager Fred Hutchinson and in one of the great upsets won the pennant by four games. It wasn't easy. Five National League teams finished above .500 that season and the Pirates, the dethroned defending champions, were only four games below that level. Obviously, the Reds knew how to win in tight competition.

In offseason trades Cincinnati landed pitcher Joey Jay (the first Little Leaguer ever to make it to the big leagues) and third-baseman Gene Freese. Jay won 21 games, while Freese drove in 87 runs. Gordy

Coleman, a big lefthanded power hitter, became the regular first baseman, and he too batted in 87 runs. Outfielder Frank Robinson had
led the team in RBIs in 1960 with 83; in 1961 his RBIs increased to
124, and he was named the Most Valuable Player in the National
League.

Everything fit into place for the Reds. The team batting average
jumped 20 points, and in a season when the earned run average of
every other pitching staff in the league went up, the Reds' improved.
Hutchinson was a strong manager, and his refurbished team was a
good ball club. It went on to win 98 games in 1962 when it was a
close third behind San Francisco and Los Angeles, which finished in
a tie for the pennant (the Giants beat the Dodgers in a playoff), and
in 1964 it lost the pennant by a game to St. Louis on the last day of
the season, after Hutchinson had to give up managing in midsummer
because of the cancer that killed him the following November.

The Reds were a capable, well-balanced team, legitimate champions. Yet they were considered hopeless underdogs, with very little
chance against the powerful Yankees. The odds amused Hutchinson,
a huge, slouching, ruddy-faced, thick-haired bear of a man, usually
quiet but with a smoldering rage just beneath the surface that made
him a figure of almost awesome respect to his players. After hearing
that some pundits not only had picked the Yankees to win but had
picked them to win in four straight, Hutch led his team into Yankee
Stadium for a practice session the day before the Series began and
said, "I read that we're not supposed to win, but I haven't told my
ballplayers yet." With memories of the Berlin crisis still fresh, there
were many arch references to the upcoming Series as a battle between
"the Reds and the Yanks."

Ford, over his hip problem, was at the peak of his form in the first
game of the Series as he shut out the Reds 2–0. It was Whitey's third
straight World Series shutout, which equaled a record set by Christy
Mathewson 56 years earlier (though Mathewson's shutouts were all in
one Series in 1905). Ford's shutout also gave him 27 consecutive
scoreless innings in World Series play, which put him third behind
Mathewson's 28 and Babe Ruth's record 29 (Ruth had been a superb

lefthanded pitcher before he switched to the outfield and became the game's best hitter).

Howard hit a line-drive home run in to the lower right-field stands of Yankee Stadium in the fourth inning to give Ford a 1–0 lead, and in the sixth Skowron hit a similar solo shot into the lower left-field stands. Otherwise, Jim O'Toole pitched very well for the Reds, as did Cincinnati's well-known relief pitcher, Jim Brosnan, who had produced the first "modern" baseball book by writing (by himself) an iconoclastic account of the game called *The Long Season.* Even as he pitched he was working on his next book, called *Pennant Race,* about the Reds' championship season in 1961.

Mantle, still incapacitated by the infection in his hip, was unable to play, and Maris was in center, with Lopez in right field and Berra in left. In the first inning, after Cincinnati shortstop Eddie Kasko hit a dinky little single to left, center-fielder Vada Pinson, who batted .343 that year, hit a long line drive to deep center, but Maris played it perfectly and hauled it in, and Ford struck out Robinson to get out of the inning. That was the biggest Red threat. Ford allowed only one more hit, although Boyer robbed the Reds of another with a great play in the eighth. It was a tight, quick, neat game, over and done with in two hours and 11 minutes.

The game the next day was slower and sloppier, and the Yankees lost, 6–2. They had only four hits off Jay, although one was a two-run homer by Berra in the fourth, moments after Coleman had put Cincinnati on top with a two-run homer off Terry. The Reds scored another on a passed ball in the fifth, another on a double and a single in the sixth, and topped it off with two more in the eighth on Yankee misplays. It was an inept day in the field for the usually impeccable New York defense. Outfielder Wally Post singled off Boyer's glove in the second. Robinson was safe on a Boyer fumble in the fourth, just before Coleman hit his home run. Second-baseman Elio Chacon scored from third base in the fifth inning when a pitched ball squirted away from Howard. Arroyo threw wildly past first base in the eighth. Post reached third base when Berra missed a try for a shoestring catch (the ball went through Berra's legs) and scored on a double to left that

Yogi couldn't get to. Only three of the Reds' six runs were earned.

Maris went hitless for the second straight game and struck out twice. Arroyo did poorly in relief. Boyer, who made some breathtaking plays at third, also made that damaging error.

Houk defended his club after the game. He insisted that his team had not played sloppy ball, no matter how bad they looked. "Those fielding plays," he said, "were tough chances, every one of them." Nonetheless, the heavily favored Yankees looked vulnerable. Mantle still could not play and was feeling so bad that he didn't even take batting practice.

RALPH HOUK:

There were plays in that game where the ball bounced a little bad, the type of plays you can make mistakes on. It's like when you see an infielder let a ball go right between his legs. You can't believe it, but sometimes the ball only has to move a little bit off line and it gets by. It was just that all those plays happened at once, in the same game.

Of course, you're supposed to be able to handle those plays. I suppose I was probably just trying to keep the writers from blasting the players.

There was a travel day before the third game, which gave Mantle extra time to recuperate, and he was in the lineup the following afternoon in Cincinnati despite his continuing pain and the fact that his wound was still draining. Thick gauze dressings were taped over the incision and he had no apparent difficulty in the game, but neither did he have to do any running to speak of. He flied out to center his first two times at bat and struck out the next two times. In the field he had to handle an easy single in the first inning and then catch a routine fly, but after that he had literally nothing to do, which was a blessing. He could trot, but he could not run hard without exacerbating the wound, possibly tearing it wide open again.

Bob Purkey, a notable junk-ball thrower, was on the mound for Cincinnati, going against Stafford, who was starting a World Series game for the first time at the age of 22. Purkey, throwing his knuckleball and other offspeed pitches, had a 1–0 lead through six innings. Maris continued to be ineffective at bat, popping up in the first, grounding out in the fourth, flying to center in the seventh. He was now oh for ten in the Series, the only regular (along with Mantle) not to have a base hit. With the Yankees still behind 1–0, Kubek opened the seventh inning with a single but Purkey got Maris and Mantle on a fly out and a strikeout, and Cincinnati had high hopes of holding the lead, winning the game and taking a significant two-to-one edge in the Series.

However, Kubek had moved to second on a passed ball and when Berra poked a two-out single into right field, Kubek came in to score and the game was tied, 1–1. It was the first time the Yankees had crossed home plate in 11 innings.

But Howard fouled out to end the inning, and in the last of the seventh Stafford ran into trouble, walking a man intentionally after catcher Johnny Edwards doubled and then giving up a two-out single that put Cincinnati back on top, 2–1. With Pinson up, Houk replaced Stafford with Daley, and Pinson flied out to end the inning.

After the first two Yankees went down in the top of the eighth, Houk sent Blanchard in to bat for Daley, and the big catcher hit another pinch-hit home run to tie the game again, 2–2. In the bottom of the eighth Arroyo made his second appearance in the Series. Jim Turner, the old Yankee pitching coach Houk admired so much, now had the same job with Cincinnati and before the Series he had jeered at Arroyo, who had played for the Reds in 1959, saying, "If Arroyo pitches, we'll beat his brains out." When Arroyo gave up three hits, two walks and two runs in two innings in the second game, letting the Reds put the game out of reach, it appeared that Turner knew what he was talking about.

But Arroyo had perfected the screwball since Turner had known him, and with it now he struck out Robinson, got Coleman to pop up and had Post hit a ground ball to third—thus dismissing three big Cincinnati hitters with ease. That put a little chill on the newly confident Reds, who had expected to tee off on Arroyo and go into the ninth inning with a lead and reasonable assurance that they would win and move ahead in the Series.

Instead, it was still 2–2 in the ninth, with Maris leading off against Purkey. When Blanchard pinch-hit in the eighth he remembered someone telling him that Purkey, the junk-ball pitcher, sometimes liked to sneak a fastball across the plate on the first pitch in order to get ahead on the count before going to his knuckleball and his other offspeed stuff. Blanchard went up to bat looking for the fastball on the first pitch, got it and hit it out of the park. In the ninth Purkey was more cautious with Maris, and he fell behind on the count, two balls and one strike. He then came over the plate with a slider, and Maris blasted it deep into the right-field stands for a home run, his first hit of the Series, to put the Yankees ahead, 3–2. That shook the Reds. It was the first time the Yankees had led since the first game, and the powerful New Yorkers, who had scored only four runs in the first 23 innings of the Series, had now scored in three successive innings. The vaunted Maris–Mantle power, up to now ineffective or inoperative, had suddenly exploded in Cincinnati's face. Purkey held on—he really pitched a fine game except for the home-run balls to Blanchard and Maris—and struck out Mantle and retired the next two batters on ground balls. But now the Reds had to go to the last of the ninth inning not ahead, not even tied, but losing.

Jack Reed took Mantle's place in center, as Arroyo went out to face the Reds again. He struck out Freese, leading off the inning, which meant he had now disposed of four of the most dangerous Cincinnati hitters—Robinson, Coleman, Post and Freese—on two strikeouts, a popup and a ground ball. Cincinnati's hopes rose when Leo Cardenas, batting for Edwards, hit a long double off the left-center-field scoreboard, and with the tying run on second with only one out, Hutchinson sent two dangerous pinch-hitters to bat. Dick Gernert and Gus Bell (father of Buddy) were each capable of reaching the seats. But Arroyo got Gernert on a ground ball to shortstop, and when Bell tapped back to the mound Arroyo lobbed the ball to first base and the Yankees had won. *They* had the two-to-one lead in the

Series, and they had Ford ready to pitch again the next afternoon.

It was a very big victory. After the Series, Hutchinson said, "Maris's home run in the third game, that's what did it. We were never the same after that."

RALPH HOUK:

We had a lead in games but the next day Mantle's leg was worse. That abscess just deteriorated. He had a hole in his hip this big around. I couldn't believe it. I was in the trainer's room there in Cincinnati with Dr. Gaynor, and Mickey kept insisting he was going to play. He was lying on the training table, and I looked at that hole—God, it was this wide—and all the blood and the mess it was. I said, "God-damn, man, you can't play with something like that." He said, "I'm playing." I said, "Mickey, I'm not gonna let you play. I promise, I'll use you as a pinch-hitter." He said, "I'm playing."

I got Doc Gaynor to one side and asked him about it. He said, "I don't see how he can possibly play with the pain he'll have when he moves." But Mantle wanted to play so damned bad that I said, "If he does play, is there any way it can hurt him or damage him? I mean, permanently?" Doc Gaynor said, "No, not really. If he can play with the pain of it, there's no reason why he'd pull something or hurt anything."

So I told Mickey, okay, he could play. And in the second inning he hit a ground ball to third and he ran like hell to first base, and that started to tear things open. In the fourth, he singled to left with Roger on base—that was the hit that got us started, because Roger later scored the first run of the game—but when Mickey got to first base that time the blood started coming through his uniform. I took him out. Damn, I couldn't believe he could play with a thing like that in his leg. He went into the clubhouse and they put another dressing on it, and after a while he came back to the bench and rooted for them the rest of the game. Mickey was something else. No one really knows what a tough man he is.

35

After watching Mantle leave the game in his bloodstained uniform, Ford said, "The bandages were so thick I couldn't believe the blood could come through." But Mantle said only, "It looked worse than it was. It was bleeding, but it didn't really hurt that bad." Maybe so, but those Yankees who ducked back into the clubhouse to watch the trainer apply fresh dressings to the wound winced when they saw the gaping, bleeding hole in Mantle's buttock. "It was as deep as a golf ball," Blanchard said, "with blood oozing out of it." Yet Mantle had batted twice, had hit the ball hard twice and had run hard to first base twice. In the outfield in the second inning he had run toward right to back up Maris on a long fly ball.

After Mantle left the game Maris scored on a double play and the Yankees took a 1–0 lead. They scored another run in the fifth, two in the sixth and three in the seventh when Lopez, playing for Mantle, drove in two and scored a third, to win 7–0.

Ford meantime was having a memorable, if not altogether happy, day. He retired the first six batters to face him, briskly adding two more innings to his scoreless streak, which moved him past Mathewson and tied him with Ruth. He gave up a single in the next inning but otherwise got out of it unscathed to reach 30 consecutive scoreless innings and break Ruth's record ("It's been a bad year for the Babe,"

Ford quipped afterward). Then he retired the Reds in the fourth and fifth without difficulty to extend his streak to 32.

Some baseball record books list Ruth's streak at 29⅔ and Ford's, when it finally ended in 1962, at 33⅔, adding to their legitimate full scoreless innings the one or two outs (or thirds of an inning) they had achieved in previous and subsequent innings—after or before runs were scored in those innings. Such fractionalization is patently absurd. A fraction of an inning in which a run is scored is not part of a scoreless inning. If a pitcher gives up a run with no one out in one inning, then retires the next three batters and gets the first two men in the following inning before giving up another run, he's been scored on in two successive innings. Yet if you figure it fractionally, he went five outs, or one and two thirds innings, without yielding a run, although no baseball statistician in his right mind would say he'd pitched a scoreless inning, let alone one and two thirds of the little devils. When Mathewson was scored on (with one out) in the second inning of the first game of the 1911 World Series (the first Series game he had pitched in since his three shutouts in 1905), his scoreless streak ended at 28: 27 in 1905 plus one in 1911. No one at that time said Matty had pitched 28⅓, and they were right. In 1916 Ruth pitched 13 scoreless innings (in the longest World Series game ever played) after giving up a run in the first inning. He pitched a shutout in the first game of the 1918 Series, which gave him 22 scoreless innings, and in the fourth game that year pitched 7 more scoreless innings before being scored on in the eighth. For years, Ruth was credited with 29 scoreless innings, the correct figure. Then some fractional ass, discovering that Ruth had gotten the third out in the first inning of the 1916 game and the first out in the eighth inning of the 1918 game, added those two outs to his 29 scoreless innings and decided he really had 29⅔ scoreless innings. Follow that line of reasoning a little further and you can argue that since the Cubs' run that broke the streak came as the second out was being scored, maybe the Babe really has another one third coming to him, upping his total to an even thirty. Foolish. Yet some record books still try to gild Ford's splendid record by listing it as 33⅔ scoreless innings instead of 33.

In any case, Ford clearly established a new record. Then he ran into a personal disaster. When he came to bat in the top of the sixth inning he fouled a pitch off his big toe and sat down abruptly at the plate. Although the toe was badly bruised he got to his feet again, resumed batting and topped a ball down the first-base line. Coleman fielded it, tagged Ford out and then raced across to the third-base line to tag Skowron, hung up between bases, for an odd, unassisted double play. Ford, his toe aching painfully, went to the mound in the bottom of the sixth, tried to pitch, gave up a single to the only batter he faced and, unable to go on, had to limp off the field and leave the game. Coates relieved him and pitched effectively over the last four innings to complete the shutout, stopping the Reds with one hit, a walk and a hit batsman (Coates's trademark).

The Yankees were now ahead three games to one in the Series, and the Reds looked thoroughly beaten. But Houk was worried. Mantle was out for the Series. So was Ford. Berra had been hurt in the seventh inning of the fourth game when he slid face-first into a tag at third base, cutting his eye, wrenching his neck and injuring his shoulder, and he couldn't play. Stafford had a stiff wrist. Cerv had torn cartilage in his knee a week before the season ended and missed the entire Series. Terry, who was due to start the fifth game, had been hit hard by the Reds in his earlier start. If the Reds beat Terry with Jay (who had already defeated the Yankees), the Series would go back to New York, where, if Stafford was unable to start, Coates would have to go against Purkey, who had pitched so well against the Yankees in the third game. Without Mantle and Berra, the Yankee attack was not as strong against righthanders, and Jay and Purkey were good right-handers. If Jay and Purkey both won, the Series would be tied at three games apiece, with Ford no longer available to pitch the showdown seventh game.

RALPH HOUK:

I was worried, and I wasn't making believe. We had a 3–1 lead in the Series but we were running pretty thin, and it's been proved recently that you don't always win with a 3–1 lead in games. I'd seen us come back from a 3–1 deficit in 1958 to beat the Braves. Maybe everybody else thought we had it locked up, but I didn't. I thought we could lose and then lose again, and we'd come down to a seventh game and I wouldn't have Ford. I was worried. I was plenty worried. I wanted to win that fifth game bad.

The thing was, I didn't know who I'd have playing in the sixth and seventh games if we had to play two more. Ford was out. I'd been expecting to have Whitey ready if it ever went to a seventh game, and now I didn't have him. He could hardly walk with that toe. Mantle was out for the Series, and Yogi was through, with his neck and his shoulder and his eye where that ball hit him in the face. He could hardly see. He couldn't have played anymore. We didn't have Cerv. And Stafford had that stiff wrist.

I'm telling you, people didn't realize it but we were in pretty bad shape. No Ford, no Mantle, no Yogi, and we were down to the point where I was looking around for starters. The night before that fifth game I just lay there in bed thinking about it. I didn't sleep all night. Really, I don't think I slept at all, and usually I can always sleep a little bit. I kept seeing Mickey coming off the field with the blood coming out of his pants, and that kind of upset the whole thing. To win a World Series without Mantle was pretty hard. And not having Yogi and Ford—hell, I was worried. That fifth game was a very, very big ball game. If we didn't win it, we could blow the whole Series. I wanted to win that fifth game bad.

He didn't stay worried long. Richardson opened the game with a single. After Kubek and Maris flied out, Blanchard hit a two-run homer. Howard followed with a double, and Skowron hit a long single to score Howard. At this point Jay, the Cincinnati starter, had faced six men and had given up two singles, a double, a home run and two long fly balls. Hutchinson took him out and brought in 21-year-old Jim Maloney, later a sensational pitcher for Cincinnati, but then an uncertain youngster. Lopez, playing left field for Berra, hit a triple off

Maloney, and Boyer hit a double to give the Yankees a 5–0 lead, and in the second inning Maris doubled Kubek home with another run.

But then Terry gave up three hits himself in the first two innings and in the bottom of the third came unraveled as the Reds scored three times to force their way back into the game. Robinson's huge home run over the fence in deep right center in the third was the sixth hit off Terry, and that was enough for Houk. Out went Terry and in came Daley, who had pitched only a third of an inning thus far in the series. Daley got out of the inning, but the Yankees' big lead had been cut in half.

Almost automatically, they responded in their next time at bat. Kubek singled, Blanchard doubled, Howard walked, Skowron drove in two runs with a single, and Lopez, making up for his disappointing season, followed his earlier triple with a three-run homer over the center-field fence. The Yankees led 11–3.

Post hit a two-run homer off Daley an inning later, but again the Yankees reacted. Lopez got his third straight hit—a squeeze bunt with the bases loaded—and Daley hit a sacrifice fly. Hutchinson, trudging wearily back and forth to the mound, used eight pitchers in the game trying to quench the flood of Yankee power. Daley pitched six and two thirds innings and gave up only one more hit after Post's home run. The Yankees won the game 13–5 and Houk, the rookie manager, had won the World Series.

"Gosh, I'm happy," Blanchard said after the game.

His manager, the old company commander, smiled and said, "Our thin gray line did pretty well out there today."

RALPH HOUK:

The biggest hit was the two-run homer Blanchard got in the first inning that put us ahead right away. I had John hitting fourth in place of Mickey. I had him in right field and Lopez in left, and it turned out that Blanchard had a hell of a day and so did Lopez. It was hard to make bad moves with that club.

We had so many guys who could do the job you needed them to do. We had the bench, and we had the kind of club that wouldn't quit. They were all good ballplayers. It was just that simple.

Then Lopez tripled and he hit the homer. Once we got ahead, I was going all out. "All right," I said, "this is the one we're gonna win." I would have used everybody in the bullpen to save that game. I would have used everybody on the *pitching* staff if I had to, except maybe Coates, who I had to save for the next game—if there was going to be one. That's why I made that pitching move with Daley fairly quick when the Reds got to Terry. I brought him in early, and he did a great job the rest of the way.

That was satisfying to me. I guess you always pull for the guy who maybe isn't the great big name. And Daley came in and did the job when I *needed* it, all year long. In the Series I needed it bad, and I guess that's why I remember it so well. My god, I thought, if Daley can just get them out this thing is all over. We were way ahead, but I was still on edge. I couldn't wait for it to be over. I didn't want to play another game. I was afraid to play the next game.

But we won, and what a day Hector Lopez had. He's never forgotten it. There was a camp recently in Florida, one of those fantasy camps, and I went over to it for a few days. Ford was there, and Mantle came in, and Skowron was there, but I think I got as big a kick out of seeing Hector as anybody. I think he remembered every pitch in that Series. Hector was a fellow that everybody on the club liked. He was always neat and well dressed, and he had a good sense of humor. Everybody liked him.

I was happy Hector had that World Series after the year he had. He played good before 1961 and he played good after it, but that year he just didn't have the season he usually had. He got off to a bad start, and because he wasn't hitting I had to make a decision. I wanted to catch Howard more and play Blanchard more and still use Yogi. That was one of my real tough decisions, and I felt bad because I didn't stay with Hector very long. I couldn't wait for him when things were going kind of bad for us in the spring, and I wound up putting Yogi in left field. After that, the way the club was set up, it might have made Hector put too much pressure on himself. But I had to keep Yogi in there. I had Howard, who was swinging the bat so good, and I had Blanchard, so Hector kind of ended up in a situation where he didn't play as much as he needed to or as much as he probably thought he was going to.

But he never complained. He never came into the manager's office bitching and moaning and griping. Hector was a fine person. He'd do anything, pinch-hit, pinch-run, play anywhere in the outfield. He'd even play third base, if we needed him to. And you didn't have to worry about Lopey not being in bed at night or getting into trouble or having to go look for him, or anything like that. He was a good member of that ball club. Everybody liked him.

He got married that spring to a girl from Brooklyn. Some people thought getting married might have affected Hector's play that season, but I don't know about that. I've found it works both ways. It can hurt one player, it can help another. Jim Turner always thought it hurt. He didn't want any of his players getting married—well, that is, his pitchers; he didn't worry about anybody else on the club. But let some young pitcher even mention he was thinking about getting married, and Turner would get mad. Oh, this is a funny business.

Lopez never complained. He liked being a Yankee, and he was a Yankee. I was real happy when he had that great game in the Series.

After a joyful train ride back to New York, with a steak and champagne celebration on board, the Yankees had a formal victory party at the Savoy Hilton, where Houk's managerial career had begun a year earlier. In keeping with the dignity the Yankees were so proud of in those days, the party was quiet. Not all the players were there. Mantle, feeling poorly, had gone straight home from Cincinnati, and so had Maris, Kubek, and Blanchard.

Maris, back home in Kansas City with his family, said, "I'm a little tired of baseball. I'm ready to tie up for a while."

Mantle said, later, "I don't like to pick teams, because I played on some good ones—the first team I played on, in 1951, won five straight World Series—but my favorite was the '61 Yankees. Kubek, Richardson, Boyer, Skowron—that was the best infield I ever saw. And Roger—when people think of Roger they think of home runs, but he was a great all-around player. Never threw to the wrong base, always went from first to third on a base hit, broke up double plays. And he was a great outfielder.

"We had a great team that year. John Blanchard, a hell of a pinch-hitter. Whitey Ford, won 25 games. That was a great ball team. That was a fun year."

Two days after the Series ended—the 365th day of the year that began with Mazeroski's home run—Houk signed a new two-year contract for $50,000 a year, a 30-percent raise. "For the first time in all my years in baseball I have security," he said. "I also have a hell of a chance of winning the pennant again."

He did, in 1962 and 1963. Then he moved up to the front office for a few years before returning to the dugout to manage the Yankees from 1966 through 1973, the Tigers from 1974 through 1978, and the Red Sox from 1981 through 1984.

He put in 20 seasons as a big league manager, but none ever meant as much to him as the first one, when the Yankees won it all in 1961.

RALPH HOUK:

That was the greatest year I ever had in baseball. My biggest *day* was when the Yankees kept me in 1947, which I didn't expect, and next biggest was being named manager in 1960. But for a season, it was winning the pennant and the World Series in my first year. I mean, you can't hardly top that. I certainly never made enough hits to top it. And then I got the new two-year contract at $50,000. People don't realize how much money that was then, or anyway how much it was for me.

It was just a great year, a great year. Usually during a season, no matter what club you manage or how well you do, you have a few problems off the field with some of the players, trouble they get into during the season. Except for the Duren thing in spring training, we never had any of that all year.

It was a pleasure managing that team. They played so *good*. They played so good all season.

It kind of gives you a chill when you think back. You'd like to see it all again. God, what great years those guys had. What a season that was!

PART SIX

Curtain Call

Thirty-six players appeared in at least one game for the 1961 Yankees. Their ages are as of opening day that season.

LUIS ENRIQUE (LOUIE) ARROYO, lefthanded pitcher, 34, 5′8″, 178 pounds. Appeared in 65 games. Won 15, lost 5, with 29 saves.

Arroyo was born in Penuelas, Puerto Rico, on February 18, 1927. He broke into professional baseball in 1948 with Greenville in the St. Louis Cardinals' farm system but it wasn't until seven years later, in 1955, that he reached the major leagues. He won 11 games for the Cardinals in his rookie season but the following spring was traded to the Pittsburgh Pirates. He had two unimpressive seasons with the Pirates and slid back to the minors. He returned to the big leagues briefly in 1959 with the Cincinnati Reds but spent most of that season and the next in the International League, with Havana and then Jersey City. In 1960, at the age of 33 with almost 13 years as a professional behind him, he seemed near the end of his career. But the Yankees, impressed by his relief work for Jersey City, added him to their 1960 roster in midseason. He won five and lost one as a reliever that year and in 1961, with Houk's world champions, he was the best relief pitcher in baseball. That was Arroyo's one big hurrah.

Bothered by a sore arm, he appeared in only 34 innings in 1962 and 6 in 1963, and by 1964 his playing career was over. He continued to be active in baseball, managing and coaching in Latin America. Fluent in both Spanish and English, he has long been a scout for the Yankees in the Caribbean area. He lives in Puerto Rico.

LAWRENCE PETER (YOGI) BERRA, lefthanded-hitting catcher-outfielder, 35, 5'7", 185 pounds. Appeared in 119 games. Batted .271, with 22 home runs.

Berra was born in St. Louis on May 12, 1925. A boyhood friend of Joe Garagiola, a major league catcher himself before going into broadcasting, Berra signed with the Yankees when he was 18 and played the 1943 season with Norfolk before entering the United States Navy during World War II. After the war he was assigned to Newark, then the Yankees' top farm club, and batted .314. He was brought up to the Yankees near the end of the season, hit .364 in seven games and never went back to the minors again. Alternating between catching and the outfield in 1947 and 1948, he established himself as a powerful, dangerous hitter (in 1947 he hit the first pinch-hit home run ever in a World Series). In 1949, Casey Stengel's first year as Yankee manager, Berra became the team's full-time catcher, a position he held for ten seasons before once again alternating between catching and the outfield. He was named the Most Valuable Player in the American League in 1951, 1954 and 1955. He hit 12 homers in World Series competition and holds the Series record for most hits, with 71. After the 1963 season he retired as a player and succeeded Houk as manager. He won the pennant in his first season but was fired after losing the World Series. He joined the New York Mets in 1965 as a player-coach and in 1972 succeeded Gil Hodges as manager. He led the Mets to the National League pennant in 1973 (the second manager ever to win a pennant in both leagues) but was dismissed in midseason of 1975. He rejoined the Yankees as a coach and managed the club again in 1984 and, briefly, in 1985. He then became a coach with the Houston Astros. One of Berra's sons, Tim, played pro football with the Baltimore Colts and another, Dale, was a major league infielder with the Pirates, Yankees and other teams. Berra was elected to the baseball Hall of Fame in 1971. He lives in New Jersey.

JOHN EDWIN BLANCHARD, lefthanded-hitting catcher, 28, 6'1", 190 pounds. Appeared in 93 games. Batted .305, with 21 home runs.

Blanchard was born in Minneapolis on February 26, 1933. He was signed by the Yankees when he was 18 and played briefly for the minor league Kansas City Blues before going to Binghamton, where he hit only .193. Reassigned to a lower minor league team in Joplin in 1952, Blanchard, still only 19, hit .301, batted in 112 runs and led the league with 30 homers. He was in military service the next two years but in 1955 drove in 111 runs for Binghamton and hit a league-leading 34 home runs. He appeared in one game for the Yankees late in 1955 but spent the next three seasons in the minors, where he continued to display power. Finally, in 1959, his ninth year as a professional, he made it to the Yankees to stay. In 1961 he blossomed, hitting 21 home runs in only 243 at bats, while hitting over .300. Unfortunately, that was his only really good year in the majors. His batting average fell off sharply the next two seasons and while he still showed home-run power he lacked consistency. He was traded in 1965 to the Athletics, who later that season sold him to the Milwaukee Braves. That was Blanchard's last major league season. After leaving baseball he conquered a drinking problem and later made an impressive recovery after surgery for cancer of the kidney. He lives near Minneapolis and sells heavy railroad equipment throughout the Midwest.

CLETIS LEROY (CLETE) BOYER, righthanded-hitting third baseman, 24, 6', 165 pounds. Appeared in 148 games. Batted .224, with 11 home runs.

Boyer was born in Cassville, Missouri, on February 8, 1937. His brother Ken was a star third baseman for the Cardinals and later their manager, and his brother Cloyd was a major league pitcher for five years and later a pitching coach. Clete signed with the Kansas City Athletics in 1955, when he was 18. Two years later he was traded to the Yankees and spent most of the next three seasons in the minors before becoming a full-fledged Yankee in 1960. In 1961 Houk made him a regular and Boyer responded by turning into one of the best-fielding third basemen in big league history. He was a pillar of the Yankee infield for six years before being traded to Atlanta after the 1966 season. He put in five years with the Braves, then went to Japan and played baseball there before ending his active career. He went into several business ventures but preferred being in uniform as a coach and minor league instructor. He is currently a coach with the Yankees. He lives in Florida.

ROBERT HENRY (BOB) CERV, righthanded-hitting outfielder, 34, 6', 200 pounds. Appeared in 57 games. Batted .271, with 6 home runs.

Cerv was born in Weston, Nebraska, on May 5, 1926. He graduated from the University of Nebraska, where he was a basketball star, before signing with the Yankees in 1950. He was a powerful hitter in the minor leagues and was brought up to the Yankees at the end of 1951, but during his first six seasons with the club he was a part-time player in Casey Stengel's platoon system. After he was traded to Kansas City in 1957 he became one of the best outfielders in the American League, hitting 38 homers in 1958 and driving in 104 runs. But he was bothered by recurring injuries and in May 1960 the Yankees were able to regain him in a trade. He filled in admirably as a pinch-hitter and part-time outfielder in 1960, but after that season, when the American League expanded, the Yankees lost him in the player expansion draft to the Los Angeles (later California) Angels. In May 1961, the Yankees got him back again, and he hit several important homers for New York in the drive to the pennant. Late in 1961 he sprained his knee sliding and was unable to play in the World Series. He never really recovered and 1962 was his last season. In the spring of 1963 Stengel, now manager of the Mets, persuaded Cerv to come to spring training but, unable to perform the way he was once able to, Cerv retired. He coached college baseball in Nebraska and Iowa for many years and fathered ten children. He lives in Nebraska.

TRUMAN EUGENE (TEX) CLEVENGER, righthanded pitcher, 28, 6'1", 180 pounds. Appeared in 21 games. Won 1, lost 1.

Clevenger was born in Visalia, California, on July 9, 1932. Signed by the Boston Red Sox, he won 16 games and lost only 2 for San Jose in 1953, his first year in pro ball. He went up to the Red Sox in 1954, was back in the minors in 1955 and was traded to Washington in 1956. He spent five years with the Senators, pitching mostly in relief. In the expansion draft after the 1960 season he was picked by the Angels and in May 1961 was traded with Cerv to the Yankees. His major league career ended a year later. After leaving baseball Clevenger became a very successful automobile dealer in California, where he lives.

JAMES ALTON (JIM) COATES, righthanded pitcher, 28, 6'4", 190 pounds. Appeared in 43 games. Won 11, lost 5, with 5 saves.

Coates was born in Farnham, Virginia, on August 4, 1932. After signing with the Yankees he spent seven seasons in the minors with New York farm clubs in Olean, Norfolk, Joplin, Binghamton and Richmond before sticking with the Yankees in 1959. A fastballer, he struck out 223 batters in 226 innings in his first year as a professional. With the Yankees as a spot starter and a relief pitcher, he was remarkably effective his first three years, winning 30 games and losing only 9 from 1959 to 1961, but he tailed off after that and was traded to Washington early in the 1963 season. He later pitched for the Reds and the Angels before his big league career ended in 1967. Coates now works as a high-voltage electrician in a shipyard. He lives in Virginia.

LEAVITT LEO (BUDDY) DALEY, lefthanded pitcher, 28, 6'1", 185 pounds. Appeared in 23 games. Won 8, lost 9.

Daley was born in Orange, California, on October 7, 1932. Signed by the Cleveland Indians at 18, he had a checkered minor league career, pitching for Bakersfield, Cedar Rapids, Reading, Indianapolis, Sacramento, San Diego and Buffalo, while also spending parts of three seasons in the majors with Cleveland and Kansas City. He reached big league maturity in 1959 with the Athletics and won 16 games that year and again the next before being traded to the Yankees in June 1961. Houk used Daley mostly as a starter but called on him frequently for relief work as well. He pitched the last six and two thirds innings and was the winning pitcher in the final game of the 1961 World Series. In 1962 Daley pitched almost exclusively in relief, was out almost the entire 1963 season with a sore arm and after vainly trying a comeback in 1964 was through as a major leaguer. He lives in Wyoming where he sells and services lawn-sprinkling equipment.

JOSEPH PAUL (JOE) DeMAESTRI, righthanded-hitting shortstop, 32, 6', 180 pounds. Appeared in 30 games. Batted .146, with no home runs.

DeMaestri was born in San Francisco on December 9, 1928. He began his professional career with San Jose in 1947 at the age of 18. He was an ordinary hitter, but his superb fielding moved him steadily up the minor league ladder until he reached the Chicago White Sox in 1951. He played for the St. Louis Browns in 1952, and from 1953 through 1959 for the Athletics, first in Philadelphia and from 1955 on in Kansas City. In December 1959 he came to the Yankees in the big trade that sent Roger Maris from Kansas City to New York. In his role as backup shortstop DeMaestri played little in 1960 and planned to retire after the season; he was prevailed upon to remain with the Yankees another year. After the 1961 season he did retire and went into business with his father in California, where DeMaestri now runs a beer distributorship. He lives in San Francisco.

ARTHUR JOHN (ART) DITMAR, 32, 6'2", 185 pounds. Appeared in 12 games. Won 2, lost 3.

Ditmar was born in Winthrop, Massachusetts, on April 3, 1929. He had five years in the minors and three with the Athletics before coming to the Yankees in 1957. He was used mostly in relief during his first two seasons in New York, but in 1959 and 1960 he was one of the Yankees' most dependable starters, leading the staff in games won in the 1960 pennant-winning season. But he was ineffective as a starter in 1961 and in June was traded back to Kansas City. Unable to regain his winning touch he retired from baseball in 1963 at the age of 34. Ditmar had attended American International in Springfield, Massachusetts, and after leaving baseball he returned to college, earned a master's degree in recreation and became a parks administrator. He lives in Ohio.

ALPHONSO ERWIN (AL) DOWNING, lefthanded pitcher, 19, 5'11", 175 pounds. Appeared in 5 games. Won 0, lost 1.

Downing was born in Trenton, New Jersey, on June 28, 1941. He had only half a season in the minors when he was called up by the Yankees in the summer of 1961. He started only one game and in 1962 returned to the minors, but beginning in 1963 he was one of the Yankees' top pitchers for five seasons before suffering a sore arm in 1968. He was traded to Oakland in 1969, to the Milwaukee Brewers in 1970, and to the Dodgers later that year. With Los Angeles he revived, won 20 games in 1971 and stayed with the Dodgers until he retired in 1977. The youngest member of the 1961 Yankees, Downing was the last member of the team to be an active major leaguer. He is remembered by trivia experts as the pitcher who gave up Henry Aaron's record-breaking 715th home run. After leaving baseball Downing went into sports broadcasting in Los Angeles, where he lives.

RINOLD GEORGE (RYNE) DUREN, righthanded pitcher, 32, 6'2", 190 pounds. Appeared in 4 games. Won 0, lost 1.

Duren was born in Cazenovia, Wisconsin, on February 22, 1929. Nearsighted, wild as a pitcher, but possessed of a blazing fastball, he was strikeout king in three different leagues during his nine-year career in the minors (1949–1957, with one brief appearance in the majors with the Orioles in 1954 and a slightly longer one with the Athletics in 1957). After pitching for Denver he joined the Yankees in 1958 and was a highly effective relief pitcher for two seasons. He was less effective in 1960. A heavy drinker, he was often in trouble with management, and in May 1961 the Yankees traded him to the Angels. He subsequently pitched for the Phillies, Reds and Senators before ending his career in 1965. He stopped drinking and became a lecturer, counselor and author on alcoholism, working closely with recovering alcoholics. He lives in Wisconsin.

EDWARD CHARLES (WHITEY) FORD, lefthanded pitcher, 32, 5'10", 180 pounds. Appeared in 39 games. Won 25, lost 4.

Ford was born in New York City on October 21, 1928. He was a first baseman as well as a pitcher in high school but when he signed with the Yankees at the age of 18 in 1947 it was as a pitcher. He worked his way steadily up the minor league chain in the Yankee farm system, winning 13 with Butler in 1947, 16 with Norfolk the next year and 16 the year after that with Binghamton, where he led the league in earned run average and strikeouts. In 1950 he was 6–3 with Kansas City in the American Association when he was called up to the Yankees in midseason. He was a rookie sensation, winning nine games and losing only one the rest of the year as the Yankees beat out the Tigers for the pennant. He also won the first of his many World Series victories that year (he won ten Series games in all, a record). After the 1950 season he went into the United States Navy for two years but returned to the Yankees in 1953 and immediately reassumed his role as a dominant pitcher, winning more than 70 percent of his starts through his first eight seasons. He slumped to 12–9 in 1960, Stengel's last year as manager, but rebounded in 1961 under Houk and averaged just under 20 victories a year for the next five seasons. His arm finally gave out, and in 1967 he retired. He won the Cy Young Award in 1961 and was elected to the Hall of Fame in 1974. He served as pitching coach for the Yankees for a time and still helps out in spring training, but after his career as an active player ended he turned to other interests: stocks and bonds, real estate, harness racing, public relations. He has homes in Florida and on Long Island in New York.

WILLIAM FREDERICK (BILLY) GARDNER, righthanded-hitting infielder, 33, 6', 175 pounds. Appeared in 41 games. Batted .212, with 1 home run.

Gardner was born in Waterford, Connecticut, on July 19, 1927. He was 17 when he broke in with Bristol but he labored for seven seasons in the minors before making it to the New York Giants in 1954. Later, he was sent back to the minors again and then sold to Baltimore, where in 1956 he finally became a first-string major league second baseman. He was traded to Washington, moved with the Senators to Minnesota and in June 1961 was traded to the Yankees. He was a backup infielder that season and the next before being traded to the Red Sox. His major league career ended in 1963. After many years as a coach he was named manager of the Twins in 1981. He was dismissed in 1985, caught on as a coach with Kansas City and succeeded Dick Howser as manager in 1986. He was dismissed in 1987. He lives in Connecticut.

JESSE LEMAR GONDER, lefthanded-hitting catcher, 25, 5'10", 180 pounds. Appeared in 15 games. Batted .333, with no home runs.

Gonder was born in Monticello, Arkansas, on January 20, 1936. He played for Ogden, Wausau, Clovis, Wenatchee, Temple, Monterey, Seattle, San Antonio, Havana and Richmond before the Yankees brought him up in 1960. He got few chances to play and in 1962 was sold to the Reds, who in 1963 traded him to the Mets. The Mets traded him to the Braves in 1965, and he spent his last two seasons in the majors with the Pirates in 1966 and 1967. After his career ended he became a bus driver. He lives in California.

ROBERT HOUSTON (BOB) HALE, lefthanded-hitting first baseman, 27, 5'10", 195 pounds. Appeared in 11 games. Batted .154, with 1 home run.

Hale was born in Sarasota, Florida, on November 7, 1933. He broke into the majors in 1955 with the Orioles and played five seasons in Baltimore before moving on to Cleveland in 1960. The Yankees bought him from the Indians in July 1961 and used him as a pinch-hitter and backup first baseman. He retired from baseball in 1962 at the age of 28 and returned to college, where he earned his bachelor's degree, his master's and a Ph.D. in education. He is now a school principal in Illinois.

ELSTON GENE HOWARD, righthanded-hitting catcher, 32, 6'2", 200 pounds. Appeared in 129 games. Batted .348, with 21 home runs.

Howard was born in St. Louis on February 23, 1929. He played one season for Muskegon in 1950 before going into military service for two years. In 1953 he batted .286 for the Yankee farm club in Kansas City and in 1954 batted .330 for Toronto, then still a minor league city. He also had 22 homers and 109 runs batted in and led the International League in triples with 16. The next year, 1955, he became the first black to play for the Yankees. Although he came up as a catcher, he played more frequently in the outfield for the Yankees during his first few seasons with the club, since Yogi Berra was still at his peak. As Berra slowed down, Howard began to catch more often and in 1961 he established himself firmly as the team's fixture behind the plate. In 1963, when he batted .287 and hit 28 home runs, he was named the Most Valuable Player in the American League. The Yankees won pennants in nine of Howard's first ten years with the club. In 1967 he was sold late in the season to the Red Sox, helped them win the pennant and appeared in all seven games of the World Series, his tenth. He later returned to the Yankees as a coach and had hopes of becoming their manager. That opportunity never came. Howard died of heart failure at the age of 51 on December 14, 1980. He lived in New Jersey.

JOHN PHILLIP (JOHNNY) JAMES, righthanded pitcher, 27, 5′10″, 160 pounds. Appeared in 1 game. Won 0, lost 0.

James was born in Bonners Ferry, Idaho, on July 23, 1933. He began in the low minors in 1953 and spent eight seasons pitching for Boise, Modesto, Binghamton, Birmingham and Richmond before making it to the Yankees for half a season in 1960 as a reliever. In May 1961 he was traded to the Angels, and his brief major league career ended after that season. After he left baseball he went into merchandising. He lives in Arizona.

DERON ROGER JOHNSON, righthanded-hitting third baseman, 22, 6′2″, 200 pounds. Appeared in 13 games. Batted .105, with no home runs.

Johnson was born in San Diego on July 17, 1938. In five seasons in the Yankee farm system he showed impressive power at bat (he hit seven home runs in the 1959 International League playoff) but not much finesse in the field. He joined the Yankees late in 1960 and in 1961 was given a shot at platooning with Clete Boyer at third base. But he hit poorly and played little and in June was traded to Kansas City, where he was not particularly impressive. In military service most of 1962 and 1963, he resurfaced in the majors with the Reds in 1964 and became a feared power hitter. He led the National League with 130 runs batted in in 1965 and stayed in the majors for 16 seasons in all, hitting 245 home runs despite a low .244 lifetime batting average. He later became a major league coach.

ANTHONY CHRISTOPHER (TONY) KUBEK, lefthanded-hitting shortstop, 24, 6′3″, 190 pounds. Appeared in 153 games. Batted .276, with 8 home runs.

Kubek was born in Milwaukee on October 12, 1936. He broke into professional baseball at the age of 17 in 1954, batted .344 for Owensboro that year and .334 for Quincy the next before moving up to Denver, at that time the Yankee's top farm team, then managed by Houk. He hit .331 for Denver in 1956 and in 1957 was promoted to the Yankees, where he batted .297 and was named American League Rookie of the Year. Kubek played just about every position in the infield and outfield for Casey Stengel during his first four seasons, but in 1961 new manager Houk kept him at shortstop all season long, and he was a key figure in the Yankees' success. A superb fielder and an excellent hitter, he seemed set for a Hall of Fame career. But he was drafted into the United States Army after the 1961 season and in the army suffered a neck injury that forced him to retire from baseball in 1965 at the age of 29. He turned to baseball broadcasting and has had a long and successful career with NBC and the Toronto Blue Jays. He makes his home in Appleton, Wisconsin.

HECTOR HEADLEY LOPEZ, righthanded-hitting outfielder, 28, 6', 170 pounds. Appeared in 93 games. Batted .222, with 3 home runs.

Lopez was born in Colon, Panama, on July 8, 1932. He began his minor league career in 1951 at St. Hyacinthe in Quebec and later played for Williamsport, Ottawa and Columbus before making it to the Athletics in 1955. He played third base and second for the A's, but after he was traded to the Yankees in May 1959 he was switched to the outfield. A steady, valuable player during most of his eight seasons with New York, he suffered through an inexplicable, season-long slump in 1961, before breaking out of it in the World Series. After his big league career ended in 1966 he became a recreation director in the New York City park system. He lives in Queens, New York.

DUANE FREDERICK (DUKE) MAAS, righthanded pitcher, 32, 5'10", 170 pounds. Appeared in 1 game. Won 0, lost 0.

Maas was born in Utica, Michigan, on January 31, 1929. He came up through the Detroit minor league system and had some success as a starter with the Tigers in 1955, 1956 and 1957 before being traded to Kansas City after that season and to the Yankees in June 1958. He won 21 games in a season and a half for the Yankees, mostly as a starter, but in 1960 became a full-time relief pitcher. The Angels took him in the expansion draft after the 1960 season, but the Yankees regained him in a trade in April 1961. His arm was gone, however, and after one brief, ineffective appearance his major league career ended. He died in Mount Clemens, Michigan, on December 7, 1976, at the age of 47.

MICKEY CHARLES MANTLE, switch-hitting center fielder, 29, 5'11", 195 pounds. Appeared in 153 games. Batted .317, with 54 home runs.

Mantle was born in Spavinaw, Oklahoma, on October 20, 1931. He was signed by Yankee scout Tom Greenwade for $100 and began his professional career in 1949 at the age of 17. He hit .313 for Independence in 1949 and a league-leading .383 for Joplin in 1950 and was brought to the Yankees' instructional school before spring training in Phoenix in 1951. There, his speed and power were so evident that he was kept with the Yankees, even though he was still only 19. In midseason he was sent back to the minor leagues for a month or so to get his batting eye back in shape (he'd been striking out far too often) but came back later in the season and remained as a regular outfielder and star for 18 years. He led the league in home runs in 1955 and won the rare Triple Crown (first in batting, home runs and runs batted in) in 1956, when he hit 52 homers. He won the home run title again in 1958 and 1960 and hit 54 home runs finishing second to Roger Maris's 61 in 1961. He is one of only five players in major league history to hit 50 or more homers twice (the others are Babe Ruth, Jimmy Foxx, Ralph Kiner and Willie Mays). He was named the Most Valuable Player in the American League in 1956, 1957 and 1962 and was elected to the Hall of Fame in 1974. After retiring as a player following the 1968 season, Mantle served as an instructor in spring training, invested in a fast-food chain, did public relations for an insurance company and an Atlantic City hotel-casino (for which he was temporarily barred from baseball) and worked as a baseball broadcaster on television. Mantle, his wife and their four sons live in Dallas. He also has a vacation home in Oklahoma.

ROGER EUGENE MARIS, lefthanded-hitting right fielder, 26, 6', 200 pounds. Appeared in 161 games. Batted .269, with 61 home runs.

Maris was born in Fargo, North Dakota, on September 10, 1934. A high school star in football as well as baseball, he gave up a college football scholarship to sign with the Cleveland Indians after graduating from high school. He played four years in the minors at Fargo-Moorhead, Keokuk, Tulsa, Reading and Indianapolis before catching on with the Indians in 1957. He showed consistent if not spectacular home-run power in the minors and during his rookie year with Cleveland (he hit 14 homers for the Indians while batting .235), but he was nonetheless traded to the Athletics in June 1958. He hit about the same that year, .240, but increased his home-run total to 28. In 1959 with the A's he lifted his average to .273 but hit only 16 homers. That December the Athletics traded him to the Yankees, along with Joe DeMaestri and Kent Hadley, for Hank Bauer, Don Larsen, Norm Siebern and Marv Throneberry, and in 1960 for the Yankees he not only batted .283, his major league high, but hit 39 home runs and won the Most Valuable Player award. He won the MVP again in 1961 when he hit his 61 homers, and had a third straight strong season in 1962 with 33 home runs and 100 runs batted in. But after that, persistent injuries hampered him—he missed an average of 66 games a season in five of his last six years in the majors—and his hitting fell off. After the 1966 season he was traded to the Cardinals, for whom he played two years, helping them to win pennants in 1967 and 1968, before retiring from baseball at the age of 34. In his 12 major league seasons Maris played on seven pennant winners. After leaving baseball he took over a beer distributorship in Gainesville, Florida, and ran it, with his brother's help, for the rest of his life. He died of cancer in Houston, Texas, on December 14, 1985, and was buried in Fargo, his hometown.

DANIEL EUGENE (DANNY) McDEVITT, lefthanded pitcher, 28, 5'10", 175 pounds. Appeared in 8 games. Won 1, lost 2, with 1 save.

McDevitt was born in New York City on November 18, 1932. Signed by the Dodgers, he made it to Brooklyn for one year, 1957, before moving with the club to Los Angeles. He won ten games for the pennant-winning Dodgers in 1959 but did not appear in the World

Series. In 1960 he failed to win a game and in December was sold to the Yankees. In 1961 he both started and relieved for New York before he was traded to Minnesota in June. The Twins sold him to the Athletics in 1962, his last year in the majors.

JOHN BURWELL (JACK) REED, righthanded-hitting outfielder, 28, 6'1", 190 pounds. Appeared in 28 games. Batted .154, with no home runs.

Reed was born in Silver City, Mississippi, on February 2, 1933. He was in the Yankee farm system for eight years (including two years of military service) before joining the parent club in 1961. A superior fielder, he batted well in the lower minors but tailed off in higher classifications. In 1961 he was essentially a defensive replacement, playing in the outfield in 27 games but coming to bat only 14 times all season. In 1962 and 1963 he played more frequently and won a memorable game against Detroit with a home run in the twenty-second inning. He retired from the game in 1964 to take over management of his family's farm in Mississippi, where in recent years one of his principal crops has been catfish, nurtured in special holding troughs.

HAROLD EUGENE (HAL) RENIFF, righthanded pitcher, 22, 6', 215 pounds. Appeared in 25 games. Won 2, lost 0, with 2 saves.

Reniff was born in Warren, Ohio, on July 2, 1938. He began his professional career at 18 with Kearney but spent most of the next three seasons with Modesto. After winning 21 games for Modesto in 1959 he moved up to Amarillo, Binghamton and Richmond before being called up to the Yankees in midseason of 1961. He was a useful backup man in the bullpen for the Yankees that season but was back in the minors in 1962. He rejoined the club in 1963 and was a top reliever for four seasons before losing his stuff. The Yankees sold him in June 1967 to the Mets, for whom he pitched the rest of the season, his last in the major leagues. He lives in Pennsylvania.

ROBERT CLINTON (BOBBY) RICHARDSON, righthanded-hitting second baseman, 25, 5'9", 170 pounds. Appeared in 162 games, most of anyone on the team. Batted .261, with 3 home runs.

Richardson was born in Sumter, South Carolina, on August 19, 1935. He played for Norfolk, Olean, Binghamton and Denver, where Houk was his manager, before going up to the Yankees late in 1955. He was up and down between the minors and the parent club until 1957, when he played 93 games at second base for the Yankees. He played less frequently in 1958 but in 1959 became the regular second baseman, a post he held for eight seasons. A steady but unspectacular hitter, Richardson surprised everyone during the 1960 World Series by hitting a grand-slam home run and by driving in 12 runs, a record, in the seven-game Series. His lifetime batting average in regular-season play was .266, but in World Series competition (he appeared in seven Series in all) it was .305. A very religious man, Richardson retired from the game at the age of 31 after the 1966 season to return to his home and family in South Carolina. He coached baseball in South Carolina and Virginia and dabbled in South Carolina politics.

ROLAND FRANK (ROLLIE) SHELDON, righthanded pitcher, 24, 6'4", 185 pounds. Appeared in 35 games. Won 11, lost 5.

Sheldon was born in Putnam, Connecticut, on December 17, 1936. A pitcher of note at Texas A&M and the University of Connecticut, he signed with the Yankees at the somewhat advanced age of 23 and in his professional debut with minor league Auburn won 15 games and lost only 1 in little more than half a season. He was brought up to the Yankees the following spring, was voted the outstanding rookie in training camp and made the club. He was moved into the starting rotation in June and came through remarkably well, although he was not used in the World Series. He suffered from arm trouble in 1962 and was back in the minors in 1963. In 1964 he returned to the Yankees and pitched effectively again, including a couple of innings in the 1964 World Series, but early in 1965 he was traded to Kansas City. He had one strong year for the Athletics, but that was all. He was traded to the Red Sox in 1966 and was finished in the majors after that season. After baseball he went into the insurance business and is now a claims representative in Kansas City.

WILLIAM JOSEPH (BILL) SKOWRON, righthanded-hitting first baseman, 30, 5'11", 195 pounds. Appeared in 150 games. Batted .267, with 28 home runs.

Skowron was born in Chicago on December 18, 1930. He played football and baseball at Purdue before signing a contract with the Yankees in 1951. He spent only three years in the minors, two of them with the key Yankee farm team in Kansas City, and hit well over .300 each year. In 1952 he led the American Association with 31 home runs and 134 runs batted in. He joined the Yankees in 1954 and shared first-base duties with the veteran Joe Collins, whom he superseded the following year. Although he suffered from a chronic back problem, Skowron was the Yankees' regular first baseman for eight seasons, an efficient if not flashy fielder and a strong, steady hitter, averaging nearly 20 home runs a year. Quiet and earnest, he was one of the most popular players on the team. He was traded to the Dodgers after the 1962 season and in the 1963 World Series batted .385 against the Yankees, when Los Angeles swept the New Yorkers four straight. The Dodgers traded him to Washington after the 1963 season, and the Senators traded him to the White Sox in 1964. He played two and a half years for Chicago before moving on to the Angels in 1967, his last year in the majors. He is now in sales and sales promotion in Chicago.

WILLIAM CHARLES (BILL) STAFFORD, righthanded pitcher, 21, 6'1",
190 pounds. Appeared in 36 games. Won 14, lost 9, with 2 saves.

Stafford was born in Catskill, New York, on August 13, 1939. He
was 17 when he signed with the Yankees and pitched very effectively
for St. Petersburg and Binghamton in 1957 and 1958. In 1959 he was
able to win only two games for Binghamton and Richmond, but came
back strongly in 1960 and had an 11–7 record for Richmond when
the Yankees called him up in midsummer. He started eight games for
Stengel's last team that year and had a sparkling 2.25 earned run
average. In 1961, under Houk, he pitched mostly in relief before he
was moved into the starting rotation in June. He responded strongly,
won 14 games, had the second-lowest ERA in the American League
and pitched well in the World Series. He won 14 games in 1962 and
seemed on his way to a long and successful career when he began to
have arm trouble. He was in the majors another five years with the
Yankees and Athletics but won a total of only 12 games during that
time. His big league career ended in 1967, when he was only 28. He
managed health clubs and fast-food stores and is now in sales. He lives
in Michigan.

RALPH WILLARD TERRY, righthanded pitcher, 25, 6'3", 190 pounds.
Appeared in 31 games. Won 16, lost 3.

Terry was born in Big Cabin, Oklahoma, on January 9, 1936. He
began pitching for Binghamton in 1954, when he was 18, and then
moved up to Denver, where he played for Houk for two seasons. He
had a 13–4 record for Denver in 1956 when he was called up to the
Yankees. He seemed a star of the future but was traded to Kansas City
with Billy Martin and two others in June 1957. He pitched well for
the then-lowly Athletics and in May 1959 the Yankees regained him
in another trade with the A's. He showed flashes of promise in 1959
and 1960 with the Yankees (he pitched the Yanks' pennant clincher
in 1960 but was on the mound when Pittsburgh's Bill Mazeroski hit

the home run that won the World Series for the Pirates in the ninth inning of the seventh game that year). In 1961 Terry started slowly, pitched a couple of strong games, was sidelined for a time with a bad shoulder and then in the last half of the season came on strongly. In 1962 he became the ace of the staff, winning 23 games, but was not as effective in 1963 and was a distinct disappointment in 1964. He was traded to Cleveland in 1965 and had one good season with the Indians, but that was all. He pitched for the A's and the Mets in 1966 and won only one game all year. In 1967, after pitching only three innings for the Mets, he was all through at the age of 31. A superb golfer as an amateur, Terry helped design golf courses after leaving baseball, tried without success to become eligible for the professional golf tour and worked as a club pro. He is also in the oil business. He lives in Kansas.

JAMES LEROY (LEE) THOMAS, lefthanded-hitting outfielder–first baseman, 25, 6'2", 195 pounds. Appeared in 2 games. Batted .500, with no home runs.

Thomas was born in Peoria on February 5, 1936. He began in the Yankee farm system in 1954 at the age of 18 and toiled for seven seasons before reaching the big club in 1961. In the minors Thomas displayed questionable fielding ability but impressive power at bat; in 1959 at Binghamton he hit 25 homers and drove in 123 runs. He made only two pinch-hitting appearances for the 1961 Yankees before being traded to the Angels with Ryne Duren in May for Bob Cerv and Tex Clevenger. With the Angels, Thomas was a dangerous hitter, driving out 50 home runs over the next two seasons. Then he slowed down. He later played for the Red Sox, Braves and Cubs, never quite living up to that first burst of ability with the Angels. His career ended in 1968 after he batted .194 for the Houston Astros. He remained active in baseball and is now with the St. Louis Cardinals organization.

EARL TORGESON, lefthanded-hitting first baseman, 37, 6'3", 180 pounds. Appeared in 22 games. Batted .111, with no home runs.

Torgeson was born in Snohomish, Washington, on January 1, 1924. He broke into the major leagues in 1947 with the Boston Braves, moved on to the Phillies in 1953, the Tigers in 1955 and the White Sox in 1957. After he was released by the White Sox in 1961 the Yankees signed him as a pinch-hitter and reserve first baseman. Late in the 1961 season he was taken off the active roster and made a coach. His last season as an active player was 1961. He died in 1985 at the age of 61.

THOMAS MICHAEL (TOM) TRESH, switch-hitting shortstop, 23, 6'1", 180 pounds. Appeared in 9 games. Batted .250, with no home runs.

Tresh was born in Detroit on September 20, 1937. His father, Mike Tresh, was a catcher for the White Sox for 11 years. Tresh, who had been in the Yankee farm system for four years, was a player of the future when he was called up for a look late in 1961, but after Kubek was drafted into the army Tresh became the team's first-string shortstop in 1962. When Kubek returned, Tresh switched to the outfield. He played seven full seasons for the Yankees and part of a year with the Tigers before his career ended in 1969. After he left the majors he became a college baseball coach in Michigan.

ROBERT LEE (BOB) TURLEY, righthanded pitcher, 30, 6'2", 215 pounds. Appeared in 15 games. Won 3, lost 5.

Turley was born in Troy, Illinois, on September 19, 1930. He began his professional career when he was 17 with Belleville in the St. Louis Browns' farm system, and also pitched for Aberdeen, Wichita and San Antonio. His minor league record was impressive: He twice won 20 games in a season and twice struck out more than 200 batters. After a year of military service he joined St. Louis in 1953 and in 1954, after the Browns became the Baltimore Orioles, he won 14 games and led the American League in both strikeouts and bases on balls. In December of that year, in one of the biggest trades in major league history, Turley was shifted to the Yankees in a complex deal involving 18 players. With New York, he was a strong but sometimes erratic pitcher for three seasons, but in 1958 he put it all together, won 21 games while losing only 7, and won the Cy Young Award as the outstanding pitcher in the major leagues. (Only one award was given for both leagues at that time.) After that, Turley lost his effectiveness, and probably his fastball, and by the spring of 1961 was only a shell of the pitcher he once had been. He stayed with the Yankees through 1962, vainly trying to recover his lost ability, but then moved on to the Angels and the Red Sox before calling it a career in 1963. Highly intelligent and exceptionally perceptive, Turley went into insurance and brokerage after leaving baseball and became an extremely wealthy man. He lives in Georgia.

NOTE: *Except for pitchers, all players on the 1961 Yankees other than Hale, Thomas and Torgeson threw righthanded.*

APPENDIX

THE 1961 NEW YORK YANKEES

BATTING

Player	PCT	G	AB	R	H	RBI	2B	3B	HR	BB	SO	SB	SA
* Lee Thomas	.500	2	2	1	1	0	0	0	0	0	0	0	.500
Elston Howard	.348	129	446	64	155	77	17	5	21	28	65	0	.549
Jesse Gonder	.333	15	12	1	4	3	1	0	0	3	1	0	.417
Mickey Mantle	.317	153	514	132	163	128	16	6	54	126	112	12	.687
John Blanchard	.305	93	243	38	74	54	10	1	21	27	28	1	.613
Luis Arroyo	.280	65	25	2	7	0	2	0	0	0	4	0	.360
Tony Kubek	.276	153	617	84	170	46	38	6	8	27	60	1	.395
* Bob Cerv	.271	57	118	17	32	20	5	1	6	12	17	1	.483
Yogi Berra	.271	119	395	62	107	61	11	0	22	35	28	2	.466
Roger Maris	.269	161	590	132	159	142	16	4	61	94	67	0	.620
Bill Skowron	.267	150	561	76	150	89	23	4	28	35	108	0	.472
Bobby Richardson	.261	162	662	80	173	49	17	5	3	30	23	9	.316
* Tex Clevenger	.250	21	4	1	1	1	1	0	0	0	1	0	.500
Tom Tresh	.250	9	8	1	2	0	0	0	0	0	1	0	.250
Ralph Terry	.227	31	66	3	15	5	2	0	0	1	16	0	.258
Clete Boyer	.224	148	504	61	113	55	19	5	11	63	83	1	.347
Hector Lopez	.222	93	243	27	54	22	7	2	3	24	38	1	.305

Player	PCT	G	AB	R	H	RBI	2B	3B	HR	BB	SO	SB	SA
* Billy Gardner	.212	41	99	11	21	2	5	0	1	6	18	0	.293
Bill Stafford	.179	36	67	5	12	3	2	1	0	4	11	0	.239
Whitey Ford	.177	39	96	11	17	10	1	0	0	12	17	0	.188
* Bob Hale	.154	11	13	2	2	1	0	0	1	0	0	0	.385
Jack Reed	.154	28	13	4	2	1	0	0	0	1	1	0	.154
Joe DeMaestri	.146	30	41	1	6	2	0	0	0	0	13	0	.146
* Buddy Daley	.133	23	45	3	6	2	1	0	0	1	1	0	.156
Rollie Sheldon	.125	36	56	1	7	4	0	0	0	2	24	0	.125
* Earl Torgeson	.111	22	18	3	2	0	0	0	0	8	3	0	.111
* Deron Johnson	.105	13	19	1	2	2	0	0	0	2	5	0	.105
Bob Turley	.095	15	21	1	2	3	0	0	0	0	11	0	.095
* Art Ditmar	.053	12	19	0	1	0	0	0	0	0	5	0	.053
Jim Coates	.029	43	35	1	1	0	0	0	0	1	21	0	.029
Hal Reniff	.000	25	5	0	0	0	0	0	0	0	2	0	.000
Al Downing	.000	5	1	0	0	0	0	0	0	0	0	0	.000
* Danny McDevitt	.000	8	1	1	0	0	0	0	0	1	1	0	.000
* Ryne Duren	.000	4	0	0	0	0	0	0	0	0	0	0	.000
* Johnny James	.000	1	0	0	0	0	0	0	0	0	0	0	.000
Duke Maas	.000	1	0	0	0	0	0	0	0	0	0	0	.000
Team Totals	.263	163	5559	827	1461	782	194	40	240	543	785	28	.441

* 1961 record with Yankees

THE 240 CLUB

The 1961 Yankees set a team record for home runs that was still standing
a quarter of a century later. The home runs were hit by 13 players.

Roger Maris	61 in 590 at bats
Mickey Mantle	54 in 514
Bill Skowron	28 in 561
Yogi Berra	22 in 395
John Blanchard	21 in 243
Elston Howard	21 in 446
Clete Boyer	11 in 504

Tony Kubek	8 in 617 at bats
Bob Cerv	6 in 118
Hector Lopez	3 in 243
Bobby Richardson	3 in 662
Billy Gardner	1 in 99
Bob Hale	1 in 13

Frequency:

Maris	1 every 9½ at bats
Mantle	1 every 9½
Blanchard	1 every 12
Hale	1 every 13
Berra	1 every 18
Skowron	1 every 20
Cerv	1 every 20

Howard	1 every 21 at bats
Boyer	1 every 46
Kubek	1 every 77
Lopez	1 every 81
Gardner	1 every 99
Richardson	1 every 221

PITCHING

Pitcher	W	L	PCT	ERA	G	GS	CG	GR	IP	RI	SV	H	ER	BB	SO	SH
Hal Reniff	2	0	1.000	2.60	25	0	0	25	45	45	2	31	13	31	21	0
Whitey Ford	25	4	.862	3.21	39	39	11	0	283	0	0	242	101	92	209	5†
Ralph Terry	16	3	.842	3.16	31	27	9	4	188	10	0	162	66	42	86	2
Luis Arroyo	15	5	.750	2.19	65	0	0	65	119	119	29	83	29	49	87	2†
Jim Coates	11	5	.688	3.45	43	11	4	32	141	71	5	128	54	53	80	1
Rollie Sheldon	11	5	.688	3.59	35	21	6	14	163	29	0	149	65	55	84	2
Bill Stafford	14	9	.609	2.68	36	25	8	11	195	20	2	168	58	59	101	4†
*Tex Clevenger	1	1	.500	4.78	21	0	0	21	32	32	0	35	17	21	14	0
*Buddy Daley	8	9	.471	3.95	23	17	7	6	130	20	0	127	57	51	83	2†
*Art Ditmar	2	3	.400	4.67	12	8	1	4	54	8	0	59	28	14	24	0
Bob Turley	3	5	.375	5.75	15	12	1	3	72	4	0	74	46	51	48	0
*Danny McDevitt	1	2	.333	7.62	8	2	0	6	13	6	1	18	11	8	8	0
Al Downing	0	1	.000	8.00	5	1	0	4	9	8	0	7	8	12	12	0
*Ryne Duren	0	1	.000	5.40	4	0	0	4	5	5	0	2	3	4	7	0
*Johnny James	0	0	.000	0.00	1	0	0	1	1.1	1	0	1	0	0	2	0
Duke Maas	0	0	.000	54.00	1	0	0	1	.1	.1	0	2	2	0	0	0
Team totals	109	53	.673	3.46	364	163	47	201	1451	378	39	1288	558	542	866	14

* 1961 record with Yankees   † Helped pitch joint shutout

BATTING LEADERS: 1961

Batting Average

Howard	.348
Mantle	.317
Blanchard	.305
Kubek	.276
Berra	.271

Home Runs

Maris	61
Mantle	54
Skowron	28
Berra	22
Blanchard	21
Howard	21

Runs Batted In

Maris	142
Mantle	128
Skowron	89
Howard	77
Berra	61

Runs

Mantle	132
Maris	132
Kubek	84
Richardson	80
Skowron	76

Slugging Average

Mantle	.687
Maris	.620
Blanchard	.613
Howard	.549
Skowron	.472

Games

Richardson	162
Maris	161
Kubek	153
Mantle	153
Skowron	150

At Bats

Richardson	662
Kubek	617
Maris	590
Skowron	561
Mantle	514

Hits

Richardson	173
Kubek	170
Mantle	163
Maris	159
Howard	155

Extra-Base Hits

Maris	81
Mantle	76
Skowron	55
Kubek	52
Howard	43

Total Bases

Maris	366
Mantle	353
Skowron	265
Howard	245
Kubek	244

Doubles

Kubek	38
Skowron	23
Boyer	19
Howard	17
Richardson	17

Triples

Kubek	6
Mantle	6
Richardson	5
Boyer	5
Howard	5

Stolen Bases

Mantle	12
Richardson	9
Berra	2
Five tied at	1

Bases on Balls

Mantle	126
Maris	94
Boyer	63
Berra	35
Skowron	35

Strikeouts

Mantle	112
Skowron	108
Boyer	83
Maris	67
Howard	65

PITCHING LEADERS: 1961

Games Started

Ford	39
Terry	27
Stafford	25
Sheldon	21
Daley	17

Complete Games

Ford	11
Terry	9
Stafford	8
Daley	7
Sheldon	6

Innings Pitched

Ford	283
Stafford	195
Terry	188
Sheldon	163
Coates	141

Strikeouts

Ford	209
Stafford	101
Arroyo	87
Terry	86
Sheldon	84

Bases on Balls

Ford	92
Stafford	59
Sheldon	55
Coates	53
Daley	51
Turley	51

Relief Appearances

Arroyo	65
Coates	32
Reniff	25
Clevenger	21
Sheldon	14

Relief Innings

Arroyo	119
Coates	71
Reniff	41
Clevenger	32
Sheldon	30

Saves

Arroyo	29
Coates	5
Reniff	2
Stafford	2
McDevitt	1

Games Won

Ford	25
Terry	16
Arroyo	15
Stafford	14
Coates	11
Sheldon	11

Games Lost

Daley	9
Stafford	9
Arroyo	5
Coates	5
Sheldon	5
Turley	5

Earned Run Average

Arroyo	2.19
Reniff	2.60
Stafford	2.68
Terry	3.16
Ford	3.21

Winning Percentage

Reniff	1.000 (2–0)
Ford	.862 (25–4)
Terry	.842 (16–3)
Arroyo	.750 (15–5)
Coates	.688 (11–5)
Sheldon	.688 (11–5)

Shutouts

Ford	3
Stafford	3
Sheldon	2
Terry	2
Coates	1
Ford/Arroyo	1
Ford/Daley/Arroyo	1
Stafford/Daley	1

GAME BY GAME COMPARISON OF HOME RUNS

MARIS AND MANTLE IN 1961 VERSUS RUTH IN 1927

(Where they stood in relation to the Babe after each game of the season)

Game	Mantle	Ruth	Maris
1	0	0	0
2	0	0	0
3	1	0	0
4	3	1	0
5	3	1	0
6	4	1	0
7	4	1	0
8	4	1	0
9	5	1	0
10	5	1	0
(April 24, 1961)			
11	7	2	1
12	7	3	1
13	7	3	1
14	7	4	1
15	7	4	1
16	8	6	1
17	8	6	2
18	9	6	2
19	9	6	2
20	9	6	3
(May 6, 1961)			
21	9	6	3
22	9	6	3
23	9	6	3
24	9	7	3
25	9	8	3
26	9	8	3
27	9	8	3
28	10	8	3
29	10	9	4
30	10	9	5
(May 19, 1961)			
31	10	9	6
32	10	9	7
33	10	10	7
34	10	11	7
35	10	11	8
36	10	11	8
37	10	12	8
38	10	12	9
39	11	13	9
40	13	13	11
(May 30, 1961)			
41	14	14	12
42	14	15	12
43	14	16	13
44	14	16	15
45	14	16	15
46	15	16	15
47	15	17	15
48	15	18	16
49	15	19	17
50	15	19	17
(June 8, 1961)			
51	15	19	17
52	16	20	18
53	17	21	18
54	17	21	18
55	18	22	20
56	18	22	20
57	18	22	21
58	18	22	22
59	19	22	22
60	19	24	22
(June 16, 1961)			
61	20	24	23
62	20	24	24
63	20	24	25
64	20	24	26
65	22	24	26
66	22	24	27
67	22	24	27
68	22	24	27
69	22	24	27
70	23	25	27
(June 26, 1961)			
71	23	25	27
72	24	25	27
73	25	26	27
74	27	26	28
75	28	26	30
76	28	26	30
77	28	26	31
78	28	27	32
79	28	29	32
80	28	29	32
(July 7, 1961)			

Game	Mantle	Ruth	Maris
81	29	29	32
82	29	29	33
83	29	30	33
84	30	30	34
85	31	30	34
86	31	30	35
87	32	30	35
88	33	30	35
89	35	30	35
90	35	30	35

(July 19, 1961)

Game	Mantle	Ruth	Maris
91	36	30	35
92	37	30	36
93	37	30	36
94	37	31	36
95	38	33	38
96	38	33	40
97	39	33	40
98	39	34	40
99	39	34	40
100	39	34	40

(July 29, 1961)

Game	Mantle	Ruth	Maris
101	39	34	40
102	39	34	40
103	39	34	40
104	40	34	40
105	40	34	40
106	40	35	41
107	40	35	41
108	42	35	41
109	43	35	41
110	43	36	41

(August 7, 1961)

Game	Mantle	Ruth	Maris
111	43	36	41
112	43	36	41
113	43	36	41
114	44	37	42
115	44	38	43
116	45	38	44
117	45	38	45
118	45	39	46
119	45	39	48
120	45	40	48

(August 17, 1961)

Game	Mantle	Ruth	Maris
121	45	40	48
122	45	40	48
123	46	40	49
124	46	41	49
125	46	42	50
126	46	42	50
127	46	43	50
128	46	44	50
129	46	44	51
130	46	44	51

(August 27, 1961)

Game	Mantle	Ruth	Maris
131	46	44	51
132	47	46	51
133	48	47	51
134	48	49	51
135	48	49	53
136	50	49	53
137	50	49	53
138	50	50	53
139	51	51	53
140	51	52	54

(September 6, 1961)

Game	Mantle	Ruth	Maris
141	51	52	55
142	52	52	55
143	52	53	56
144	53	53	56
145	53	53	56
146	53	53	56
147	53	54	56
148	53	55	56
149	53	56	56
150	53	56	56

(September 15, 1961)

Game	Mantle	Ruth	Maris
151	53	56	57
152	53	57	58
153	53	59	58
154	53	60	58
155*	53	60	59

(September 20, 1961)

Game	Mantle	Ruth	Maris
156	53	60†	59
157	54	60†	59
158	54	60†	59
159	54	60†	59
160	54	60†	60
161	54	60†	60
162	54	60†	60
163*	54	60†	61

(October 1, 1961)

* In both 1927 and 1961 the Yankees played one tie game, which added one game to the 154-game schedule in 1927 and one to the 162-game schedule in 1961.

† Ruth's season ended with the 155th game.

INDEX